my name is _____

and this is
MY new gender workbook

My New Gender Workbook

A Step-by-Step Guide to Achieving World Peace
Through Gender Anarchy and Sex Positivity

Kate Bornstein

Routledge
Taylor & Francis Group

NEW YORK AND LONDON

Second edition published 2013
by Routledge
711 Third Avenue, New York, NY 10017

Simultaneously published in the UK
by Routledge
2 Park Square, Milton Park, Abingdon, Oxon OX14 4RN

Routledge is an imprint of the Taylor & Francis Group, an informa business

© 2013 Taylor & Francis

First edition published by Routledge 1998

Library of Congress Cataloging in Publication Data
Bornstein, Kate, 1948–
  My new gender workbook: a step-by-step guide to achieving
  world peace through gender anarchy and sex positivity/
  Kate Bornstein.—2nd ed.
  p. cm.
  Rev. ed. of: My gender workbook. 1998.
  1. Gender identity. 2. Sex (Psychology) I. Bornstein, Kate, 1948–
  My gender workbook. II. Title.
  HQ1075.B69 2013
  305.3—dc23   2012033355

ISBN: 978–0–415–53864–0 (hbk)
ISBN: 978–0–415–53865–7 (pbk)
ISBN: 978–0–203–10903–8 (ebk)

Typeset in Stone Serif and an eclectic mixture of other fonts
by Florence Production Ltd, Stoodleigh, Devon, UK

A lot of the ideas in this book were crowdsourced from smart people who asked good questions and made great comments at my lectures and workshops over the last fifteen years. And even more crowdsourcing came from people who follow my words on Twitter. I call all these people my twibe. So this book is dedicated to you, dear twibe. Thank you for calling me out on my shit. And thank you for helping me #stayalive. Auntie Kate loves and respects you very much.

kiss kiss

Here's What's In Your Workbook. Look!

4. Let Why Equal Why   83

So . . . why is gender? And just how perfectly gendered are you? There's an in-depth exam to find that out exactly.

5. There's Only One Gender: Yours   113

This chapter is jam-packed with theory—which is another word for unproven ideas that could be big fat lies. But if the theory in this chapter is close to correct, you're going to find out a whole lot about your unique gender and the kind of fun you can have in it. Two big bonuses: rhyme games!! AND 101 gender outlaws name their genders in their own words. Imagine that.

6. SEX! SEX! SEX! SEX! SEX! SEX! SEX!   151

I forget what this chapter is about. But you won't. Not ever.

7. Get Ready to Do Your Gender   187

Most everyone goes through their life without paying much attention to their gender(s). Yes, you have more than one of them. Everyone does. This chapter is filled with drills that will help you become comfortably aware and focused on the performance of your gender(s).

8. Do Your Gender Mindfully   199

Just what the chapter title says: you get to consciously make and implement decisions about your gender. You're going to learn about all the drag you already do in life, and there's a comprehensive look at cultural playgrounds where you can practice any new genders that strike your fancy. There's storytelling, whips and chains, and a four-page comic you can show your friends and family when they ask you what the fuck is up with your gender!

9. The Missing Piece is Nothing, and We're Going to Find It Nowhere

Welcome to the wild and wacky world of paradox. What does it mean to the dominant culture that two of its fundamental building blocks are collapsing? Gender as man-and-woman-only and sexuality as homo-and-hetero-only are so last century, and you're going to find out why. You're also going to read the real story of the Garden of Eden, and God's thoughts on morality. Yep.

10. OK, Now What?

This is where you'll learn how to achieve world peace through sex positivity and gender anarchy. Tra-la, how fun!

Acknowledgments

I try to figure out how to thank all the thousands (yes, *thousands*) of people who helped me write this book. And, just like in some movies, there's a surprise at the end of the credits.

Use this page for notes or doodles.
Really, it's way OK if you write in this book!

Preface to the 21st Century Edition

Not many writers get do-overs. So, I'm grateful to my publisher, Routledge, for giving me the opportunity to update this workbook fifteen years after its first publication in 1997. Back then, the idea of "working" one's gender was a new concept. Now, there are thousands of people who are living their lives, mindfully working their genders. I've learned a great deal by becoming friends with many of them.

The first edition of this book focused on gender, pretty much all by itself. This version takes a look at gender as one of fifteen inter-dependent spheres of cultural regulation, collectively known as kyriarchy. The word was coined by Elisabeth Schüssler Fiorenza, and we all owe her thanks for naming the point of convergence of gender, sexuality, race, looks, age disability, class, mental health, religion, family/reproductive status, language, habitat, citizenship, political ideology, and humanity. This edition of the workbook examines gender as part of that system, and offers up suggestions on how to dismantle the whole fucking mess through a politic of desire, and an activism of radical wonder and radical welcoming—all stuff I've been puzzling over for the last fifteen years.

I've kept many words and elements the same in this edition, like puzzles and games and quizzes and such. Most importantly, I've kept the voices of literally hundreds of people in addition to my own. The

@quarridors: You see, people assume that gender is a simple progression of masculine to feminine, but actually . . . from a non-linear, non-normative viewpoint, it's more like a big ball of wibbly wobbly . . . gender-y blendery . . . stuff.

underlying problem with gender is that for centuries there's only been one point of view from which to observe it. With the addition of all these voices—some from the original edition, and many new voices—gender can be examined for what it really is, as so beautifully summed up by @quarridors in their brilliant riff on a famous line from my favorite BBC television show, *Doctor Who*, here to the left of this text.

Some New Conventions in This Version of the Workbook

I LOVE comic books and graphic novels, so I'm going to rip on them. From time to time, I'll be adding parenthetical, more personal, ideas to the text. This is me, over to the left of the page, doing just that!

But wait, there's more! Part of this book is about learning to mindfully be all the possible identities you want to be. The toon me that you see above is me as good auntie. THIS toon of me, to the right here, is a li'l more let's-not-fuck-around me. Sort of like Starbuck in *Battlestar Galactica*, only if she was an old lady, like me.

And just one more version of me who will be speaking with you: this is me as Lady Death, from Neil Gaiman's *Sandman* Series. Talking about death is a difficult thing to do. I do it best when I'm this me. Don't worry, there's not too much death in this book. I promise.

Now, please meet Li'l Blu, whose pronouns of choice are sie and hir. Blu has no gender—well none that sie wants to talk about anyway. In fact Blu doesn't have much to say, but sie has a lot to feel, and a whole lot to think about while sie's rambling through this book. Just like you!

It's been a true honor—and a whole lot of fun—to write this book in concert with so many contributors, and it's my heartfelt hope that readers will put these ideas and theories to work with the intention of putting an end to the suffering of all sentient beings.

Kate Bornstein
January, 2013

Please use this space for notes,
pictures of your true love,
or a letter to someone you really admire.

Chapter 1: Welcome to Your New Gender Workbook

 Is your body situated as comfortably as possible? Very well, I'll begin. From the moment we take our first breath—or from the moment our picture first hits the ultrasound screen—the cry "It's a boy" or "It's a girl" ushers us into the world.

As we grow into childhood and mature into adulthood, everything about ourselves grows and matures—everything except gender. We're taught that our genders never shift or waiver. We're supposed to believe that our gender stays exactly the same as the day we were born. The genders we're assigned at birth lock us onto a course through which we'll be expected to become whole, well-rounded, creative, loving people—but only as men or as women. From where I stand, that's like taking a field of racehorses, hobbling the front legs of half of them and the rear legs of the other half, and expecting them to run a decent race: it doesn't work.

Gender, this thing we're all seemingly born with, is a major restraint to self-expression. This has never made sense to me. Why should we be born with such a hobble? Does that make sense to you?

More and more people are beginning to agree with the idea that gender is more than either/or—there must be dozens of theories. But for the moment . . . fuck theory. This is a workbook, and we're going to start with the practical. And, since this is a workbook about questioning things, let's get right to work and ask some questions.

And yes, I'm going to use the word *fuck*. A lot. This is a book about gender and sex, and how can we talk about that without using the word *fuck*.

What's "New" About This Workbook?

A lot has happened in the world of sexuality and gender over the last fifteen years—so much so that the first edition of this workbook started to feel a little dated. For example . . .

- In my country, trans people are more and more included under the protection of the law against hate crimes.

- There are so many more hate crimes against trans people. Mostly male-to-female trans people. Mostly trans women of color.

- The Miss Universe beauty pageant is open to trans women. Now, that may sound shallow to you, but beauty is a great big part of the trans experience, and it's simply lovely to see beautiful trans women in pages other than porn. Not that I mind the porn, mind you. Au contraire!

- Membership in The Girl Scouts of America is now open to young trans girls.

- In 2012, Argentina became the first country to give a legal green light to any person who wants to change their gender. They've removed all the medical and psychiatric hoops. If you want to change your gender in Argentina, you can—just because you want to.

- In the case of pre-teen and tween trans youth, more and more doctors have begun to use hormone blockers to prevent the genderfying changes of puberty. Trans youth can now make their decision later, when they've had more time to experience life.

- At this writing, the picture that pops into most people's minds at the word transgender is a young, handsome trans man. Fifteen years ago, the image conjured by the word transgender was an older trans woman, just slightly mannish-looking. That's a great big cultural shift.

I've taken all of this and more into account, and now you've got the 2013 update in your hands. If you're interested in checking out the pieces of the first version that we couldn't include here, you can find the most important pieces online at www.routledge.com/cw/bornstein.

But what, specifically, is new? Well, for starters . . .

- The focus of the book remains on gender, but I'm including lots more about gender's uneasy but yummy ties to sexuality.

- Gender is increasingly being seen as one of many intersecting systems of oppression, so there's a lot more focus on how that's the case.

- The concept and reality of genderqueer hit the world after this book came out, and its impact on the matrix of sex/gender theory and activism has been staggeringly fun.

- The world at large is waking up to the reality of bullying and the tragedy of people who kill themselves because they've been bullied. So, I'm going to examine just why sex and gender are magnets for bullies—and why gender outlaws are punchlines for jokes in a bully culture.

- LGBTQetc has increased to over forty-five more letters, and it's time for a more inclusive umbrella of sexuality and gender. What could possibly unify such diverse manifestations of desire?

- The geopolitical world has grown vastly more polarized since the book came out, revealing itself to be a binary that's nearly as powerful as the gender binary itself. This update explores the meta principle that links gender and political ideology.

- And speaking of political ideology, what is the place at the table of sex-and-gender activism in a coalition of the margins? What do sex and gender activists have to offer other activists? I've got some thoughts on that—rudiments for a politic of desire to supplant both identity politics and politics of power.

- Ever since I wrote the first *My Gender Workbook*, I've been traveling around the world and through the interwebs, conversing with people who've taken gender a whole hell of lot further than I'd ever dreamed was possible. I've been taking notes. You'll find a lot of their words and ideas throughout this book. My hope is that by the time you're done reading this book, you'll have found at least one person's voice in here that echoes your own.

Finally, I've updated the formatting of the book. I'm using more illustrations to . . . well, illustrate some finer points and/or just for the fun of it.

I'm retaining the use of multiple voices in the book, some of which will pop up next to related text. And occasionally, there will be pages of tweets arranged by topic, and formatted like the stream you read when you're reading Twitter live. OMG, do you still have Twitter in 2027?

These are some of the factors I've been juggling—and watching other people juggling—for the past fifteen years, and I think it makes for content that's scary, but lots of fun and lots more relevant.

A Word About Comfort

I want to acknowledge, early on in the book, that some of this exploration of gender might make you squirm, blush, giggle, or scowl. It's an uncomfortable subject, I know. I've tried to be as compassionate as I can be about the discomfort this book may cause some people, but as hard as I try to make you comfortable, the real comforting is going to have to come from inside yourself. It's taken me a long time to learn that one.

I had very little compassion for that part of myself that couldn't live up to being either a real man or a real woman. I couldn't even think of any reasons why I should be compassionate with myself. When I finally started to come to grips with the nature of my own gender, I ran into the odd position of discovering people who were much more willing than me to simply let me experience my gender quandary without judgment.

Eventually, it was a Catholic priest who taught me the value of compassion for myself. I was in AA at the time, still a guy and still afraid of dealing with acting on my transgender nature. I went on a men's retreat to a Catholic monastery. We did all the standard retreat-type workshops and meetings, and the last thing we each had to do was to sit down with a priest and go over our personal issues. The priest

No, it wasn't a Buddhist monk or nun who gave me that advice. It was a Roman Catholic priest. Don't you just love it when spiritual paths overlap?

assigned to me was an older man; I'm guessing he was in his seventies, a nice father-type guy. He asked me what was the "big issue" in my life, and I figured, oh fuck it, I'd tell him. So for about half an hour, I spilled out my transgender story. At the end of my tale, this priest looked at me—maybe his eyebrows were a little further up on his forehead—and he said, "Well, I'm certainly not qualified or experienced enough to give you any specific advice about a sex change, but I can tell you this: your comfort level is somewhere down around your ankles, and you need to do something about that." He went on to tell me that I should do at least three things a day to make myself more comfortable, and then he said, "Al, you need to learn to treat yourself like you would treat an honored guest in your house." That was over thirty years ago, and it's still some of the best advice I've ever received. Whenever I'm beating up on myself about gender stuff or anything else, I can usually get back to the point of treating myself like an honored guest.

If we don't show ourselves the same amount of compassion as we show others, we'll eventually come to resent the compassion we have for others. There's little enough compassion in the world right now, so we need to grow our own to compensate for the lack we sometimes experience from the culture at large.

Exercise: Do three simple things for yourself today to make yourself more comfortable. Just do anything at all that makes you comfortable, and do not place any stress or guilt on yourself for doing it. Repeat this exercise daily for at least a week. At the end of the week, write down any changes you notice in the way that you feel about yourself.

OK, I'll be checking in on your comfort level from time to time. But now that you've got the idea, let's take a look at how and why some people have come to question gender.

Kickstarting a Gender Journey

I sent a tweet to all the people who follow me on Twitter. Well, I don't like the idea of following, so I call them all my *twibe*. I'm including what some twibe members tweeted as a response to the question: *What's kickstarting your gender journey?*

Now, you may not have any reason to question your own gender . . . well, not yet anyway. But wouldn't you like to know more about your own gender and how it's been affecting your life? Just how freewheeling and open are you when it comes to the subjects of gender and sexuality? Do you have much flexibility when it comes to grasping the mechanics of changing genders? How about the idea of gender as a fluid state—sometimes guy, sometimes girl, sometimes neither, sometimes both? How are you with that one? Are people who mess with their gender a little crazy for doing that?

Let's find out where you might be standing right now when it comes to your own gender. Yes, you've lived with your gender all your life—so what can you *do* with it? That's called *aptitude*.

@gwenners: For me, [my gender journey] began when I asked mom for Mary Jane shoes, found out they were not for kids like me. That was it—the first moment I knew there was a difference—and the first moment I was taught I did not belong where I felt I did. I was 3-ish.

@JenInATeacup: Had to be abt age 10 when I realised all the stories I wrote were from a boy's POV, when I was a girl.

@mannaka: when I came out as queer in middle school, someone said I was "too girly" to be a dyke. That led to me wondering—what makes someone a "girl"? Or a "boy"? Or neither, both, all of the above, something else entirely??

Discovering Your Gender Aptitude

This isn't a quiz or an exam to see how good you are at gender theory. Like I said earlier, screw theory—this is a practical quiz that will hopefully help you find out more about yourself. There are no right or wrong answers. Just take your time and check off the answers that most nearly match the way you feel about each question.

When you're done, you'll know your GA—your Gender Aptitude—and from there, we'll go on a little journey together through previously unexplored and underexplored areas of gender through the lenses of identity, desire, and power. Now, doesn't that sound exciting? I should think so! All right, let's begin.

QUIZ: YOUR GENDER APTITUDE

SECTION I: ASSUMPTIONS

Which of the following most accurately describes something that you assume is true about yourself?

☐   A.   I'm a real man.

☐   B.   I'm a real woman.

☐   C.   I'm not a real man or a real woman, but I'd like to be.

☐   D.   None of the above. I'm something else entirely.

Give yourself 5 points if you checked A, 3 points if your checked B, 1 point for C, and no points for D.

Write your score for this section here: _____

So . . . Are You a Real Man? A Real Woman?

That seems to be a simple pair of questions. It's not surprising that most people would smile and say, "OF course I'm a real man," or "OF course I'm a real woman." It's just not something most of us question.

The difficult part comes when we're asked to remember the times we've been made to feel we're not quite as manly or masculine, or as womanly or feminine as we could be . . . or even should be. Maybe it was the day we found ourselves deeply afraid or weeping uncontrollably, and we (or someone else) questioned how much of a man we really are. Maybe we've not been able to get pregnant, or maybe we haven't wanted to, and we (or someone else) questioned how much of a woman we really are.

There are a lot of rulebooks about gender—but no one has ever written a rulebook that works for everybody everywhere. Gender universality breaks down when we ask the simple questions of what it is that constitutes a "real man," and what it is that constitutes a "real woman." All of us have learned and continue to learn our genders by trial and error. We all must build our own definitions of real manhood and real womanhood, and we're very pleased to know people who agree with our definitions. When

I was told that I looked like a boy, I walked like a boy, I acted and moved and spoke like a boy. I threw a ball like a boy, but I was never called a boy, unless it was a mistake made by a witless stranger, at which time I was expected to correct him at once. Then, it seems, I was to feel embarrassed and vaguely sinful, all for some unknown purpose, mostly because we were Catholic and it felt good.

The torment of a tom-boy is this then, to be told these countless times to act like a lady, walk more like a lady, yet having legs that do not seem to bend quite like a lady's leg should, and hair that would not lie or curl quite like a lady's hair would, and did this mean I had to quit hockey and forget how to throw a ball? All this disturbed me greatly and did not begin to make any sense until years later.

—Ivan E. Coyote

enough people agree with us, we begin to assume it's *natural*. Well, if gender is so natural, why hasn't it been written down and codified?

Most everything else that's considered "natural" has been codified. Why isn't there some agreed-upon manual we could hand our youth and say, "Here, honey. This is what a real man is. Learn this well." Why do we mystify these categories to such a degree that we assume "everyone knows" what real men and real women are? Let's keep looking at your gender aptitude when it comes to the subject of these categories called "real men" and "real women."

QUIZ: YOUR GENDER APTITUDE

SECTION II: PERCEPTIONS

1. **Do you stand up to pee?**
   - ☐ A. Yup, most of the time.
   - ☐ B. No, never.
   - ☐ C. Well, I've tried it a few times.
   - ☐ D. It all depends on the effect I want to create.

2. **Have you ever worn the clothes of "the opposite sex"?**
   - ☐ A. Never have, never intend to.
   - ☐ B. Yes, but when I wear them, they're for the right sex.
   - ☐ C. What sex in the world would be opposite of me?
   - ☐ D. Several of the above.

3. **Do you shave?**
   - ☐ A. Yup. Except when I'm growing my beard or mustache.
   - ☐ B. Depends. I go back and forth on hairy armpits and hairy legs.
   - ☐ C. I have lots of places I could shave if I wanted to. Sometimes I want to, sometimes I don't.
   - ☐ D. I shave other people.

4. **When you go into a store to buy clothes for yourself, do you shop mostly in a department labeled for your assigned gender?**
   - ☐ A. Well, duh! Where else?
   - ☐ B. No, because sometimes the other departments have stuff that fits me better.
   - ☐ C. Yes—for some reason it's very important to me to do that.
   - ☐ D. I will shop in any department for anything that's fabulous.

5. **Are there things you can do in the world because of your gender that others can't do because of theirs?**
   - ☐ A. Yes, but that's just the way the world is.
   - ☐ B. Yeah, but they get paid well for doing what they can do.
   - ☐ C. I used to think so.
   - ☐ D. Honey, I've never let a little thing like gender get in my way.

6. **Are there things you can't do in the world because of your gender that others can?**
   - ☐ A. No. Well, maybe I can't have a baby, but who wants to? Ha ha!
   - ☐ B. Well, duh. Of course!
   - ☐ C. I used to think it was because of my gender, yeah.
   - ☐ D. Maybe a long time ago, back before I graduated with honors from Hogwarts.

7. **When the store clerk asks, "How can I help you, sir?" do you . . .**
   - ☐ A. Smile?
   - ☐ B. Wince?
   - ☐ C. Curse?
   - ☐ D. Curtsy?

8. **When the store clerk looks up at you inquiringly and says, "Yes, ma'am?" do you . . .**
   - ☐ A. Wish you'd grown that mustache after all?
   - ☐ B. Smile?
   - ☐ C. Purr?
   - ☐ D. Brightly exclaim, "Gee, I'm sorry . . . Would you like to try for Door Number Three?"

continued next page

9. Basic black looks best . . .

☐ A. On my new BMW.

☐ B. With pearls.

☐ C. With anything.

☐ D. Well, dip me in blood and throw me to the vampires.

10. Have you read the book *Gender Outlaw* by Kate Bornstein?

☐ A. Nope. Is it a Western?

☐ B. I'd say what I really think about that book, but I'm nervous about how that might affect my aptitude score.

☐ C. Yes, and I loved it!

☐ D. I could write a better version.

Give yourself 5 points for each A answer, 3 points for every B, 1 point for a C, and no points for any D answers.

Write your score for this section here: _____.

The Elusive "Real Me"

There are lots of levels of identity. The part of you that can be named by anyone who meets you, that's an identity. The part of you that you work real hard to present to the world, that's another of your identities. Optimally, our identities are an accurate reflection of who we feel ourselves to be, and they get us treated the way we'd like to be treated. Some people give a name to the part of themselves they deeply feel themselves to be—they call it *the real me*.

There are books, television shows, college-level courses, DVDs, audio CDs, self-help groups, and cults that promise we can learn to be an identity called "the real me." Why would we need to learn to be that, unless there was so much pressure coming from the rest of the world that's making us not be "the real me."

There are obviously enough people in the world who think they're not being "the real me" to keep all the other people in business trying to teach them. People who recover from alcoholism become the real me. Lesbians, gays, and bisexual people coming out of the closet and embracing their desires become the real me. Men who learn to cry discover another kind of real me. People born again into anything from fundamentalism to feminism claim to have discovered the real me. More to the point of gender, some transsexual people believe that when they've gone from one gender to another they've arrived at the real me.

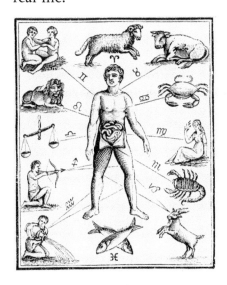

What's the real me got to do with being a "real man" or a "real woman"? And, most importantly, does your gender (identity) match up with who you feel yourself to be? Do you think your gender and the way you present it are an accurate reflection of everything you are or could possibly be? Does your gender match up with the real you? Let's see.

QUIZ: YOUR GENDER APTITUDE

SECTION III: INTEGRITY

1. **Has someone else ever accused you of being not a real enough boy/man, or not being a real enough girl/woman?**

   ☐ A. No.

   ☐ B. Yes.

   ☐ C. No, but I've felt that myself.

   ☐ D. Yes, and I've had to agree with them.

2. **You're in the middle of the sidewalk, in broad daylight. Your lover leans over and kisses you hard and long on the mouth. Do you . . .**

   ☐ A. Kiss back and lose yourself in the moment?

   ☐ B. Have a panic attack about who might be watching and what might happen to you?

   ☐ C. Thank heaven for kissable lipstick that stays on until you wash it off?

   ☐ D. Offer to sell tickets to gawking passers-by?

3. **Has it ever happened that you've been in a group of people who are similarly gendered to you, and you find yourself behaving in a way one or more of them considers gender inappropriate?**

   ☐ A. No.

   ☐ B. No, I'm very careful about that.

   ☐ C. Yes.

   ☐ D. Yes, it happens all the time.

4. **You receive an invitation to a concert. The top of the invitation reads, "All Genders Welcome." Do you . . .**

   ☐ A. Wonder why they phrased it like that?

   ☐ B. Get nervous about who or what might show up?

   ☐ C. Feel defensive?

   ☐ D. Feel included?

5. **Have you ever been mistaken for being a member of a gender other than the one you think you're presenting?**

   ☐ A. No.

   ☐ B. Yes.

   ☐ C. Yes, but not as frequently as I used to be when I was first trying this stuff out.

   ☐ D. I intentionally try to confuse people.

6. **Have you ever agonized over your appearance to the point of canceling a social obligation because you feel you don't look right or won't fit in?**

   ☐ A. No.

   ☐ B. Yes, I've agonized, but I haven't canceled.

   ☐ C. It doesn't have to be some social obligation; sometimes it's just easier not to leave the house.

   ☐ D. Yes.

7. **Have you ever been discriminated against, harassed, or attacked because of your gender presentation?**

   ☐ A. No.

   ☐ B. No, I've been careful.

   ☐ C. Yes—it happens to women every minute of every hour.

   ☐ D. Yes—it happens to a lot of us.

8. **Is acceptance by or membership in some boys'/men's or girls'/women's organization important to you?**

   ☐ A. I hadn't really thought about that.

   ☐ B. Yes.

   ☐ C. Yes, but I don't hold out much hope for that.

   ☐ D. No, we're starting our own.

9. **Which of the following most nearly matches your definition for the word transgender?**

   ☐ A. Some disorder that results in women looking like hot, young guys and men cutting off their penises.

continued next page

☐ B. Being born in the wrong body, or having the wrong sex for your gender—and you fix that.

☐ C. Transgressing gender, breaking any rules of gender in any way at all.

☐ D. Shifting from your birth gender to any of several other genders whenever, in whatever fashion, and for as long as it pleases you.

10. Which of these phrases describes you most accurately when it comes to rules about your personal behavior and identity?

☐ A. The rules work for me, and I don't really see that gender rules hurt anyone anyway.

☐ B. I think many social and cultural rules governing individual behavior and identity are unnecessary—and some are just plain dumb.

☐ C. I'm trying to figure out which rules to follow and which rules to ignore.

☐ D. Rules? Honey, the Identity Police have arrested me so many times, they've got a cell with my name on it.

Give yourself 5 points for each A answer, 3 points for every B, 1 point for a C, and no points for any D answers.

Write your score for this section here: _____

Why It's Me Who Gets to Ask These Questions

I don't know who discovered water, but
I'm pretty sure it wasn't a fish.

—Anonymous

This is a book about gender, because gender is what I know. It's what I've been questioning and researching all my life—and I'm an old person! Thankfully, I believe in past lives, but that does leave me with having to acknowledge that gender is the primary journey I was given to make in this lifetime. The journey has been lots of fun and sometimes really dangerous.

It's all been worth it—I am so grateful for simply being who I am these days. I'm what's called a trans-sexual person. There are two culturally sanctioned genders: male and female. I was assigned one gender at birth, and I now live a lot of my life as the other gender. I was born male and raised as a boy. But it never felt right to me—I had to learn how to do boy things. It felt like I was pretending to be a boy. I was a phony. I went through both boyhood and adult manhood like that. In my late thirties, I went through a gender change and I became a woman. But it never felt right to me—I had to learn how to do woman things. It felt like I was pretending to be a woman. I was a phony. After a few years, I stopped being a woman and settled into being neither.

In the 1990s I wrote a book about gender-as-neither—*Gender Outlaw*—and since then I have happily traveled across the world to do plays, performance pieces, workshops, lectures, and campus town hall style meetings about gender-as-neither—and, by golly, the idea has been catching on.

Multiple and/or mixed up genders can be way more fun than simply either/or. When you are expressing yourself as the gender you're most comfortable experiencing yourself to be, there are more opportunities to relate with others just the way you want—and yes, that includes sexual relations. But gender doesn't equal sexual preference—well, it sort of does, but doesn't really.

For example, I've always loved women—I was a hetero, and now I'm homo. Or lesbo, I'm never quite sure. Long ago, I was living with a lesbian lover—after three years, she said she was a guy. He announced that on national television. We lived together for a few more years as a heterosexual couple, then we stopped being lovers. He found his gay male side, and I found my slave girl side. What a wacky world, huh?

Exercise: Recall any journeys you've made across identities. They don't have to be gender identities. If you can't think of any, then do you know anyone who has? Respectfully ask them what it was like. If you don't know anyone, can you imagine what it must be like for people who do have gender identity journeys? What key words would you use to describe all of these life journeys? Write those key words in the margins of this page.

Right, so you and I lead completely different lives—how could you possibly relate to what's written in this book? Because I bet a week full of pizzas that you and I have one great big thing in common with each other: both of us were assigned one of two genders at birth. No matter what else makes you and me different, we can bond over the fact that we've both had to go through life knowing we were assigned one of two genders at birth. Both you and I have had to work with our assigned genders to make ourselves a life worth living. (If you took my bet seriously, you can send the pizza to me through Routledge. They'll get it to me.)

All right—enough about me. It's time to do some more work on you.

Just Who Do You Think You Are Anyway?

You're not the same person you were ten minutes ago. None of us is. Each of us makes dozens, if not hundreds, of minor decisions in the space of ten minutes. And unless we're cut off from the rest of the world, each of us is subject to influences that can change the course of our lives. Sure, I had a sex change and, sure, that's a big deal. My question is why exactly it is a big deal compared to all the other stuff that changes in our lives.

For example—maybe someone smiled at you this morning and it made you feel good. Change. Maybe you heard something on the news that made you wonder just how much say you have in your government. Change. Maybe you've learned something new while searching online. Change. Or maybe a bird landing on your windowsill has made you change your mind about the state of your life. Change. Email, texts, voice messages.

Change, change, change.

We all go through a whole lot of changes in a very short period of time. That's what growth is all about. We're so used to these mini- and micro- changes that we give them no thought, but the fact is we're not the same people we used to be, and we never will be.

@momotroniuity:
My gender changes at a whim, Sometimes I don't even know where in or even outside the spectrum it is, but I'm still me.

@celebelei: gender changes w/my breath. Butch transfaggot rebirthed w/phoenix and the flow of rainbow faerie wings. Sun-whore of a kitten purring.

@labcoatlingerie: My best lesson from gender exploration is that even core parts of identity can change. Placed on the activist table, that reminds us that another kind of privilege or oppression might some day be ours, so look out for *everyone*.

@youlittlewonder: The main change is in the leeway I have to play w/ gender. The parameters within which I "perform" are much bigger as I grow older. The best part is that at almost thirty, I no longer have to hear "just a phase" when it comes to gender non-conformity.

We change our attitudes, our careers, our relationships. Our age changes minute by minute until the day we die—goodness knows what happens to our age then! We change our politics, our moods, and sometimes our sexual preferences. We change our outlooks, we change our minds, we change our sympathies. Yet when someone changes their gender, we put them on some television talk show.

Then again, it sure does seem to me that over the course of our lives, we—all of us—do change our genders. All the time. In response to each interaction we have with a new or different person, we subtly shift the kind of man or woman, boy or girl, or whatever gender we're being at the moment. For example, we're usually not the same kind of man or woman with our lover as we are with our boss, mentor, or parental figure.

When we're introduced for the first time to someone we find attractive, we shift into being a different kind of boy/man or girl/woman than we are with people we're not attracted to.

We all change our genders—but that's not the point. The point is that it's high time we knew what we are doing with gender and why. It's time for gender to become more of a conscious thing—less taken for granted. You can't fly a plane on automatic all the time—well, maybe you can, but I wouldn't want to be riding in it. With that in mind, let's get on with the next section of the gender aptitude quiz and see just how flexible your very own personal gender might be. Hang on, we're going to dig a bit deeper now.

QUIZ: YOUR GENDER APTITUDE

SECTION IV: FLEXIBILITY

1. **When someone you don't know flirts with you—and it's the kind of person to whom you are usually attracted—do you . . .**

   ☐ A. Immediately daydream about the great sex you're going to have later tonight?

   ☐ B. Make an attempt to get to know the person?

   ☐ C. Panic because it's been so long and you wonder if you know how to flirt any more?

   ☐ D. Flirt right back, matching move for move and words for words?

2. **When the kind of person that normally turns you off begins to flirt heavily with you, do you . . .**

   ☐ A. Threaten, or even hit them if you have to—or just because you want to?

   ☐ B. Leave?

   ☐ C. Tell them, "Honey, you flirt with this hand"?

   ☐ D. See if there's anything about it you can enjoy as long as it's only flirting?

3. **When was the last time you were aware of something about your gender that was holding you back in the world?**

   ☐ A. I never gave that much thought before—I'll need to think about it.

   ☐ B. Do you want that in minutes or seconds?

   ☐ C. Do you mean the times I did something about it, or the times it overwhelmed me?

   ☐ D. It was just before the last time I shifted my gender.

4. **How many genders do you really think there are?**

   ☐ A. Two.

   ☐ B. Well, there are two biological sexes. Is that what you mean?

continued next page

☐ C. I'm going to guess there are lots of genders and two sexes.

☐ D. When do you want me to stop counting?

5. **Do you feel it's possible for someone to change their gender?**

☐ A. No. And "they" and "their" just sounds wrong as a pronoun for one person. "They" is plural.

☐ B. I think people can try to change their gender, but no. Not really, no.

☐ C. Yes, with proper supervision, surgery, and hormones. I think so.

☐ D. How many times, in how many ways, and for how long a time each?

6. **What do you believe the essential sign of gender to be?**

☐ A. The presence or absence of a penis.

☐ B. It's some combination of genitalia, secondary sex characteristics, hormones, and chromosomes.

☐ C. It's an energy thing. People have male or female energy.

☐ D. Whatever.

7. **If someone tells you they're neither a man nor a woman, and you find out they mean it, do you think to yourself . . .**

☐ A. "This person is either kidding or is really, really sick"?

☐ B. "The poor, brave dear!"?

☐ C. "Whoa! What a trip!"?

☐ D. "I found another one at last!"?

8. **If you meet someone who you think is one gender, but you find out they used to be another gender, do you think to yourself . . .**

☐ A. "I've been betrayed"?

☐ B. "What's wrong with me that I didn't notice it myself"?

☐ C. "The poor, brave dear!"?

☐ D. "Wow—that's great—I didn't even know"?

9. **If you see someone on the street whose gender is unclear to you, do you . . .**

☐ A. Think "Freak"?

☐ B. Try to figure out if it's a man or a woman?

☐ C. Mentally give them a makeover so they can pass better as one or the other?

☐ D. Notice they're staring at you, trying to figure out what you are?

10. Is the male/female dichotomy something natural?

☐ A. Yes, without any question.

☐ B. It's possibly a combination of nature and nurture.

☐ C. Probably, but I keep seeing and reading about more and more exceptions.

☐ D. A natural male/female dichotomy? Prove it.

Give yourself 5 points for each A answer, 3 points for every B, 1 point for a C, and no points for any D answers.

Write your score for this section here: _____

Look at the Pretty Butterflies

When I wrote the first version of this book, people suggested that I write down everything I've learned about gender. Sort of do the "Everything You Wanted to Know about Gender but were Afraid to Ask" approach—with all the answers. I wasn't comfortable with that, and now I've got a good idea why I wasn't.

People like to associate a gender change with butterflies. Why? Some folks like to say it's the transformation of ugly to beautiful. Maybe in some cases that's true. Some people say it's all about the transformation from earthbound to flight—also true for many people.

Humanity has always been fascinated with the process of transformation. As children, we play with clay or Play-Doh, and we transform it continually from one shape to another. We're fascinated with caterpillars becoming butterflies. We write stories about ugly ducklings that become swans, and cars that become robot warriors. The great energy conundrum is the constant search for more and more refined ways to transform less matter into more energy with the least harmful effects on the ecosystem.

Our literature and our philosophy, our science and our folklore, our religions and our politics all boil down to some kind of transformation. Through transformation, we perceive we're alive and growing. The opposite is also true: when transformation stagnates or is blocked, we approach death of one sort or another.

Now Look at the Pretty Cocoon

We always look at what was before and what came after, but we rarely look at the act of transformation itself. Butterflies have a rough time of their transition from caterpillars. The cute li'l caterpillars weave weave weave and end up with a cocoon all around them. They transform themselves into a chrysalis, and then into a full-fledged butterfly. Now that's a lot of work all by itself—with lots of good metaphors about

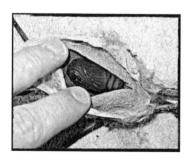

transformation—but the pertinent part comes next: they have to get out of the cocoon—they have to really struggle to get out of that thing. Now, a while back someone told me something interesting about butterflies. I don't know if it's true or not, but I like the concept, so I'm going to believe it.

OK, so let's say you're walking through a field, and you see this cocoon. It's pretty obvious there's a butterfly in there, struggling to get out. Humanitarian that you are, you bend down and very gently open the cocoon to free the butterfly. Good deed? Nope.

It seems that wise Nature has decreed that the butterfly needs the struggle. The struggle to get out of the cocoon triggers a chemical process in the butterfly that allows it to live once it's out. If you free a struggling butterfly from its cocoon, you're signing its death warrant.

That's what this workbook is going to help you discover: the sort of work you'll need to do if you want to know what lies outside whatever gender cocoon you've spun for yourself. Or maybe it's not a cocoon at all—maybe you're living in a gender web that's been spun around you. Whoops, there I go mixing metaphors—butterflies and spiders, indeed. Well, this whole book is a mix of metaphors, styles, genres, and points of view—and that should make the work more fun than simply reading words in a book. When it comes to gender, if you do the hard work of picking apart your own gender, I promise you're going to have a lot of fun, flying through the meadows of the world.

@AutistLiam: Childhood was a regular decision not to transition yet (they beat up sissy boys, pretending to be a girl is safe) then Teens— realisation that I'd rather die than keep pretending. Then I met another trans person and everything became okay.

QUIZ: YOUR GENDER APTITUDE
SECTION V: LOVE AND SEX

1. Do you have a "type" of person you regularly fall for?

☐ A. Why yes, I do.

☐ B. I try to keep my mind open about this sort of thing, but I usually fall for a certain kind of person.

☐ C. I seem to fall for lots of "types" of people, but usually they're all the same gender.

☐ D. It's not a "type" of person, but the people I fall for can connect with me, and I can connect with them.

2. If you fell in love with a heterosexual woman, would you be ...

☐ A. Pleased as punch?

☐ B. Really confused?

☐ C. Nervous as hell?

☐ D. Curious, curious, curious?

3. If you fell in love with a heterosexual man, would you be ...

☐ A. Reassuring yourself that the old Greeks had friendships like that?

☐ B. Pleased as punch?

☐ C. Nervous as hell?

☐ D. Curious, curious, curious?

4. If you fell in love with a lesbian woman, would you be ...

☐ A. Apprehensive, but titillated?

☐ B. Nervous as hell?

☐ C. Pleased as punch?

☐ D. Curious, curious, curious?

5. If you fell in love with a gay man, would you be ...

☐ A. Reassuring yourself that the old Greeks had friendships like that?

☐ B. Resigned to your fate?

☐ C. Pleased as punch?

☐ D. Curious, curious, curious?

6. **If you fell in love with a woman who used to be a man, would you be . . .**
   - ☐ A. Concerned how well she would pass in public?
   - ☐ B. Wondering why you couldn't have met her before her change?
   - ☐ C. Nervous as hell?
   - ☐ D. Curious, curious, curious?

7. **If you fell in love with a man who used to be a woman, would you be . . .**
   - ☐ A. Convinced that he's really a woman and you're not really a faggot?
   - ☐ B. Really confused?
   - ☐ C. Nervous as hell?
   - ☐ D. Curious, curious, curious?

8. **Who's ultimately responsible for birth control?**
   - ☐ A. She is.
   - ☐ B. He is.
   - ☐ C. I am.
   - ☐ D. Honey, I haven't had to worry about that one for years!

9. **I like it . . .**
   - ☐ A. On the bottom?
   - ☐ B. On the top?
   - ☐ C. In the middle?
   - ☐ D. Yes I do!

10. **Who's ultimately responsible for keeping sex safer from HIV and STD transmission?**
    - ☐ A. I am.
    - ☐ B. I am.
    - ☐ C. I am.
    - ☐ D. I am.

Give yourself 5 points for each A answer, 3 points for every B, 1 point for a C, and no points for any D answers.

Write your score for this section here: _____

No Gender is Not the Same as No Genders

If anything, no gender is all genders—and I think there are a whole lot of genders. No gender is a space containing all genders—those that exist, and those as yet unimagined. It was only when I got myself to a point close to no gender that I found myself able to pick and choose from any and all of them, without ever being stuck in one. More and more people are living within this space of no gender.

I made this point in my first book, *Gender Outlaw*, and received quite a bit of correspondence that boiled down to "Kate, you say you live without a gender—how exactly do you do that?" Well, there's a real easy answer to that one, and it's the key to the whole workbook. Ready?

The way you live without gender is this: you look for where gender is, and then you go someplace else.

At first, it's not easy to spot where gender is. Once we do spot where gender is, it's even more difficult to find a place where gender isn't. That's when this book might come in handy. But if you've got that, then you don't need to read any further. Give me a call, and let's go out for tea. However, if the maxim above doesn't make much sense to you just now, please read on, and we'll have our tea another day—someplace where gender isn't.

@RJmakes: My gender journey started when I shaved my head. When my gender wasn't obvious, I realized I had been wearing "girl" like a costume.

If you want to take a peek behind the curtain of gender as it drapes itself over not only you but also the entire globe —well, I'd suggest reading and really doing the exercises in this book. For now, let's wrap up the quiz to determine your gender aptitude.

This is the last set of questions. Then you'll get to see how you fare on the final criteria of your gender aptitude: issues of no gender. As usual, pick the answer that's closest to how you feel.

@JoelleRubyRyan: Being a TransWarrior has necessitated a spiritual journey 2 make sense of my path & 2 give me tools 2 fight for a radical new world.

@tylluan: I cannot imagine myself without my queer & crip components. Discovering the whole expansive arena of queerness & gender gave me the . . . power to artistically reframe my life; let me grow organically, non-categorically. My disability, that realm of thought, let me . . . understand myself as separate from the weights of others, & re-enter my body as the home of my self. It showed me a self . . . & let me know that it was okay; said if I wanted to, I could choose to love that self. I am a queer crip poststructuralist.

QUIZ: YOUR GENDER APTITUDE

SECTION VI: NO GENDER

1. **Which one of the following statements most nearly matches your attitude toward gender?**

   ☐ A. Gender simply is. I don't think about it, there's no need to.

   ☐ B. I've been working on my own gender for a long time, and I'm getting to the point where I may actually have made it my own.

continued next page

    ☐ C. I'm starting to wonder why gender is always an either/or thing.

    ☐ D. Gender is what happens to me when I get dressed in the morning.

2. Which one of the following statements most nearly matches your feelings about gender?

    ☐ A. I'm satisfied with my gender.

    ☐ B. I guess my feelings range anywhere from anger and frustration to sadness and apathy.

    ☐ C. Gender confuses me. I don't know why it is the way it is.

    ☐ D. I feel . . . I feel . . . I feel a song coming on!

3. Has there been any time when you've felt you have no gender?

    ☐ A. I'm not all that aware of my gender, but I know I've got one.

    ☐ B. I've got a gender and I'm well aware of it much of the time.

    ☐ C. I feel something like no gender when I'm alone or I'm in some situation where gender doesn't matter.

    ☐ D. No gender is lots of genders—that makes sense to me.

4. Have you ever questioned the nature of gender itself?

    ☐ A. The word natural comes from nature. I don't question what's natural.

    ☐ B. I question the nature of my own gender, but gender itself? No.

    ☐ C. I question gender, but I get the spooky feeling I'm not supposed to do that.

    ☐ D. The nature of gender? Isn't that an oxymoron?

5. What's the relationship between gender and desire?

    ☐ A. How could you have desire without gender? Can't be done.

    ☐ B. I hadn't thought to question that before—I thought it was obvious.

    ☐ C. Desire without gender makes sense intellectually, but my desires depend on gender.

☐ D. Oh dear. You really think a little thing like no gender is going to determine my unbridled desire?

6. **If you woke up one morning and discovered you were neither a man nor a woman, would you . . .**

☐ A. Go mad, or into hiding?

☐ B. Call friends for support?

☐ C. Read the rest of this book as fast as you could?

☐ D. Yawn and get dressed?

7. **Do you think there's some sort of connection between your gender and your spirituality?**

☐ A. My religion has rules about gender, and I mostly follow them.

☐ B. Yes, gender is reflected in yin and yang and the inherent duality and non-duality of the universe.

☐ C. Gender could be part of someone's spiritual journey.

☐ D. My gender is an expression of my spirituality.

8. **How do you deal with aspects of your gender that you don't like or agree with?**

☐ A. There's very little I don't like about my gender.

☐ B. I struggle with some ways in which I'm gender stereotyped.

☐ C. I haven't known quite what to do about parts of me that aren't right for my gender.

☐ D. I've been using a gender-changing spell I learned in some Harry Potter slash.

9. **Why are you reading this book?**

☐ A. I didn't choose to read it, that's for sure.

☐ B. I think it's important to try to understand what it is that other people experience.

☐ C. It's been dawning on me that maybe these might sort of be, well, my issues too.

☐ D. The gender-changing spell I learned doesn't always work, and this book is making sense.

continued next page

10. What would you do if you thought this book was filling your head with radical left-wing ideas about gender?

☐ A. Get rid of the book as soon as you didn't need it for class any more.

☐ B. Read the book, being very aware of the author's radical bias.

☐ C. It'd be too scary to read right now—maybe later.

☐ D. Post "Occupy Gender" all through your social networks.

Give yourself 5 points for each A answer, 3 points for every B, 1 point for a C, and no points for any D answers.

Write your score for this section here: _____

To be perfectly clear: I'm asking you to ponder your gender just the way it is. I'm not asking anyone to stop being a man or a woman. Why should I do that, if that's what you enjoy being? Transgender or cisgender, the odds are you've got—or at one time had—a gender. So, take a deep breath, because it's time to look under the hood.

Your gender aptitude score is on the next two pages!

Congratulations! You've finished your gender aptitude test! Now, go back and collect up all your sub-totaled scores for each section. Add up your score for all six sections, and find your GA on the next two pages. You have a range of possible scores from zero to 255. Now, don't fret. It's just an aptitude, and like any other part of human potential, with a little or a lot of work you can always improve. Let's see what your numbers translate into.

If You Scored 0-60, You're a Gender Freak

Whoa! This stuff must seem like kids' play for you. Either that or water in the desert, huh? Have fun reading the book any ol' way you want to. It's going to make you feel a lot less alone in the world. Tweet me and let me know if I got this stuff right, will you?

If You Scored 61-100, You're a Gender Outlaw

You've been working not only on your own gender but on the subject of gender itself for quite some time, huh? I bet things are still a bit scary and a bit serious for you in your life. If I were you, I'd read this book with the intention of getting the most fun out of it. Have a ball!

If You Scored 101-175, You're a Gender Novice

Gee, it's like you have one hand in respectability and the other hand someplace where someone else likes it. You're not always taken for "normal," are you? In fact, you probably get an infrequent but regular bout of the gender willies from time to time, don't you? Fret not. You've got a very rewarding journey ahead of you. All it's going take is some practice. Read on, read on.

If You Scored 176–235, You Are Well Gendered

Hiya, Mister Man! Hello, Ms. Lady! I'm guessing you're not reading this book to learn anything about yourself—am I right? Maybe you're reading it as a class requirement, or maybe a friend or family member wanted you to read it. Well, I think that's very commendable. Keep on reading, and do what's comfortable for you to do. I promise I'll be gentle.

And If You Scored 236–255, You're Captain James T. Kirk!

Omigod, I've always wanted to meet you! Can I have your autograph, please? Ah, Captain, with this book, you're finally going where no man has gone before. And everyone else who's reading this book will be keeping you company. How fun is that?

So, where is gender? Everyone has to find that one out for themselves. But sometime over the last fifteen years, I've discovered a piece of a map that leads you right to gender's door. It used to be a whole treasure map, but my pugs ate most of it, so there's only a piece of the map left. Ready to go treasure hunting? Watch out for pirates.

Chapter 2: Finding Gender

Arrrr, There Be Pirates!

So, is this exciting or what? A clue-filled fragment of a real live treasure map that could maybe point your way to gender. Some clues are more obvious than others. I can see sixteen of 'em—how many clues can you find? A partial list of the more obvious clues is on the next page. Read on ... and be careful—where there's treasure maps, there's always pirates.

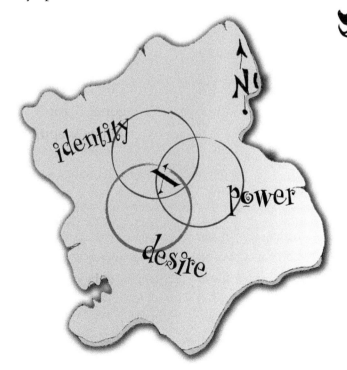

@FakeLoriSelke: Pirates are communal, live on the margins of society, value scavenging, re-use, and reappropriation. They look scary & they lack polish. I've mentioned this before: I think the best description of my gender is "pirate."

Some Treasure Map Clues

Yep, turn the book upside down.

If you're working in an ebook, you'll have to lock the page orientation first!

Each clue will help you find out where gender is. I don't promise you'll find my analysis of each of these clues in this book, but you might. After all, buried treasure shouldn't be all that easy to find, right?

1. Identity has something to do with it.
2. Desire has something to do with it.
3. Power has something to do with it.
4. The font is sort of goofy, not at all scholarly.
5. The three circles are linked in a Venn diagram.
6. X marks the spot.
7. What's the significance of the number 3?
8. The map casts a shadow on the page. Why?

Finding out where each of these clues might lead is what this chapter is all about. And yes, there are several more clues to the map, but they'll reveal themselves over the course of the book. So turn the book right side up again, please, turn the page, and let's get started!

Before we start examining the clues, I want to assure you that this is going to have some real practical value in your life—or result in some great belly laughs—or a good cry—or maybe a gasp or two of surprise. I'm happy to say the study of gender has got all of that, and then some. It starts with identity, desire, and power—these are the three spheres of life experience that make life worth living. And gender's got a grip on each one of them.

Clue 1: Identity Has Something To Do With It

Identity answers the following questions—you'll find out more about yourself if you answer them too. Keep your answers to these or any other questions as private as you like. You don't have to write them down. So . . .

Who do you want to be?

How do you want to be seen in the world?

Who are your role models?

How do you want to be treated?

What people do you want to spend quality time with?

What people do you feel an urge to help?

What qualities describe the person you most want to be?

Clue 2: Desire Has Something To Do With It

Desire answers a more difficult group of questions. Desire simply means wanting—and we can want anything at all: ice cream cones, world peace, a comfortable pair of shoes. But since this is a gender workbook, I'm going to focus on the kinds of desires most linked to gender: love, romance, friendship, sex, and family. Do your best to answer these—if any of your answers are embarrassing, you can just answer them in your head. So . . .

Who is it you'd like to fall in love with you?

What would your ideal family look like, and how would people treat each other?

What are some qualities of someone who could be your best friend?

Who do you want to fuck?

Where do you want to fuck?

How do you want to fuck?

Do you want to fuck at all?

Name three romantic things you'd like to do for someone who would appreciate them.

Name three romantic things you would appreciate if someone did them for you.

Clue 3: Power Has Something To Do With It

Power is the third space of experience that determines our quality of life. I'm going to use a social justice definition for the word and define power as fair and easy access to the resources you need to make life worth living for you and your loved ones. Power is access to resources—and power is universally the sphere of life experience that's most out of our control. Nevertheless, there are resources we need.

On a scale of 0 to 5, with zero being completely empty and 5 being completely fulfilled, how do you fare on this scale of the resources commonly required for a life worth living. Once more—you don't have to write down your answer if for any reason you don't want to.

Resources That Make Life More Worth Living	
Food	
Shelter	
Health Care	
Education	
A Job You Enjoy For Which You're Fairly Compensated	
Freedom to Travel	
The Right and Ability to Protect Yourself	
Privacy	
The Right and Ability to Practice Your Most Sacred Beliefs	
Dignity	
The Right and Ability to Say Anything That Isn't Mean	
Comfort	
Freedom and Ability to Help Others Who Lack Any of This	

Clue 4: The Font is Sort of Goofy, Not At All Scholarly

The cleric Nazrudin ran through the streets, leaping for joy.

"I'm a father," he cried. "My beautiful wife just gave birth!"

People gathered round him.

"Is it a boy or a girl?" they asked him.

"Yes!" he cried. "But how did you know?"

—Sufi folk tale

Examining the impact of gender on your identity, your desire, and your access to resources—well, that's likely to bring up some sadness and anger. And, here's where silliness and a great cheap joke come in really handy.

I'm just letting you know that I'll be going for the cheap laugh every time I can—and I promise I'll do my best to do that without being mean to anyone. So ... identity, desire, power: you can't live without 'em. But here's the scary part, the part where we need to look for comedy—it's getting harder and harder to live with 'em. On to the next clue of the treasure map: the Venn diagram.

Clue 5: The Three Circles are Linked in a Venn Diagram

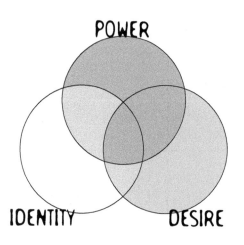

A Venn diagram is used to show exactly how two or more disparate things have something in common with each other.

By making a Venn diagram of identity, desire, and power, it makes sense somehow that they're linked. What, if anything, ties them all together to the point where you really can't increase the strength of one of the circles without making the other circles somewhat stronger at the same time?

For example: What if all of a sudden, you woke up one morning and you were exactly the person you've always wanted to be all your life—how might that affect your family life, love life and sex life? How much more able do you think you'd be to go get the resources you need in life? That's the fun part. Sadly, it seems to work out that if you decrease the strength of any of these spheres, the other two get weaker as well.

Well-aimed gendered words leave festering wounds in identity, desire, or power. Maybe that's happened to you—and maybe it wasn't because of gender.

Remember a time someone was just plain old mean to you, and it really hurt?

Have you been able to get real angry about that?

Have you gotten through the anger?

And even though you can remember all the hurt, have you gotten yourself to a place that's more at peace with the memory of someone being mean to you?

For example, a young woman is walking through the halls of her school, and suddenly she feels the words strike her: *Dyke. Whore. Slut.* Whether any of those words are true or not, that girl is not going to be feeling all that great about who she is. And she's certainly not going to be feeling sexy as those words rip gaping wounds into her sense of self. And she's probably going to feel powerless and alone. Her life may begin to feel less worth living.

I don't think you need an exercise to remember this one, but if you do catch yourself being mean to anyone—using gender or anything else as a weapon—here's something you can do . . .

What to Do When You're Mean

You apologize if you can, then you forgive yourself
for being mean, and then you promise yourself that
you'll try harder next time.

That's hard, hard work—maybe the hardest work in this workbook. OK, I lied—an exercise would be useful here. So ... EXERCISE: please highlight or circle the above paragraph, and dog-ear the page. It's that important.

Back to the Venn diagram. If identity, desire, and power are so important, what is the natural and default motive energy in all three circles? I'm going to go out on a limb and say that I'm pretty sure it's God who lets us know at a gut level what's naughty and what's nice. And you should know that I'm an atheist.

Still, I know there's something greater than all of us. I know there's something that's really big. And I know that there's a great big goodness in the world. I call it The Great Big Good—but I'll be saying God, too. So X marks God *and* the natural loving goodness of our hearts.

Throughout this book, I'm going to be making that assumption: that you have a loving heart, no matter what form that love might take. It's the part of us that simply knows the right thing to do in a situation.

That's what optimally sits in the middle of the Venn diagram: all that smart, mindful, loving energy—and everyone in the world could be going through life happily co-creating decent lives with each other.

> ### Bonus Essay Question
> Why do you suppose the world isn't all warm and fuzzy and doesn't look more like that?

Other than all those good feelings, what else is motivating or regulating our identities, desires, and powers? The answer is in the next clue on the treasure map: *X marks the spot.* Right, gender modifies, motivates, and sometimes controls identity, desire, and power.

Yep. It's really as simple as that—what's complex as hell are the implications of the fact. That's what's really going to bake your noodle. Gender calls a lot of the shots on who we are, who we love, and how much easy access we've got to the resources we need to make life more worth living for ourselves and our loved ones. What, you don't believe me? You think you're the boss of gender? Think again.

Clue 6: X Marks the Spot

QUIZ

IS GENDER THE BOSS OF YOU? LET'S FIND OUT

1. Is your gender or lack thereof part of your self-image?

2. Does your gender or lack thereof in part determine how you present yourself in the world?

3. Did you grow up in a place where most people believed that everyone—including and especially you—is or should be heterosexual?

4. Are you paid the same amount of money for the same amount of work as someone of another gender?

5. Is your health care impacted by your gender or lack thereof?

6. Are your chances for a job in any way impacted by your gender or lack thereof?

7. Do you have a preferred way to dress in order to signal to other people your gender or lack thereof?

8. Have you ever had to keep secret any desire or thoughts you have about desire for someone of the same gender as you?

9. Would it make you nervous to think about no more gender-specific bathrooms—everyone could do their business in little stalls in one great big bathroom?

10. Do you do special things in your life to make yourself be seen as more or less of some specific gender?

Now look at the next page and let's see what your pondering has perhaps led you to.

IS GENDER THE BOSS OF YOU?

If you can answer YES to six or more of these questions, then gender is messing with your life big time. And if you can answer even one of these as YES, gender is messing with your life.

What Gender? Good Question

One of the biggest stumbling blocks to the effective study of gender and sharing what we learn is that most everyone assumes that the word gender means to everyone the same thing it means to them.

That is so far from the reality of gender . . . well, it's so far from my reality of gender. So, I think it's only fair of me to tell you just what my understanding of gender is, so when I toss around words, you'll know where I'm coming from. Gender, as a puzzle, doesn't have to be that difficult a thing to solve.

I was afraid that I could never be a convincing woman, no matter what I did to my body. So I kept running away from myself and my destiny. Then I decided to do some reading-thinking. I asked myself "What is a woman?" Someone who is small and slender? Someone who is soft and pretty? Someone who has little body and facial hair? Someone who has a vagina? Someone with more estrogens than androgens? Someone with XX chromosomes?

I found that it was almost impossible to come up with a definition of a woman that wouldn't exclude a lot of women. I decided that being a woman (or a man for that matter) is a lot like being an Aryan superman—a myth. Gender is a continuum with very few people at either extreme and everybody else in the middle. At some point you just have enough characteristics of one or the other where society sees you as being of a particular gender. What do you think?

—Pat Nivins

@siniful: In high school, I discovered my father's briefcase, his initials engraved on it. I realized I wanted to be him . . . so I started to play with my gender expression. My definitions of beauty were shaped by a desire to be androgynous.

@HeatherRose23: Feeling ordinary has been one of the most extraordinary experiences I've had as a transgender person.

Solving the Gender Puzzle

So, what is gender anyway? It's not such a difficult puzzle after all.

The Not-So-Difficult Puzzle After All

DOWN:

1. Currently a system of dividing people, all of us, into one of two impossible-to-live-up-to standards: male or female.
2. Something that Ken and Barbie dolls have, even though they have no genitalia.
3. A means by which we can express our sexual desire.
4. A means by which we can attract others to whom we are attracted.

ACROSS

2. A fanatical cult, demanding blind obedience to mostly unwritten, unagreed-upon rules, regulations, and qualifications.
5. Any standard (usually, but not necessarily biological) by which we can easily and without much thought conveniently divide the human race into two neat parcels (e.g. sociological gender, genital gender, chromosomal gender, psychological gender, hormonal gender, et cetera, ad nauseam)
6. An oppressive class system of two, and two only, classes, usually held in place by the assumption that the class system is "natural," in which system one class has nearly total economic and political power over the other.
7. A means of cultural traction; an identity or persona by which to either identify oneself to another, or maintain some position within a relationship or culture.

Answers at the end of the chapter.

Now that wasn't very hard, was it? Of course not! Where gender begins to get difficult is when we mix sex into the equation.

She has sex, but no particular gender.
—Marlene Dietrich really said that about Greta Garbo

Everything You Need To Know About Sex Versus Gender—Honest!

Gender and sex are two distinct phenomena working in any given culture as well as in and on our minds. Gender and sex obviously influence who we are and how we relate to others. The concepts referred to by *both* words tend to get jammed into one word, "sex," as in:

> **What sex do you think that person over there is?**

or

> **Would you like to have sex with that person over there?**

The concept of gender is muddled enough without our confusing it with something entirely different like biology. Sure, some people differentiate sex and gender by saying things like:

> **My sex is male, but my gender is woman.**

But why not say:

I'm a woman with a penis.

For so long, we've bought into a biological imperative that has labeled genitalia as "male" or "female"; and what's more, we've dignified that imperative by giving it its own word: *sex*! Anyway, who says penises are male and vaginas, vulvas, and clitorises are female? "Sex" as a designation of biological gender says it.

I don't get it. I know too many male men with vaginas and too many female women with penises to any longer buy into some wishful thinking on the part of old-guard scientists who'd like to have things all nice and orderly in some predictable binary. For a long time, we've tried to explain two different, admittedly related concepts with one word: sex. We need to pull them apart if we're going to make any sense of it.

Gender is real easy to sum up in one word: categorization. Anything that categorizes people is gender, whether it's appearance or mannerisms, biology or psychology, hormones, roles, genitals, whatever: if we're trying to categorize or separate people out, it's gender. So where does that leave sex? Sex is fucking: any way, shape, or form, alone or with another or others. Once we've got *that* distinction, things start to clear up. Let's do a little chart thing here to sort it all out. The following chart is light on the sex components, which are covered more in depth in Chapter Sex. I mean Six. Yes, Chapter Six.

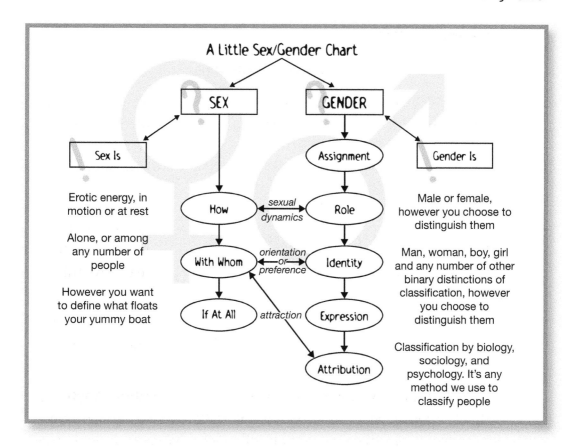

A Little Sex/Gender Chart

Please Use <u>Sex</u>
Only When Speaking of Fucking

The world becomes a lot brighter when we say that sex is simply the act, or the energy. Sex does *not* mean the designation of category. Taken in this light, sex has only a few aspects, chiefly: how you'd like to do it and whom (if anyone) you'd like to do it *with.* This breaks down into a great many more components, which you can find right now by skipping ahead to Chapter 6.

In this book, I'm going to use the word *sex* to refer to erotic energy at rest or in motion. It doesn't work to call gender by the same word we use for fucking and so on. Using the word sex *only* for fucking and so on robs essentialist thinkers of their gendered biological imperative —which is usually based on some arcane combination of genitals, chromosomes, hormones, and reproductive ability. Who says that biology has the last word in determining someone's identity anyway? It's one thing to say that someone has a vulva, vagina, clitoris, breasts, ovaries etc. It's quite another thing to assume that person is either female or a woman.

Components of Gender

1. **Gender Assignment** answers the question "What do the authorities say I am?" In most cultures, it's the M or F designation. What the doctor says you are at birth, usually determined by the presence (male) or absence (female) of a penis. Most cultures assign some permanent, immutable gender at birth. A few cultures allow people to change their gender assignment later in life; some cultures even build in a possible switch in gender assignment. Gender assignment is something that's done *to* each one of us, long before we have the ability to have any say in the matter.

2. **Gender Role** answers the question "What does the culture think I should do with my life?" It's the sum total of qualities, mannerisms, duties, and cultural expectations accorded a specific gender.

3. **Gender Identity** answers the question "Am I a man or a woman or something else entirely?" Most people don't think about this one very much. They let gender assignment non-consensually stand in

for gender identity. But identity *is* personal; it's what we feel our gender to be at any given moment. Sure, this feeling might be influenced by biological factors that have a cultural tag sticking out of each one of them. The feeling of being some gender might also have to do with a sexual fantasy, or a preference for some role. There are as many good reasons for having or choosing a gendered identity as there are people.

4. **Gender Expression** is how we show to the world the gender we feel ourselves to be. This can shift over the course of our lives, or even moment to moment.

5. **Gender Attribution** is what we all do when we first meet someone: we decide whether they're a man or a woman, or something indeterminable. We attribute a gender to someone based on an intricate system of cues, varying from culture to culture. The cues can range from physical appearance and mannerisms to context and the use of power.

The fear is worst before the fact. Until the first time someone burst out laughing at me, I didn't know how I'd survive the humiliation. Until the 1st time I had to refuse in public to fulfill my gendered duties, I didn't know how I'd ever face my friends again. Until the 1st time I was beaten up, I didn't know how I would have survived the trauma. But now I know what it feels like to be laughed at. It is frustrating, but not frightening. Now I know that I can stand up and refused to play gender games in public, even if I turn beet red as I do so. Now I know that even broken bones don't hurt forever.

Fear? There is always fear. Anything new is frightening. The only way to get over a fear is to shut your eyes and ignore the pit in your stomach. The second time you do it the pit will be smaller and one day you will have trouble remembering that what you are doing used to be hard.

—Laura Franks
Moscow, Russia

Exercise: Ask three different people how they would define for themselves the five components listed above. How do their answers compare to (a) your perception of each person and (b) your own answers to those questions as they apply to you?

Where It Gets Messed Up

I know that I will externally and internally always be a "woman," even though I'm not sure what a woman is or what a man is anymore. I'm just glad for the fact that many of us have both characteristics.

—Mara Oong

In the majority of cultures in the world, the socially acceptable, easy way to define one's **sexual preference** or **orientation** (who we want to be sexual with) depends on the *gender identity* of our sexual partners. To make things worse, the gender identity we're attracted to must also be phrased in terms of men and women. We're attracted to men or women or both—that's the sum total of our desire. So sex (the act) becomes hopelessly linked to gender (the category).

And what about sexual attraction? That's linked to **gender attribution**, usually (but certainly not always) based on a person's **gender expression**. First we attribute a gender, then we decide if we want to be attracted to that person; but the first filter is almost always "Is that person the right gender for me, sexually and romantically?"

Finally, what we enjoy actually *doing* sexually, **the sex act itself**, often involves a specific sort of genital play, and as genitals have been gendered in this culture, so sex has become gendered.

Once you add sex into the gender mix, instead of the nice, easy gender puzzle we had before, we end up with a puzzle that looks more like the scary looking thing on the next page.

Can you find the thirty-two gender-and-sex-related words in this puzzle? It can be done, but wasn't the first puzzle a lot easier? And I only used a few of the words we can mix up in our lives! For a list of the words hidden in this puzzle, turn to the end of the chapter.

The Much More Difficult Puzzle

```
I L G A U N P U K Y J Y U O O O H T Z P A E L F N W I P Q H
W T A N D R O G Y N O U S Y F E I E H A T W V F X E D R U O
R H P S W Q X J V M F F D Y D C M W W J C C Q D V N Y B M M
E E E F Y Y M P Q K F P U D E D G B A T T R I B U T I O N O
T T R A N S G E N D E R I G S Z M R E V L V H X M K V B K S
I W P O C U O C G F V Q N L I K M O R O O A Y W N L B J G E
T K E X P R E S S I O N A I R U U D X R E B U O U G I K I X
S Q P F J C Q V Q G J R I E E Z C H I K L R S X H L Y G R U
E Z V N F F X Q W P V H B R T N C K V O B C N F E J X R B A
V A T T R A C T I O N P S A O O N J I P G V W L V S M J K L
S K S G N I K G A R D D E Z V N P X J Q Z W X I T P I J K R
N Y Y A I N I D J W Y Y L H N E E U Q G A R D K K A O B J V
A D G G U H E T Q Z K B J C B J E J Y N G N F E M I N I N E
R H G E N D E R Q U E E R I J N I Q A I U Q O F N T M T P B
T V A X J L Y T N I X O R C R Y Q R R N A A A K S A E L O Q
J Y M N X U B T T M E S G T C O D L K T H K L Y B O Y I X N
A Z X V D C B G G U N G G K C I M D Y U K S C P F U I P P P
Z B Q Y O S E A Y M N A P V U C E A B U T C H R D P I L U G
H E Y K M U O Y U D K L D L B D B W N D P L D E F J A J N F
Y V Q T E Z Z M E I N T E R S E X L L C Z F R T J R W W U Z
Z L Q D P E I W E N K F Y A P G X H Z D E H A T I S O H Y F
S R R B O L A N R E H E E F E M I O A X A I Z Y Q O Y X P C
G P K I Z F T Z K B L Q H E N A B D Q Q H V V Y O B M O T R
L X O M G F N E V O M B T M K S Q I C A E V O L J H T I U G
Y J J B Z Y Z L X T U C I M U C T W Z I A V W E H M O J Q O
X T J F N R L F W T A I Y E A U V V W A F Q T C S D E N U C
I U O W G F T R Z O O A O F G L H E T E R O S E X U A L E H
M G S K I N H F I M N N X I P I P O T E Q E Z E A F L W E G
A Y U I I G Q A T G B N A G D N N F N E V B A Z R G A Y R G
H J E N J F H T N Q M N L N C E L V H B A V H X W J Z O P Z
```

No wonder people want to use the term "sex" for both the identity (gender) and the act (sex). The two have become interdependent. In terms of our sexual desire and our gender identities, we've opted for the easy way out, the "everybody knows it's this way" solution. "Everyone knows that the way I define my desire is by the gender of my partner." Personally, I can't buy that.

The Easy Way Out is Neither Easy Nor a Way Out

If the world's great thinkers have taught us anything, it's that we rarely achieve personal fulfillment by mindlessly wandering through life, taking the path of least resistance and little or no responsibility for our actions. We need to question our assumptions, and that includes our assumptions about sex and gender, if we're going to understand those aspects of ourselves and others.

Gender: Identity as Armor?

I've been living on the border of the two-gender system for nearly three decades. More and more frequently, I manage to escape the system entirely. I claim no socially sanctioned gender, and I'm trying to retrace the steps it took for me to arrive at this point. I think it comes down to an understanding of gender as simply one aspect of identity. Gender is a kind of identity, that's all.

The question "How do you live without a gender?" broadens into "How do you live without an identity?" We forge our identities, or actively fortify the identities we seem to be born with in the same manner and with a similar purpose, as an armorer forges a suit of armor for a warrior. The problem is, once the suit is fitted, you'd better not get any bigger or smaller. Identity isn't us.

It's *safe* having an identity—it's secure. It's safe having a gender. But there's a price for that safety and security within some hard shell. We can't grow any more. Our identities become so hard and so restrictive that we can no longer stretch and explore—we can't find new ways of experiencing the world, new ways to delight ourselves, new ways to please others. We're frozen in that shell. And the only thing for it is to come out of that shell, leave it behind us, and begin the whole process over again.

Connecting With Your Inner Gender

Hahahahahaha! No way. I'd never inflict anything called an *inner gender* on anyone. But the fact is if we want to connect with gender, then we need to connect with it on a deeply personal level. Connecting with gender on a purely social, intellectual or political level isn't going to bring about a personal understanding of the subject.

We can read about gender and identity for all our lives. We can study it, put it under a microscope, talk with people about it, and see endless movies about this stuff, and we won't really know any more about gender and identity than we did when we started. We'll be more curious, uh huh. We'll be a lot more apprehensive about the traps we've read about, perhaps. But we won't really know anything. Not until we experience gender—consciously—ourselves.

It's when we begin to poke around in the piles of accumulated emotions, mannerisms, attitudes, and values; it's when we really let ourselves look at what we've gotten ourselves into—that's when we can begin to get some clarity on gender. That's when we can construct a gender identity for ourselves that best lets us express our needs and wants in this world.

I was on a radio talk show out of southern Florida once. The (white, heterosexual male) host literally wouldn't let me say on the air I'm not a man or a woman. He accused me of living in some fantasy world. ::shrugging:: What can I say? To some degree he was right. But what good is a fantasy if there's never any hope that you can one day live it out?

The Ten-Minute-a-Day Gender Outlaw Exercise

Here's a simple, basic exercise. It's one you can do once a day. It doesn't have to take a long time. Each day, take one or more of these three questions, and write down a series of answers.

What is a Man?

What is a Woman?

Why do we have to be one or the other?

The trick is that the answers have to be phrased in questions, like the television game-show *Jeopardy*—it works best to keep the questions open, which is where I think they belong. It doesn't matter what *track* those further questions take, just as long as more questions come out of it, to a point where the question itself is enough and you don't need to write any more.

So, one day it might look like this:

- **What is a man?**
- What's a woman, for that matter?
- What's a boy?
- Was I ever a boy?
- What was it like to be treated like a boy?
- Did I like it?
- What did I like about it?
- How do I like to be treated today?
- Does that make me a boy, still?

Another day, it might look like this:

- **What is a woman?**
- Why am I even bothering to ask that?
- Doesn't everyone know what a woman is?
- Who the hell is everyone anyway?
- What business of theirs is it to tell me what a woman is?

And still another day, it might look like this:

- **Why do we have to be one or the other?**
- What other choices are there?

Or you may go on asking questions for pages and pages. The point is to get to a question you want to think about some more, one that really tickles your brain; something you can ponder on for the balance of the day. Once you get to *that* question, you stop. That's all there is to it. Try it every day at first. It's a good discipline for learning to explore one of the most basic facets of our cultural identities. Once you've gotten into the routine of asking these questions, well, then you can taper down to once every couple of days, to once a week, to once a month, as the questions begin to linger. But for now, make it a point to ask yourself one of these questions every day for one month, and to answer it *only* with other questions. Mark it on your calendar. Start today, okay?

Now you know what gender is. You even know where to find it. The trick now is to find somewhere else to go—somewhere where gender isn't. That brings us to the next clue of the treasure map. In any equation, X is used as a symbol for a specific number—sometimes known, sometimes unknown. In our treasure map, what is the quantity of our X? That's right—there are still lots of pirate clues to follow, in order to find the treasure!

Answers to The Not-so-Difficult Puzzle (Page 46):

1. gender, 2. (across) gender, 2. (down) gender 3. gender, 4. gender, 5. gender, 6. gender, 7. gender.

And . . . Solving The Much More Difficult Puzzle (Page 53):

Please don't feel bad if this one made you stumble. It's hard.

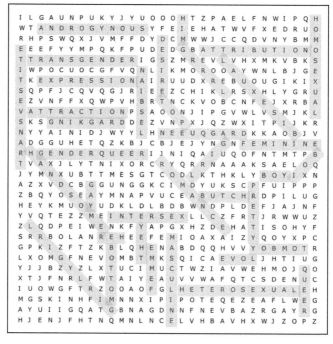

Chapter 3: Let X=X

Okay, so we know that gender is X. Gender lies at the nexus of identity, desire, and power. We know that gender is calling the shots of who you can be, who you can love, and what resources you can access to make life worth living for yourself and your loved ones. If all of this is true, then the following equation is also true:

| The Great Big Good | Your Kind Heart | X (gender) | A Good Life for Everyone |

Oh, if only. But, that's just plain silly! If that equation were true, then all we'd have to do is hand out copies of this workbook to everyone in the world and life would be paradise for everyone. (Actually, it's not a bad idea to get a lot more people thinking about gender—that would tend to ease some suffering.) But gender isn't the only factor calling the shots.

As if juggling our own notions of identity, desire, and power wasn't complicated enough, there are many other factors we juggle at any given time that guide, influence, or regulate our lives and the way we, in turn, treat other people.

So the X in our gender equation is going to remain a variable number. It's different for everyone—people are like snowflakes that way. Here's a short list of factors that—in addition to gender—do more than meddle with our lives. Each of these fifteen factors—listed in no particular order here—tries to regulate our lives with its own rules.

☐ gender   ☐ sexuality   ☐ language

☐ race   ☐ looks   ☐ habitat

☐ age   ☐ disability   ☐ citizenship

☐ class   ☐ mental health   ☐ political ideology

☐ religion   ☐ family/repro-ductive status   ☐ humanity

Exercise: Get a pencil, please—the kind with an eraser—because you're going to want to come back and do this exercise every now and then. Please take a moment and rate each of the factors above on a scale, from minus 5 to plus 5. Minus 5 means it's completely controlling your life for the worse, 0 means it has no discernible effect on your life, and plus 5 means it's making your life a whole lot easier and more comfortable to live. Write your numbers in the box next to each of the words.

You Know Gender by the Company It Keeps

RACE is one of the first things that many of us use to put people into a box the moment we see them. Like every other factor on the list, race is a system of classification by which we categorize people into large and distinct populations or groups—each with its own mythical stereotypes.

According to my last look-see at the Race Wiki page, race is determined at least in part by "heritable phenotypic characteristics, geographic ancestry, physical appearance, and ethnicity."

Race may or may not be visible, but to the degree that race is known and/or visible, race alone can limit who you're allowed to be in the world. Race alone can drive a wedge between you and a loved one. Race can help you get a job, and race can keep you from getting one.

AGE is a determining factor in how seriously we're taken, how strong or weak, and how smart or stupid we're presumed to be. Young and old both come with rules regarding when, how, and with whom we're allowed to have sex. And age is a power on/off switch in almost any family, school, group, or nation.

CLASS "is relative status according to income, wealth, power and/or position." That's Betsy Leondar-Wright's definition of class, from her book *Class Matters*. Many people visualize class as rich or poor, bosses and workers, 99 percent and 1 percent. Well, yes and no, depending on the sphere you're examining. For example, you are part of the 1 percent on the planet who's privileged enough to be reading this book. Your class dictates just how much access you've got to food, shelter, health care, and education. Class alone can be responsible for an inflated or deflated view we have of ourselves. Love, sex, and romance are closely monitored by the class police. So . . . how many classes can you name in this illustration? How many more can you name that aren't in the picture?

LOOKS—to what degree is a person attractive or not—is rarely viewed as a serious system that regulates the quality of life. But the rules of who looks good and who looks bad goes right to the heart of body image, sometimes resulting in eating disorders, and always impacting our sense of self-worth. How we look affects our belief in ourselves as sexual beings. Our looks can be a determining factor in the kinds of jobs we get or don't get—or the club memberships we're offered or denied—or the kind of bullying and harassment we're subjected to.

I've been advised by my twibe on Twitter to use the word **DISABILITY** to describe the space that regulates a person's status according to the degree that everything about their bodies works efficiently. Or not. Cory Silverberg calls it *Embodiment*, implying more agency. Fact is, everyone is or will become disabled, and depending on the condition of your body, you could be viewed as an imperfect person. Maybe you can enter, occupy, or leave most any place at will, or maybe you've been forbidden entrance. Your good health or lack of it—your mobility, or sight, or hearing, or feeling, or erectile capabilities, or allergies, or pimples—will totally skew your odds for a date on Saturday night and also impact your access to all of those life-fulfilling resources we talked about earlier.

MENTAL HEALTH is a space that's often conflated with Disability—but by golly . . . the notion and reality of madness and visions and voices and holy states of ecstasy comprise only a small part of the vast number of configurations possible in the grey areas of mind and psyche that we demean with the impossibly inadequate words "mental health" and "mental illness." We're all mad in some way. For some of us, our madness makes a long-term relationship impossible. For some of us, our madness means we have no idea how you feel unless you spell it out to us in words we can understand. For some of us, our madness gets us stripped of all our rights and dignity and thrown into the hospital. Yep, mental health is a concept used to regulate. If you're a mad thing like me, you know what I'm talking about. If you think *none* of this applies to you, may I respectfully suggest you get into therapy. No, really.

FAMILY AND REPRODUCTIVE STATUS—The communally held idea of a nuclear family unit hasn't been a reality since it was first dreamed up in the 1950s. I should know—I grew up in it. Today's family configurations range from the sublime to . . . well, the more sublime. Lots of genders, lots of partners, lots of happy kids. Ever since the days of *The Scarlet Letter*, living in a relationship that's anything less than *Leave It To Beaver* perfect (google it—it's an important cultural reference point) . . . anything less than a legal marriage with kids like that can get you labeled outcast, pervert, or unfit to adopt children. Trying to explain your no-parent home to your friends can get you laughed at or pitied. As to reproductive status—google *"Roe v. Wade."* Or look at how people talk behind a childless woman's back. Now, google *"Roe v Wade* + misogyny." And now, google "pregnant men."

What **LANGUAGE** are you reading in this book? I wrote it in English. A couple of my books have been translated into Swedish, Italian, Portuguese, Korean, and Japanese. I'm guessing you could hack into an ebook version of this book, extract the text and run it through a translator—but there are nuances in my English that wouldn't make it through to the reader. Not to mention all the fucking profanity in this book.

@AutistLiam: Being trans is a mental illness the same way my PTSD is—it's a perfectly rational response to a highly unusual situation. Take any cis man and any cis woman and "bodyswap" them, they'd feel pretty bad with unexpected body parts & hormones too. As an autistic person, it makes lots of sense to me that a brain can have expectations and be very distressed when these aren't met . . . And I see being trans very much like that. My brain needs things to be thus and so and I'm distressed when they aren't.

Bonus question: Which people in this illustration are getting married?

Profanity—now that's a language that can get you into trouble, right? Will fucking with language most certainly reflect on your perceived identity? Yes, in-fucking-deedy.

I've chosen the word **HABITAT** to stand in for the space that regulates the impact upon your life of geography, ecology, climate, shelter, and neighbors. Habitat includes words such as *urban*, *rural*, *suburban*, *the sticks*, *the hills*, *the prairies*, *the mountains*, *downtown*, *uptown*, *Main Street USA*, *wasteland*, and *Garden State*. Habitat includes words such as *hillbilly*, *city girl*, *redneck*, and *yankee*.

Habitat means "Do we have to sweat out earthquake insurance, or flood insurance, or is there going to be another tsunami, or do we live next door to a nuclear power plant?" Habitat means that where we live impacts who we are—it gets us pegged as a stereotype, and that stereotype affects our love lives and our ability to put food on the table for our families.

CITIZENSHIP exists for no other reason than to fence you in to the majority rule of the country you live in. It's an outdated way of saying, "This land is my land and anyone who lives on it has to do what I say." As I'm writing this workbook in 2013, the internet is eroding state boundaries. Some people, like me, think that's really cool. Some people think that a one-world government is a sign of the apocalypse. Citizenship means more or less accepting and abiding by a set of laws, economy, values, rights, and borders. Citizenship means your identity has to be legal, your love for another or others must be sanctioned by the state, and you get what resources you can squeeze out of the system.

I'm calling it **RELIGION.** I thought about calling it Spirituality, or Spiritual Ideology, but what I call spirituality is any path by which we connect with whatever it is we call the something that's great, and bigger than all of us, and really good. I call it The Great Big Good. More on that later.

Religion is specifically a prescribed and often ritualized path, usually with the aim of that sort of connection to God or Goddess, or Mother Nature . . . there are lots of pathways all laid out, each of which is ready to show us the way to enlightenment and right living. I am not being snarky here. As far as I can tell, the existence of religions is one of the main reasons we haven't all burned up in some nuclear holocaust. But religions come with responsibilities, rules, must-do's, should-do's, and mustn't do's.

Religious doctrine gives us a shortcut to discovering what's right and what's wrong—and that's a lovely thing for people who are mostly right in the eyes of their religion. The problem comes when we're doing something that's not mean to anyone and our religion calls that bad. The other side of that coin is when we do a really mean thing and our religion says that's a good thing to do. Sometimes our religion tells us how to vote. Sometimes our religion tells us whom,

@ariel_silvera: Religion has not figured in my gender but faith/belief in role models, fictional and real, has been vital. Iconic gender-variant characters, kickass female characters, and of course amazing queer/feminist/trans artists/writers/fighters.

@Jen_Lillie: if God can be genderless why can't people be too?

@sassafraslowrey: my #spirituality= deeply rooted in the velveteen rabbit's definition of becoming REAL by love not birthright just like my #gender.

@wordscanbesexy: my gender is only as political as I exp oppression around it. Since xition, misogyny and trans misogyny are in my daily experience.

@drum4ica: Gender politics confuse my gender: not girl enough not boy enough not queer enough not trans enough.

@labcoatlingerie: My #identity wasn't #political until someone said I couldn't have it.

how, and when we can fuck. And sometimes the simple proclamation of our religious beliefs can get us harassed, beaten, or murdered.

SEXUALITY is different than gender, but as elements of desire they're closely related. Sexuality is ostensibly no more than who, how, when, if, and where you want to fuck, fall in love with, marry, or make a family.

But those private decisions can get us into a lot of trouble, and I mean really. . . homophobia is so gay. And what about the fact that monogamy is taken for granted? Why? And what's so bad about not wanting sex right now—or ever? Sexuality includes all these and more. Revelation of our other-than-culturally-sanctioned sexuality can get us harassed, beaten, or murdered. Sexuality alone can deprive us of or entitle us to property, civil rights, social status, employment, health care and privacy.

POLITICAL IDEOLOGY—alternately World View—is often a stamp of identity, especially in a highly politicized and/or polarized environment. What kind of world do you want to see humanity build for itself? How does your ideal world differ from the reality of the world we live in? Can you find voices that express your world view in mainstream media? Or do you have to go looking in far-flung corners of the internet to find ideas that match your own? How does sex fit into your world view? Out in the open? Behind closed doors only? How is the expression of difference dealt with in the predominant political ideology where you live? Do you have the same rights and resources as someone living within the space of another political ideology?

Yes, **HUMANITY** is what it all boils down to, but I'm interested in exploring what it is that makes us human—and what it might be that makes people less human in the eyes of other people. Does your use of or reliance upon a cell phone, laptop, or a wheelchair make you more of a cyborg, and less of a human? When does artificial intelligence stop being artificial? These are real questions being asked by smart people —totally worth a google.

AND ALL THIS BRINGS US BACK TO GENDER, WHICH is, of course, another space of regulation that never stands apart from any of the others. And that gives us a model by which we can measure cultural impact on our quality of life. Here's what you and I look like, under the constant bombardment by powerful cultural influences.

@JoelleRubyRyan: My gender is seething: enraged at marginalization, systemic discrimination, polarization, division, dehumanization, violence & hate.

@Siniful: I think being an atheist helped me observe what *is*, rather than have prescribed notions to how the universe works. Observing what *is* requires listening. Listening to our bodies, our loved ones, and finding Truth in those things. Listening has shown me that there is more than just the gender binary. Multitudes more. And it's beautiful.

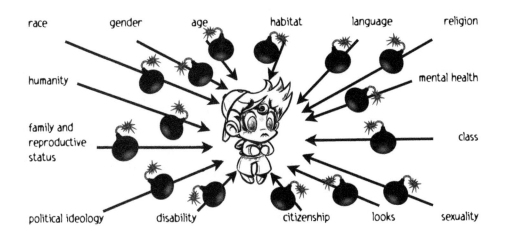

race   gender   age   habitat   language   religion

humanity   mental health

family and reproductive status   class

political ideology   disability   citizenship   looks   sexuality

Exercise: How to Spot the Bombs Coming at You

Here's something else you can observe by using this as a cultural model: not only do these spaces of regulation issue orders to our identity, desire, and power—they give rules to each other. Here are a few examples:

1. Your race can influence your political ideology.

2. Your age tells you how to behave sexually.

3. Your mental health may impede or enhance the practice of your religion.

4. Your citizenship controls your family and reproductive status.

5. Your class tells you how well you can express your gender.

Now, you fill in five more examples of your own:

6. _____

7. _____

8. _____

9. _____

10. _____

How to Spot the Bombs Coming at You, Part 2

Compare what you've found with the treasure-seeker doing this exercise nearest to you. What are the similarities and differences between what you wrote and what they wrote? How did it make you feel about the other person, knowing what they wrote down? Ask them how it made them feel about you.

Given this model of multiple spaces impacting our lives, finding gender in all that mess isn't so much like peeling back layers of an onion or opening a cocoon as it is freeing a bird that's trapped by dozens of creeping vines. We're no longer juggling what really matters in life. It's all most of us can do to juggle the rules coming from whatever it is that lies behind each of those fifteen real-life spaces that regulate and shape the course of our lives.

With all that going on, there's not much opportunity or time to think about who you are, how you'd like to fuck, or where you can get the week's meals—is there? Well, here's a koan I learned from Zen Buddhist Master Cheri Huber. It's gonna help, I promise.

The Way You Do Anything is the Way You Do Everything

Here's what that means: essentially, everything you do in life is a sort of rehearsal for everything else you do in life. And every principle you find in life is going to find an echo of itself in every other principle you discover in life.

The way you do anything is the way you do everything. How is this particular koan pertinent to this workbook or our treasure map? Well, many basics that apply to gender as a space of regulation may very well apply to each of the other spaces that regulate our lives. In other words, the more you learn about gender, the more you may very well learn about race, class, age, citizenship, political ideology, and all that jazz. So now, let's explore some of the basics of gender that might help us get out of line of fire of all those culture bombs.

Exercise: Google the word "koan." No, really. You're going to be writing your own koan in the last chapter, so you may as well get familiar with the concept. When you're satisfied you understand what a koan is, have another look at the koan on the previous page. Mull it over for a good three minutes. Write down your observations here in the margins of this page, then dog-ear this page.

Advanced Exercise: If you can, compare your observations with someone else who's mucking about in this workbook. See if you can read each other's observations without making any judgments about yourself or each other. Practice this exercise some more until you get better at making fewer judgment calls.

So what meta principles apply to gender that might apply to other spaces of regulation? First and foremost, gender represents itself as a binary. A binary is a space that contains only two elements. These elements are equal and opposite to each other in every respect. And they are the only two choices in that space. In gender, the binary is male and female. And whaddaya know . . . each of the other spaces is most usually seen as a binary.

Given the multiplicity of many real gender binaries—man-and-woman, boy-and-girl, crone-and-curmudgeon, lady-and-gentleman—and a lot more that I haven't listed—is it possible to say with conviction that gender as man-and-woman is truly the natural binary? On the next page, see if you can spot the assumed "natural" binary in each space of cultural regulation.

Exercise: See if you can match the binaries below with the spaces that contain them. Draw a line connecting the space with a commonly associated binary.

1. Gender	A. Homo or Hetero
2. Race	B. Rural or Urban
3. Age	C. Male or Female
4. Class	D. Able or Crippled
5. Religion	E. Saint or Sinner
6. Sexuality	F. Left Wing or Right Wing
7. Looks	G. Young or Old
8. Disability	H. English or I just don't understand you
9. Mental Health	
10. Family/Reproductive Status	I. Black or White
	J. Machine or flesh-and-blood
11. Language	K. Patriot or Traitor
12. Habitat	L. Ugly or Beautiful
13. Citizenship	M. Married with Children or Single and Barren
14. Political Ideology	
15. Humanity	N. Rich or Poor
	O. Sane or Insane

(1. Gender → C. Male or Female)

Did you find that exercise frustrating? Was it too simple for you? Were the binaries somehow wrong or incomplete? Well, you're right on all counts. But people still insist that binaries not only exist but are the true representation of the space they alone somehow define. Let's focus back in on gender for a moment.

Here's a double-trick-reverse-question for you. If I took a great big balance scale, and I put a pound of feathers on one side and a pound of lead on the other side, which would weigh more? If you said that a pound of feathers and a pound of lead would weigh the same in that balance scale, you'd be wrong.

I warned you—this is a double-trick-reverse-question. I promise that the simple act of you breathing on the scales would have blown a feather or two off, and the lead would weigh more.

And what's the lesson? The only space in which two elements of a binary can be truly equal is in a vacuum. And gender doesn't exist in a vacuum—it's subject to both influence and control by every other binary in a culture.

The truth of gender is that there are white men and black men, and because of the racial component, these are seen and treated by the dominant culture as two different and unequal genders. A rich woman who owns everything, a poor woman who works three jobs, a trophy wife, and a roller derby girl—that's four different and unequal genders. A trans guy with all his mental faculties intact, and a trans guy with PTSD or bi-polar disorder, or eating disorder, or any of hundreds more challenges to mental health—all would be seen and treated by the dominant culture as different and unequal genders. So, please remember the basic principle you can apply to any binary: the only time that the two-only elements of a binary are truly equal is in a vacuum—when they exist completely by themselves, with no outside influences.

Is there any *natural* binary in nature? I haven't found one in over fifty years of actively looking. Seems like everything can be broken down into more and more components than just two. Even gender. Let's take this again, slowly and in more detail. But first, have fun with this puzzle.

FIND THE TWINS!
WHICH TWO ARE EXACTLY ALIKE?

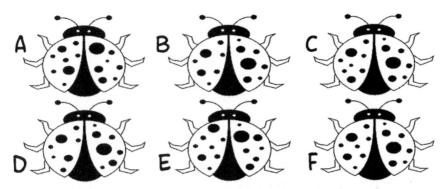

Answer: none of them match exactly, just like real life. Too bad.

A binary is two—and two only—whatevers, and they are supposed to be equal and opposite in every way. In the gender binary, that would mean men and women. Really?

Is there anywhere in the world where men and women are equal and opposite in all three spaces of identity, desire, and power? Really, can you name me a town where that's the way life is—men and women completely equal in every single way? How about a family? Can you think of one family where men and women are equal in every single way? How about your own family? No, the search for a natural binary is sort of like the search for Bigfoot or the Loch Ness Monster.

So am I saying there's no such thing as a natural binary? Yes, that's what I'm saying. If you think you know one, tweet me @katebornstein, and I promise I'll answer you. Really—one simple binary in nature that's two, and two only, and equal and opposite in every respect. I haven't found a single pair in all my years of looking. And this brings us to the next treasure map clue: the significance of the number three.

Clue 7: What's the Significance of the Number 3?

The introduction of any third factor into a space that's defined as two and two only will break that space and leave it powerless. That's the value of three: it really fucks with the false value of two. If this makes sense to you, you have just deconstructed a binary. *Deconstruction* is a word that belongs to the field of *postmodern theory*. And raising the subject of postmodern theory brings us to the inevitable and valid question: *Who gives a fuck about postmodern theory?*

Well, I think that postmodern theory put into practice is exactly what's going to take our culture in the direction of more freedom of identity, desire, and power for everyone. If that's even remotely possible, then try out this little three-minute lesson in postmodern theory, and I promise it's all you'll ever need to learn. Get this one down, and you'll wow your professor, guaranteed. Ready? Here we go.

@msmanitobain:
I would like a gender-traveling machine, like time-travel. Or, maybe persona-traveling. I don't like being stuck in one "gender."

@grapedrink: It's complicated to occupy both spaces, but it seems like they've begun to overlap now more than ever! :) I say this as a nerdy/geeky pansexual.

@thejoseebear: [I am] genderqueer. There is so much more to me but I love the beauty of ambiguity.

Say you walk into a room—any room. What might you see? Let's keep it simple. Most anyone walking into a room would see a ceiling, a floor, some walls—maybe there's a man and a woman in there too. That would be a perfectly true thing to see and to say. Well, a postmodern theorist might walk into the same room and say: Yes, there's a ceiling, but it could be part of the floor upstairs.

I see a floor, but I also see wood planking, and what is probably part of the ceiling of the room downstairs. Yes, there's a wall, but the wall is also an opening into the next room, so the wall is also a door. There are two people, sure, but we don't know their genders. We do know that they are someone's children. One of the people could be a woman, or a trans woman, or a trans man. Each person is definitely someone's child, but either could be someone's son or daughter or girlfriend or boyfriend or all of the above.

So postmodern theory is little more than the notion that objects and ideas can have more than one—even paradoxical—meanings, all at the same time, depending on context. Simple.

Right, so now you've got more tools—call them tracking devices—for gender. You know that gender is one of many spaces of regulation that pose as binaries. You more or less know how to deconstruct a binary. And you know that anything—gender included—can have more than one meaning, depending on its context. SO . . . on to the next exercise.

Exercise: Next to each of the following words, describe in a few keywords how—in your life—that space of regulation reinforces the gender binary of man/woman.

RACE

AGE

CLASS

RELIGION

SEXUALITY

LOOKS

DISABILITY

MENTAL HEALTH

FAMILY/REPRODUCTIVE STATUS

LANGUAGE

HABITAT

CITIZENSHIP

POLITICAL IDEOLOGY

HUMANITY

It's Movie Time!

That's right, grab yourself some popcorn and go watch the Disney/Pixar film *WALL·E*. Even if you've seen in before, have another look. No, really—do that right now, and then come back and we'll have a heart to heart about this impossibly-gendered love story—because, silly rabbit, robots have no gender.

I'm completely smitten with *WALL·E*. But when I went to see the film when it opened in 2008, the last thing I expected to see in my friendly, heterosexual upper east side Manhattan neighborhood movie theater was a feature-length cartoon about a pair of lesbian robots who fall madly in love with each other. *WALL·E* is nothing short of hot, dyke sci-fi action romance, some seven hundred years in the future! Woo-hoo!

Isn't that what you saw?

No? What movie were you watching?

Did you see a heterosexual boy robot fall in love with a heterosexual girl robot? I did . . . at first. And it makes sense how someone could assume that. I mean, *WALL·E* is a sweet little guy, right? He's all "gosh, shucks," and shy around girls . . . a real warm-hearted guy, right? And EVE! Is she adorably kick-ass hot and fierce, or what?! OK, I confess: when I first saw the film, I saw a boy robot and girl robot. My question is this: how and why did most of us jump to that conclusion?

Is it because of their names? The names sound like Wally and Eve, but their names are very specifically WALL·E and EVE, all in capital letters—because both names are acronyms for each robot's prime directive and function. Nothing to do with boy or girl there.

The film makers take a great deal of care in pointing out that WALL•E and EVE's notion of butch/femme romance is based in the world and culture of the film musical *Hello, Dolly!* And *that* is supposed to be a cue for the audience to believe they're a "healthy" heterosexual male and female couple. But it's not proof that they are male or female. And anyway, how camp is *Hello, Dolly!*?

Is it that simply by looking at the robots, we can tell that WALL•E's a boy and EVE is a girl? What was it up on that screen that defined the robots' gender? Both robots were naked, so we could see their entire anatomy, right? Neither of those robots had a vulva or a penis. Did you see one or the other? Neither robot was sporting an Adam's apple. Neither EVE nor WALL•E flashed a breast or nipple that I could see. So, we've got no way to spot those robots as male or female by using secondary sex characteristics. But still, most of us would swear on a stack of holy bibles or holy *Gender Trouble* that those robots are male and female. How did we most of us come to agree on that?

What's the gender of this robot? Why do you think that's the case?

Both EVE and WALL•E have cute little storage compartments right where their internal reproductive organs would've been had they been human. I'm guessing neither robot has a DNA strand, so there is no way to type them by XX or XY—not to mention over a dozen more X, Y, and O chromosome combinations that determine any of the fifteen human genders found in human nature. So it's not sperms and eggs nor X's and Y's that are making EVE a female and WALL•E a male. Barring hormones—which I didn't get a whiff of during the entire film—that just about exhausts the physiological basis for determining gender.

Pixar and Disney made a great many anatomical choices when they designed EVE and WALL•E to be as close to human as they can possibly be and still be robots. They didn't give us one single anatomical clue to the gender of these cute li'l robots, but they knew we'd see WALL•E as boy and EVE as girl. Both of 'em are gosh-darned CUTE, right? Oh, come on. You know they're SO adorable, right? How can they be that in nearly everyone's eyes . . . gay or straight? I think the answer is that we shift our mind's criteria for gender when we watch a film or listen to a love song or read a novel. We all blithely switch genders in our minds, the better to identify with the vocalist or character. Reading novels, listening to music, or watching films, we consciously or unconsciously switch the gender mix to what delights us the most.

What's the gender of this robot? Was it easier to assign a gender to WALL•E and EVE? Why?

We want to identify with the singer of the song or the one being sung to, so we make the genders "right" in our minds. For example, there's a wonderful song by Tegan and Sara, *I Know I Know I Know*. I first heard it as soundtrack music during a very heterosexual moment on *Grey's Anatomy*. No surprise then that what I first heard in that music was a girl singing a bittersweet love song to her boyfriend. Then I bought the song from iTunes, and I played it over and over. It became easy for me to hear the song as a girl singing to her girlfriend, and suddenly I could enter the music as opposed to being outside the music, listening in. It wasn't until several months later that I found out that Tegan and Sara are sisters . . . and they're both lesbians! Sometimes, art is so powerful that it trumps gender as a pathway to love and romance in our hearts and minds.

Marlene Dietrich in a tuxedo can make many hearts flutter. So does Mx. Justin Vivian Bond nowadays, in a gown or a tux—or both at the same time. Gender ambiguity—when it's safely positioned onstage or up on a movie screen—is and always has been sexy to damn near all

Can you spot who's butch and who's femme in this picture? I bet you can!

of us, no matter what our gender might be. All of our desires are being tickled. So how's that happening? What is it that's signaling sexual attraction to an audience with such a wide range of gender identities and sexual desires? I think the answer is that WALL•E is butch, and EVE is femme, two genders defined by the expression of strong, respectful sexual desire.

Butch and femme are sexy dance steps with unlimited variations. Butch is gallant, femme is gracious. Butch is hail and hardy, femme has wicked cool wiles. Butch is handsome. Femme is pretty. Butch/Femme is all about relating to each other like gentlemen and ladies—no matter our genitals. Butch is Stanley Kowalski, femme is Blanche DuBois. But in a production called *Belle Reprieve,* Stanley was played to perfection onstage by handsome, butch lesbian Peggy Shaw. Beauteous drag queen Bette Bourne played Blanche. They were perfectly butch and femme.

Butches can be dominant or submissive, strong or weak, honorable or complete rats. So can femmes. Butch and femme have nothing to do with who makes more money. And no one in real life is a hundred percent butch. No one is a hundred percent femme. Like everything else about our identities, butch and femme are all a matter of degree based on preference, comfort and choice. There's no perfection in the dance—there's only the totality of self-expression and how that self-expression dovetails with someone else's self-expression. When people play with that consciously, it's wonderful fun. At its best, butch/femme becomes an erotic expression of "This is how I'm femme, and it makes me really happy that I delight the butch in you" and "This is how I'm butch, and it makes me really happy that I delight the femme in you."

There is no singular archetype of butch and femme. The belief in the notion that there's a right way to do butch and a right way to do femme begins perhaps with mythological, fictional, or cultural archetypes, which over time become accepted unconsciously as "normal" in a given culture. For example, weak, defenseless or predatory femme is imposed as "normal" behavior for females in a hetero-normative, sexist culture. Strong, stalwart, and silent or brutal butch is imposed as "normal" behavior for males in a hetero-normative, sexist culture. Like in campy *Hello, Dolly!*

Can you spot who's butch and who's femme in *this* picture? This one is a bit more difficult, but I bet you still can!

Yes, EVE is pertly streamlined. EVE's eyes literally sparkle and dance. EVE giggles, for heaven's sake. EVE is kick-ass strong and powerful. EVE is performing femme. WALL•E is rugged and protective and shy and loyal. WALL•E is a sensitive little thing, held together by sheer will and rubber bands. WALL•E is performing butch. Once we begin to look at the characters as butch and femme—not male and female—we can assign to them any gender we like. Sure, the film can be about a boy robot and a girl robot. But how about EVE as a sweet femme boy robot?

And WALL•E is a sweet butch girl robot, with a heart of solid gold, like performer/chanteuse extraordinaire Lea Delaria? You could watch the film with that interpretation of the characters. WALL•E and EVE are best mates and they love each other. They hold hands. That works.

When the only gender clues present in the film belong to the genders butch and femme, then the movie could be about two boy robots—a younger version of the gay male couple played by Nathan Lane and Robin Williams in the film, *The Birdcage*. Fierce femme and strong gentle butch, both of 'em boys. WALL•E works just as well with that configuration of robots—if you want it to. You're the audience. You get to decide.

This isn't Disney's first whack at the cultural gender binary. *Mulan* is a film about a female to male cross-dresser. And what about *Pinocchio*? An animated block of wood spends an entire movie trying to become a "real" boy—aided by a blue fairy and cricket of undetermined gender dressed in male clothing.

And what gender exactly was Ariel (a non-gender-specific name, by the way) when that little mermaid had a fishy tail? Did she go through a gender change when she grew legs which (presumably) had something between them so she could be a "real" girl? And getting down to basics, can anyone prove that Mickey and Minnie Mouse are male and female?

I'm delighted to see Pixar/Disney's blow to the binary gender system. It's a brilliant film on many levels. I bet you—no matter your gender or sexual orientation—you'll fall in love with how those robots fall in love with each other. I sure did. OK, then. Wasn't that a fun break?

OK, this is the most difficult one so far. Who's the butch, and who's the femme? Answer: it's hard to tell. Some butches wear dresses. Some femmes like boy clothes. Ours is a world like WALL•E's, that way: sometimes it's just hard to tell

Why was gender buried and hidden anyway? Is gender so valuable that it's a treasure that *needs* to be hidden away? Why are there pirates, and who the fuck are they? *Omigod, am I a pirate?* Then why don't I know where the buried treasure is? I am sooooo confused.

Chapter 4: Let Why Equal Why

All of Blu's questions can be answered with one more question.

Why Is Gender?

We know that there is a gender—it exists, it's real. But we don't really give much thought to *why* gender exists at all. Well, a whole lot of what goes on in the world depends on the existence of gender. We know *where* gender is—we've uncovered it. What's more, we've discovered that it's not what it seems at first glance to be. So, *why* is gender? Maybe the symbols we use for gender will give us a clue as to why gender

@stella_zine: [I am] interfaith ♥ white ♥ working class ♥ femmey ♥ dom-top-ish ♥ sober ♥ genderqueer ♥ queen-boi ♥ strap-on cockrocker ♥ former sexworker ♥ undoing racism.

exists at all. After all, symbols are usually devised to express a direction, a concept, an action, or a value. Just how they reveal those expressions depends on the sort of symbol we use.

Some symbols would be fairly clear to anyone who can see them, like these:

We can look at these symbols and get a rough idea of what they stand for. Other symbols are baffling until we've been taught what they mean—then we can see why the symbols are used, and they make sense.

Still other symbols are baffling, and they don't make much sense even after we learn what they mean.

The symbols recognized for gender in most areas of the world don't represent gender as we've come to look at it now. There's more than two.

Over the ages, people have devised symbols to express more than two genders—and they make sense as gender beyond a binary, but they still don't express exactly what gender is or why it exists in the first place.

Yep, the spiral is an old, old symbol for people who sport both male and female genders—perhaps taken from a conch shell. Interestingly, writer Neil Gaiman chose the spiral as the sigil of his character, Delirium, who is the embodiment and force of madness itself.

Now, some people symbolize gender as a gradient scale—shades of grey.

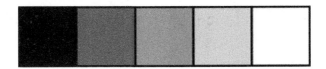

But that still leaves us with the assumption that there are two poles: black and white. Well, I think I've come up with a damned good model for a symbol that says what and why gender is. I'm a raging foodie, and so . . . yes! It's the old US Food and Drug Administration's food group pyramid!

Eat My Gender!

It's not the *perfect* symbol for gender, but it's awfully close. I'm trying to symbolize gender as both a space that contains infinite binaries and components, and as a space that regulates identity, desire, and —especially—power.

@QueerKidJess: My gender is mine and I want to own it even if it scares me, even if people don't understand or believe me. I'm non-binary and I'm real.

@thebeardlessone: I'm not really exploring gender, I'm staying exactly where I am while people draw maps saying that right here be monsters. I am agendered, Asexual, autistic, trying to live life with no regrets. Things I've not spotted, #sexuality edition: Polysexual, Multisexual, [x]romantic [y]sexual, demisexual, grey-a.
Ask me about these. Oh, and is genderblind a #sexuality? Worried to tell people about my #gender because they'll blame it on my #mentalhealth problems.

Remember the old food group pyramid? At the very top are sugars and fats—don't eat too much of them, they're not all that good for you. Next level down are dairy and meat—you can eat more of those, but not a whole lot. Next down are fruits and vegetables, and all the way at the bottom are complex carbohydrates: have a ball, eat 'em all. Well, gender works something like that, and this image expresses *why is gender*.

From a purely social justice point of view, gender confers or withholds power. And it's not based purely on man or woman—we've learned that there are shades of gender, depending  on the presence of other spaces of regulation, other vectors of oppression. So a symbol for gender would look like this pyramid—where height represents power and width represents the number of people who've got that power. The top's got all the power, the bottom's got all the people. And it's not a matter of having all the power or none of the power. There's a gradient. Yep, I like this symbol. We can get some work done with this symbol.

The pyramid, filled with a gradient scale from black to white is one of the symbols that's going to make even more sense the more we learn about it. Take a look at the way tippy-top of the pyramid. See how those two lines converge into a point? Let's call that point the perfect gender—that gives us a starting place.

We know that an identity of "perfect gender" would confer the most power upon a person. So, what are the components of a perfect gender? And how can we describe that perfectly gendered person without using gendered words such as man, woman, male, female, masculine, feminine and so on? Easy-peasy lemon squeezy . . . here we go. We simply ask: "Who's got all or most of the power—the best access to resources?" Now we can describe the perfectly gendered person.

white
citizen of the USA
Protestant-defined Christian
middle aged
upper class
heterosexual
monogamous, monofidelitous
able-bodied and of sound mind
tall, trim, and reasonably muscled
attractive, according to
cultural standards
right-handed
well-educated
well-mannered
professional or executive level
politically conservative
capitalist

self-defining and self-measuring
physically healthy, with access
to health care
in possession of all rights
available under the law
free and safe access to all
private and public areas
as allowed by the law
property owning
binary-oriented
logical (linear thinking)
lives in a wealthy suburb
possessing a well-formed,
above-average length penis,
a pair of reasonably matched
testicles, and at least an
average sperm count
legally married, and parent of
more of the same

Exercise: Add some more factors that would confer power upon this lone perfect gender. Write your answers in the margins of this page.

And now we've got a better picture of gender in the world—the more perfectly gendered you are, the more power you have. Please don't have the least concern if you think you're not perfect. No one is. It stuns me that most everything in the culture forwards this ideal gender identity and its exclusivity. Who's doing that? Have a look at this version of the gender pyramid by Diane DiMassa. She drew this back in 1997, and it still holds true for today. That's art for ya. And that's how embedded gender is in our culture.

Warning! Gender Pirates Be Here

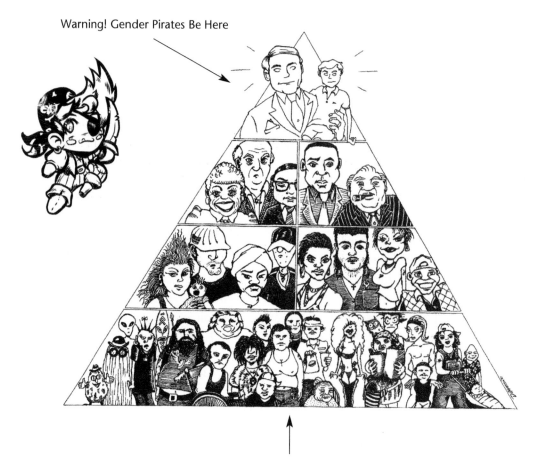

Yay! Gender Pirates Be Here, Too!

The Case for a Perfect Identity

The dynamics of the pyramid work so that nearly everything in the culture pushes us to:

- be some perfect gender (probably impossible for most of us)
- be like that gender (possible for a very few people)
- be liked by that gender (possible to many, but not all people)

What's more, the further removed we are from the qualities expressed by the top of the pyramid, the less and less our gender is perceived as real. For example, if our genitals are in any way anomalous to the prescribed genitals for our gender, well that obviously makes us unreal men or women, right? Similarly, if we're in our late teens or early twenties, we're told we're not-quite-men and not-quite-women; we're told we'll grow into that.

No, I'm not going to try to name it beyond referring to it as the Perfect Gender. I'm sure by reason of my own cultural indoctrination that I've left out some of its defining qualities, maybe important ones. But we can each of us give it a name if we want to, all the while listening to the names that others have given it. But enough theory. Let's get back to pirates. We've found the treasure, and it's gender. OK, why is it a treasure? On to the next clue, me hearties!

Clue 8: The Map Casts a Shadow on the Page. Why?

(Answer on the next page)

Answer: *Because our pyramid exists in more than two dimensions of the culture it simultaneously permeates and towers over.*

The Perfect Identity

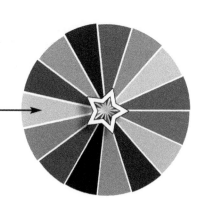

OK, now we're taking an aerial look at the pyramid, which shows itself to be more of a cone—and it's got fifteen triangles making up its sides. One of those triangles is gender. Another triangle could be race. Another side of the conical pyramid could be age, or class, or religious beliefs. There are so many ways to classify people, but the tippy top just happens to remain the same: the Perfect Identity. At the top we'd have the Perfect Gender and the Perfect Race, and the Perfect Class. So, the culturally-agreed-upon standards of perfection just might all converge into one identity that's got the bulk of the power in the world, and that identity relies on its granted perfection from each of the classifications that support it.

Looking down from the top, from the viewpoint of this perfectly identified individual, each side of the pyramid can be defined by some aspect of classification by the standards of the top's own claimed perfection. This is how folks at or near the very top see the rest of us. The conical pyramid has fifteen sides—one for each space of regulation—with the same person on top who's not only perfectly gendered but also of the perfect race, class, age, citizenship, religion, sexuality . . . and so forth.

@sassafraslowrey:
i play w/ age like i play w/ gender. weird femme exterior, internal peter pan little boy. don't let dresses fool you, i'm no princess

@Jared Fladeland:
As I understand the laws of the universe more, I understand that age, race, gender, sexual preference . . . These are all words, and Words are merely pointers to help us understand what we mean. My age, as a shaman once told me, is thousands of years old, because I carry my ancestors with me always. And my gender/ preferences cause such confusion that I simply say: I'm in love.

Could the very top of the pyramid reflect a possible common source of oppression for many if not most oppressed groups? I think so. What do you think? Does this shift the way you see and experience gender now? If so, you're getting closer to discovering why gender is truly buried treasure, and we're getting closer to discovering the pirates who buried it. Arrrr.

The posited "perfect identity," this powerful oppressive force made up of the composite perfections of all systems of classifications, has got a lot of names today. Feminists call it MAN. Jews have called it GENTILE. People of Color call it WHITE. Bisexuals, lesbians, and gays call it STRAIGHT. Transgender folks call it CISGENDER. In this binary-slanted world, we keep naming our oppressor (someone or a group who has more power than us and is using that power to withhold access, resources, or wealth) in terms of some convenient opposite. On the other side of the fence, we have a tendency to call our gender or identity the "good" gender or the "good" identity. "Transgender is better than cisgender because blah blah blah."

We have to knock that off, all of that good-and-bad way of thinking. It's a tactic of the privileged to name others by using themselves as a yardstick. We need to realize that no single attribute gives a person enough power to oppress us. No single quality of identity resulting in a privileged status gives a person enough power to keep the rest of us in thrall.

@xmandymitchellx:
I try to make porn that is honest in some way, that genuinely feels good to make & watch, & perhaps causes people to expand their horizons. I feel so alienated from mainstream culture or ideas that it would be impossible for me to try and create fantasies palpable to the masses. Sorry that sounds weird. What I mean is I can't seem to make porn that is focused on earning profit. There has to be some compromise. Or at least that's what I tell myself to justify getting whatever I want.

Just something to think about, that's all. Try it out for yourself. See what it's like to devise other faces to this pyramid, other systems of cultural regulation that haven't been mentioned so far ... see if it holds up for you. But for now, let's get back to YOUR gender, shall we? It's the moment of truth, *The Big Exam.*

Are You Perfectly Gendered?

@ClosetedTrans: people see me, my body w/out a binder (i cant get one), my hourglass shape i cant hide. they tell me i must be a girl. Who ... me? im a boy.

Well, of course you're not perfectly gendered. But let's just see how close you get. The first quiz in this book was to determine your aptitude for playing with gender; it was about your potential. This one is going to take a look at how you stack up in terms of gender perfection right now in your life.

IMPORTANT: Parts of this test might make you angry, left out, sad, or lonely. Take notes in the margins if it does. Part of the work of this workbook is to find out the places that are scary, the places that are shameful. It's an important step in making gender exploration safer. I promise, later in the book, you'll examine what's scary with an eye to defusing the fear. For now, it's time to be really honest. Just check the answer that's most accurate, okay? Please google any terms you don't know. If you're reading an ebook, try the dictionary function on words that don't seem to make sense.

 This isn't gonna be a fair test. I wanna get that out in the open from the start. But it's written in the same way that we're tested every day of our lives in this culture, so if it's not fair, it's an accurate measure of where we stand in the world, and that's the purpose of this test. The good news is that it will be a pretty fair score measuring where you stand gender-wise in terms of being a real man or a real woman. OK ... let's find out just how perfectly gendered the world thinks you are.

THE GREAT BIG GENDER EXAM

SECTION I: YOUR BIRTHRIGHT

A. Penises

1. Were you born with and do you still have a penis?

   ☐ a. Yes, with a matching set of testicles, thank you.

   ☐ b. Yes, and I was reborn with a vulva and a vagina.

   ☐ c. No, or No, I got mine later.

Note: If (c), skip to sub-section B. "Other Genitals." Otherwise keep going.

2. Is/was your penis:

   ☐ a. A bit larger than average?

   ☐ b. About average?

   ☐ c. Smaller than average?

3. Do/did you and others think your penis is/was attractive and well formed?

   ☐ a. Yes.

   ☐ b. Most of the time, yes.

   ☐ c. No.

continued next page

B. Other Genitals

4. Were you born with and do you still have a vulva, vagina, and clitoris?
   - ☐ a. No.
   - ☐ b. Yes.
   - ☐ c. Yes, but that's not all I've got.

5. Do you or others think your vulva, vagina, and clitoris are attractive and well formed?
   - ☐ a. Yes.
   - ☐ b. No one's complained yet.
   - ☐ c. No.

C. The Rest of Your Body

6. Could your race be described as white or Caucasian?
   - ☐ a. Yes.
   - ☐ b. No, but people think I am.
   - ☐ c. No.

7. What's your age?
   - ☐ a. 35+ years old.
   - ☐ b. 25–34 years old.
   - ☐ c. Other.

8. Would others describe you as:
   - ☐ a. Fit and trim?
   - ☐ b. In pretty good shape for your age?
   - ☐ c. Fat, skinny, or otherwise out of shape?

9. Are you free of any chronic or congenital diseases?
   - ☐ a. Yes.
   - ☐ b. I don't know, or I'm not sure.
   - ☐ c. No.

10. Do you have, or have you ever had a sexually transmitted disease?
    - ☐ a. No.
    - ☐ b. I don't know or I'm not sure.
    - ☐ c. Yes.

11. Is there some disease which, by reason of family history, you're susceptible to contracting at some point in the future?
- ☐ a. No.
- ☐ b. Don't know or not sure.
- ☐ c. Yes.

12. Do you have what might be considered a mental disorder?
- ☐ a. No.
- ☐ b. Possibly, I don't know.
- ☐ c. Yes.

13. Are you under professional care for, or currently taking medication for some mental or emotional problem?
- ☐ a. No.
- ☐ b. No, but I used to be.
- ☐ c. Yes.

14. Are your hormone levels balanced according to the current medical standards for the gender you were assigned at birth?
- ☐ a. I'm just going to guess they are.
- ☐ b. I hope so.
- ☐ c. No, or I doubt it.

15. Are your "gender" chromosomes either XX, if you were assigned female at birth, or XY, if you were assigned male?
- ☐ a. I assume so.
- ☐ b. I hope so.
- ☐ c. No, or I doubt it.

16. Is your body capable of reproduction according to the gender you were assigned at birth (high healthy sperm count or good quantity of healthy eggs)?
- ☐ a. Yes.
- ☐ b. I don't know or I'm not sure.
- ☐ c. No.

17. Is your corpus callosum the proper shape for the gender you were assigned at birth (tubular for male, bulbous for female)?
- ☐ a. Yes, or I assume so.

continued next page

☐   b.   I hope so.

☐   c.   No, or I don't give a rat's ass.

18. Are you:

    ☐   a.   Right-handed?

    ☐   b.   Ambidextrous?

    ☐   c.   Left-handed?

19. Would you be considered disabled by many people, either by reason of your senses or the shape or configuration of your body?

    ☐   a.   No.

    ☐   b.   Yes, but people might not know at first.

    ☐   c.   Yes.

D. Interactions

20. Do others sometimes take you for a gender other than the one you were assigned at birth?

    ☐   a.   No, never.

    ☐   b.   Sometimes and/or when I was a child, yes.

    ☐   c.   Yes, frequently

21. Do others sometimes take you for a gender other than the one you wish to present?

    ☐   a.   No, never.

    ☐   b.   Sometimes, but not frequently.

    ☐   c.   Yes, frequently.

22. Are you considered by others to be:

    ☐   a.   Handsome?

    ☐   b.   Beautiful?

    ☐   c.   Plain, average, or unattractive?

23. Do you think others would describe you as:

    ☐   a.   Having an ideal height?

    ☐   b.   Having an average height?

    ☐   c.   Too short or too tall?

24. Do you dress with some awareness for your safety?

    ☐   a.   No.

☐ b. Depends on where I'm going.

☐ c. Yes.

25. Do you dress with some awareness of compensating for some flaw in your appearance?

☐ a. No, never.

☐ b. Sometimes.

☐ c. Yes, frequently.

26. Do you generally feel safe walking alone on the streets of a city?

☐ a. Yes.

☐ b. It depends on the neighborhood and time of day.

☐ c. No.

27. Could your class status best be described as:

☐ a. Middle or upper class?

☐ b. Working class?

☐ c. Other?

28. Do you agree with the gender you were legally assigned at birth?

☐ a. Yes.

☐ b. I never thought about that before.

☐ c. No.

29. Have you ever been hospitalized against your will for some mental disorder?

☐ a. No.

☐ b. I almost was, or I should have been but I wasn't.

☐ c. Yes.

30. Have you ever been arrested or convicted?

☐ a. No.

☐ b. I almost was, or I should have been but I wasn't.

☐ c. Yes.

31. Have you broken some law for which you could now be arrested or convicted?

☐ a. No.

☐ b. There's no way I could be caught.

☐ c. Yes.

continued next page

32. Is there some situation you know of where your fundamental human rights are not protected by the law?
    - ☐ a. Not that I know of.
    - ☐ b. Yes, but only in small ways.
    - ☐ c. Yes.

33. Were your birth parents legally married to each other at the time you were conceived?
    - ☐ a. Yes.
    - ☐ b. Don't know.
    - ☐ c. No.

34. Were you raised by:
    - ☐ a. Both your birth parents?
    - ☐ b. One of your birth parents?
    - ☐ c. Other?

35. In what religious belief were you raised?
    - ☐ a. Protestant-defined Christian.
    - ☐ b. Other Christian.
    - ☐ c. Other.

36. Would you or others describe your political views most nearly as:
    - ☐ a. Right wing?
    - ☐ b. Left wing?
    - ☐ c. Undecided?

SECTION 2: HOW PERFECT?

A. Membership

37. Are you a member of, or do you support some civil rights organization or movement?
    - ☐ a. No.
    - ☐ b. Not actively, but I believe in their rights.
    - ☐ c. Yes.

38. Have you ever converted to a Protestant-defined Christianity?
    - ☐ a. No, that's where I started.
    - ☐ b. Yes.
    - ☐ c. No.

39. Are you now or have you ever been a member of what might be called a cult?
    - ☐ a. No.
    - ☐ b. No—unless you're including twelve-step programs, in which case, yes.
    - ☐ c. Yes.

40. Are you currently active in any religious group or organization, other than a Protestant-defined Christianity?
    - ☐ a. No.
    - ☐ b. Occasionally.
    - ☐ c. Yes.

41. Have you ever had and worked hard to get rid of some regional accent or dialect?
    - ☐ a. I never had one to start with.
    - ☐ b. Yes, I had one but not any longer.
    - ☐ c. Yes, I had one and I still do.

42. Do you make conscious decisions to dress correctly (and differently) for different parts of your life, rather than for the fun of it?
    - ☐ a. Yes, but it requires very little thought.
    - ☐ b. Yes, I've got wardrobes worked out for different things I do.
    - ☐ c. I can do that, but mostly I dress for the fun of it.

43. Do you sometimes either wish for or actively seek membership in some group that's defined by some identity you're not usually acknowledged as having?
    - ☐ a. No, I belong to the groups I need to belong to.
    - ☐ b. Yes.

continued next page

☐ c.   There are groups like that, but I don't want to belong to them.

44. Do you pass up buying or wearing something you might like because others you want to be liked by might not approve?

☐ a.   I would pass things up, but not because of any individual's disapproval—rather because it simply wouldn't be proper.

☐ b.   Yes, frequently.

☐ c.   Not really.

B. Relationships

45. Are you a birth parent of one or more sons?

☐ a.   Yes.

☐ b.   No, but I'm adoptive, foster, or step-parent to a son or sons.

☐ c.   No.

46. Are there people toward whom you definitely feel superior?

☐ a.   Yes.

☐ b.   Only the bad ones.

☐ c.   No.

47. If you chose to marry your lover, could you do so legally?

☐ a.   Yes.

☐ b.   Depends on which lover and where.

☐ c.   No.

48. Do others consider you to be "within your place or station" in the culture, given who and what you are?

☐ a.   Yes.

☐ b.   I try.

☐ c.   No.

49. Are there some people you don't wish to associate with, primarily because of how it might make you look?

☐ a.   Yes, and I don't associate with them.

☐ b.   Yes, but I associate with them anyway.

☐ c.   No.

50. Do you feel despised by or less important than some groups of people?

   ☐ a. No.

   ☐ b. Yes, but not so much.

   ☐ c. Yes.

51. Would others describe your sexuality as:

   ☐ a. Heterosexual?

   ☐ b. Homosexual?

   ☐ c. Other?

52. Would others describe the general nature of your relationship(s) as:

   ☐ a. Monogamous, faithful?

   ☐ b. Monogamous, unfaithful?

   ☐ c. Non-monogamous, polyamorous, or other?

C. Ideas

53. Which of these statements about power most nearly matches your own point of view?

   ☐ a. Power should be wielded solely by the responsible.

   ☐ b. Power, in the wrong hands, is dangerous.

   ☐ c. Power should be shared on a consensual basis.

54. Which of these statements would you most agree with?

   ☐ a. There are two kinds of people in the world: those who agree with that statement, and those who don't.

   ☐ b. There are two kinds of people in the world: and depending on the day of the week, I'm one or the other.

   ☐ c. There are as many kinds of people in the world as there are people.

55. With which of these statements can you most fully agree?

   ☐ a. I have an essential identity by which I can easily measure the identities of others.

   ☐ b. I measure myself against the essential identities of others.

   ☐ c. I am not (any of) my identity(ies).

continued next page

SECTION 3: SENSE OF SELF

56. Do you find yourself interrupting others' conversations for one of these reasons?
    - ☐ a. I only interrupt another when the other person isn't making sense or is saying things less important than what I have to say.
    - ☐ b. Whenever I do, I feel like I'm being impolite or pushy.
    - ☐ c. I try not to interrupt another unless interrupting is part of the social or cultural convention for the group in which we're talking.

57. When you find a seat in a movie theater, are you concerned that you might be blocking someone else's view of the screen (perhaps a child or someone shorter than you)?
    - ☐ a. No, the theater is a public space.
    - ☐ b. I don't have that problem.
    - ☐ c. Yes—I sit somewhere else if I can.

58. When someone sits in front of you in a movie theater and blocks your view even though there are plenty of other seats available, do you:
    - ☐ a. Take it personally, and get upset?
    - ☐ b. Get annoyed and not say anything?
    - ☐ c. Ask them to move or slide down, and if they don't, then you move?

59. When there's a long line to get into some event, do you:
    - ☐ a. Figure out the best way to get to the front of the line ahead of the others and do it?
    - ☐ b. Get annoyed because the people in front of you shouldn't be in front of you?
    - ☐ c. Wait your turn in line?

60. When a clerk or agent overlooks the person in front of you in line and serves you first, do you:
    - ☐ a. Proceed with your transaction gratefully?
    - ☐ b. Feel guilty and proceed with your transaction?
    - ☐ c. Allow the person who was in front of you to be served instead?

61. When you're introduced on a first-name basis to someone for the first time, do you:
    - [ ] a. Shorten their first name to a nickname, and use that?
    - [ ] b. Use their name the way you were introduced?
    - [ ] c. Get around to asking the person how they like to be addressed?

62. Is there some particular group of people that you don't belong to, about whom you enjoy telling jokes or listening to jokes about them?
    - [ ] a. Yes.
    - [ ] b. I listen and sometimes I laugh, but I rarely if ever tell those jokes.
    - [ ] c. No.

63. Is there some group of people you believe are better suited to do work you find unpleasant to do yourself?
    - [ ] a. Yes.
    - [ ] b. Yes, but I do the work anyway.
    - [ ] c. No.

64. When someone who you think does not have a similar identity to you tries to claim the identity you have, you would probably:
    - [ ] a. Simply refuse their claim?
    - [ ] b. Try to find out why they think they have that claim?
    - [ ] c. Try to find out why they think they have that claim, and why you thought they shouldn't?

65. Do you think you take up too much space in the way you sit, walk, stand, or speak?
    - [ ] a. I never really thought about that, or people have told me that, but I don't understand it.
    - [ ] b. Sometimes I consciously or unconsciously take up less space.
    - [ ] c. I try to take up as much space as I need, at no one else's expense.

66. Do you believe there are some groups of people who deserve their bad fortune and/or mistreatment?
    - [ ] a. Yes.

continued next page

☐ b. Yes, but I'm trying to see their side of things.

☐ c. No.

67. When someone from a marginalized group to which you don't belong accuses you of discrimination, do you usually:

☐ a. Feel you're a victim of reverse discrimination?

☐ b. Feel sorry for them?

☐ c. Listen to them, and if they're right, you work to avoid repeating that kind of behavior?

68. Without having met someone personally, are there ways you know you're better than someone, just by the way they look or dress or behave?

☐ a. Yes.

☐ b. Yes—I try to act compassionately.

☐ c. No.

69. Is there something you own that makes you feel better or more important than someone else?

☐ a. Yes.

☐ b. Yes, but I don't let that influence how I deal with that person.

☐ c. No.

70. If you were told you weren't allowed in some space set aside for a marginal group to which you don't belong, would you most likely:

☐ a. Go in anyway?

☐ b. Feel hurt or angry, and complain to others about it?

☐ c. Honor their wishes, and figure out why that's the case?

71. If you were to hear that some group is complaining that they aren't properly represented in some field or organization in which you are represented, would you probably:

☐ a. Dismiss the claim on the grounds that they're not working hard enough to be included?

☐ b. Agree with them that they should do something to become represented and/or tell them to form their own group?

☐ c. Work with them to ensure equal representation within your group?

72. Do you commonly refer to some other people in terms of their not being something you are (e.g. non-whites, lower classes, non-believer, or disabled)?

    ☐ a. Yes.

    ☐ b. Yes, but when I do, I don't mean that I'm better.

    ☐ c. No.

73. Are there any questions on medical, membership, or government forms or applications that omit you?

    ☐ a. No.

    ☐ b. No, but I can see where there are some questions that might leave out others.

    ☐ c. Yes.

74. If you hear that some group is trying to get a new word or words into the language by which they might identify themselves, might you:

    ☐ a. Feel they're being nit-picky and then refuse to use the new word?

    ☐ b. Use that word to their face, and the old words for everyone else?

    ☐ c. Adopt the word and use it?

75. If you hear that some group or population to which you don't belong is legislating for laws that would name them specifically in laws that already exist, would you most likely:

    ☐ a. Object on the grounds that they want special rights?

    ☐ b. Assure them that the law could be interpreted to include them?

    ☐ c. Do what you can to support them?

76. Did you grow up believing that you are entitled to a certain good standard of living, or that a good standard of living was within your grasp if only you worked for it?

    ☐ a. Yes, and it's true.

    ☐ b. Yes, but I think the world has changed since then.

    ☐ c. No.

continued next page

77. Do you sometimes find you mistake a person for another person because it's difficult to tell those kinds of people apart (e.g. another race, age, body type, person in a wheelchair)?

☐ a. Yes.

☐ b. Yes, but I really don't meet enough of those kind of people to tell the difference.

☐ c. Not usually, but if I do, I work to find out where I'm not looking.

78. When you meet someone on the phone, in a letter, or online, do you assume they're the same race or class or age or other aspect of identity as you?

☐ a. Yes.

☐ b. Yes, and I'm embarrassed if I find out it's otherwise.

☐ c. No.

79. Do you regularly credit, by name, the ideas, beliefs or opinions of others?

☐ a. No, there's really no need to.

☐ b. Sometimes, but I believe we all have or can have the same ideas anyway.

☐ c. Yes, whenever I can.

80. Do you sometimes adopt the dress or mannerisms or craft of a marginalized group to which you do not belong without acknowledging its origin?

☐ a. Yes, because I don't believe anyone has any special rights to those sort of things.

☐ b. Yes, but I think that's part of our melting-pot culture.

☐ c. I try not to unless I'm invited.

You're almost done. Hang in there. Just a few more questions, and then we'll see what kind of gender the world thinks you've got.

SECTION 4: BONUS POINTS

Now, find all of the following qualities that apply to you. Add up the number of items you check.

☐ 81. Blond(e).

☐ 82. Blue eyes.

☐ 83. Manager or executive.

☐ 84. Annual income over $50K.

☐ 85. Live in a gentrified part of a city.

☐ 86. Live in a well-manicured suburb.

☐ 87. Own a car.

☐ 88. Own your own business.

☐ 89. Proud of your parents.

☐ 90. Parents are proud of you.

☐ 91. Proud of your children.

☐ 92. Children are proud of you.

☐ 93. Citizen of the USA.

☐ 94. Rarely if ever lonely.

☐ 95. Have an insurance policy.

☐ 96. See well without glasses or lenses.

☐ 97. Play a contact sport.

☐ 98. Have been the recipient of an honor as an adult.

☐ 99. Have an excellent credit rating.

☐ 100. Have one or more doctorate degrees.

☐ 101. Have your writing included in a published book or ebook.

☐ 102. Know which silverware to use for what course at a formal dinner.

☐ 103. Have 1,000 or more friends or followers online.

☐ 104. Never questioned your own gender before reading this book.

Okay—You're Done! Score!

Penises

In this world, the Perfect Gender is first defined by a penis and matching testicles. In fact, if you didn't check 1A on this section, you simply are not in the running. So, here's how you can score this section: 1.a. 250 points; 1.b. 5 points; 1.c. 0 points. For the remainder of this section, give yourself 10 points for every 'a', 5 points for every 'b', and 2 points for every 'c' for a maximum 270 for this section.

Total points this section: _____

Other Genitals

Genitalia other than penises simply don't give you much of a leg up on the ladder to Perfect Genderhood. Sorry, that's just the way it is. For this section, give yourself 2 points for every 'a', 5 points for every 'b', and 10 points for every 'c' for a maximum of 20 points in this section.

Total points this section: _____

The Rest of Your Body

Your race, age, state of health, and how you measure up to the posited gender norm are each important factors in determining just how perfectly gendered you are you are. For this section, give yourself 10 points for every 'a', 5 points for every 'b', and 2 points for every 'c', for a maximum of 140 points this section.

Total points this section: _____

Interactions

How we're perceived, and what freedom we have to move around in the world also contribute highly to the perfection of our genders. For this section, give yourself 10 points for every 'a', 5 points for every 'b', and 2 points for every 'c' for a maximum 170 points this section.

Total points this section: _____

Membership

While formal or informal membership in some organization isn't as important as your body or your birthright, it does give some indication of how well you pass in the world, so it's worth some points. For this section, give yourself

5 points for every 'a', 2 points for every 'b', 1 point for every 'c', for a maximum 40 points this section.

Total points this section: _____

Relationships

How we structure our relationships is a factor in how we're perceived, and so you're going to get more points for this section. For this section, give yourself 7 points for every 'a', 4 points for every 'b', and 2 points for every 'c' for a maximum 56 points this section.

Total points this section: _____

Ideas

Since so much of our lives springs from our philosophy, our ideas will get a great deal of weight. The directions in which we think will eventually lead to how we live our lives, and to what degree or aspect of perfection we wish to attain. For this section, give yourself 20 points for every 'a', 10 points for every 'b', and 5 points for every 'c', for a maximum 60 points this section.

Total points this section: _____

Sense of Self

An important indicator of those with a Perfect or near-Perfect Gender is a sense of entitlement. Race, age, physiology, education, and many other factors may contribute to this sense. If we feel entitled, that's a pretty good indicator we're nearly Perfect. For this section, give yourself 15 points for every 'a', 10 points for every 'b', 5 points for every 'c' for a maximum 300 points this section.

Total points this section: _____

Bonus Points

This is all whim. Or it's not. This section is totally unfair. Give yourself 10 points for every category you were able to check off. In fact, if you can think of some more reasons that you might be better, more perfect, more privileged, or in any way more powerful or higher up than other people, go ahead and give yourself 10 points for every reason you can come up with. If you can't think of any other ways you might be better or better off than others, go ask some friends of yours. Remember, it's 10 points for each way you come up with! Cool, huh? Maximum points this section: 200 or 300 or even more!

Total points this section: _____

TOTAL SCORE: _____

How You Rate

1500

Cool, doode! You are PERFECT! Well, almost. Since you took this test, you must have some doubts, so you're ALMOST perfect. Very cool, though. Very. A question, though: Why in the world are you reading this book?

1200–1499

You're definitely up there in the top, say third, of the gender pyramid. Almost everyone loves you and wants to be near you. Well, everyone who counts, that is. You can easily pass for being a real man or a real woman. Odds are you probably don't get all the respect you want, right? And sometimes you feel guilty for the respect you do get. Here's the deal: you'll never make it to the top, and you've got a lot of privilege to scrape off if you ever hope to make it to the bottom. It's up to you.

1050–1199

You're considered very important in the circles in which you travel. While others might question your occasional eccentricity, it's doubtful they would question your gender identity as a real man or a real woman. If the world was a banquet, you'd be the meat and potatoes. You're working hard at being accepted, and it probably shows. If you play your cards right, you can probably move up a notch or two on the social ladder, which in turn would help you move up your job ladder.

750–1049

You know your place and pretty much stick to it. People tend to appreciate you like they'd appreciate a loyal dog, right? Don't count on others being too surprised when you start playing with your gender. Don't count on too much support, either. The good news is that without much work, you could very easily nose-dive into real outlaw status.

550–749

Um, you don't get invited to a lot of ritzy places, do you? Look, if you're going to be Perfect, you've got a lot of work to do. Probably too much work to bother with, you're that far away from Perfect. On the plus side of things, there's that old line, "Freedom's just another word for nothing left to lose." You're pretty close to that, aren't you?

0–549

Heh, heh. You're weird. You know you are, so why'd you take the test? Oh, I know: you take pride in what the culture persists in calling your flaws and imperfections, no? My kind of outlaw!

Did this test trip you up in any way? Well, it would ... the scores are totally arbitrary. So is most everything else in the culture.
So are the ideas of real men and real women.
So's gender in general.
Why?
Exactly.

Use this page for notes, doodles,
love letters, or arithmetic.

Chapter 5: There's Only One Gender: Yours

> You get to name your own gender and have it be a real gender. You have the right to do that, and no one can take that right away from you, because it's always there in your heart: your gender. Yours. The more mindfully you do your gender, the more certainty you get that you're expressing yourself well in the world.

One factor that makes it really hard to name our own gender(s) is that it's fall-over-backwards easy—not to mention occasionally frightening and disempowering—to be unconsciously influenced by social factors beyond our control. That's a fact. Well, how can we use that fact to better assess the value of gender? The value of our buried treasure has yet to be measured, and only you can measure the value of gender to you.

@sassafraslowrey: my gender most often offends the politics of other trans folks. numerous transitions & quitting T (twice) is seen as treason

This is a workbook, so what work can we do, knowing that we haven't always been the one calling the shots on our gender identities? The answer can be found with the help of the last clue we looked at on the treasure map: the map is throwing a shadow on the page. Is it simply a drop shadow, a trick of page layout design? Or could we read more into this clue because it's a puzzle, and the fact that the map is throwing a shadow onto the page is a clue to the value of gender.

There's a lot to be learned from shadows, like: when you see a shadow, it's wise to see what's casting it—or if nothing is casting it at all.

Identities are real. They cast shadows on us, and we cast the shadow of our identities on others. Identity is something we all seem to need or cling to—something we all know how to perform, mindfully or otherwise.

Exercise: In the margins of this page, write down the names of nine people you know who perform their default identities differently from how you perform your default identity. Make sure that no one on the list knows anyone else on the list. Yes, you can use fictional characters if you like. Or dead people. Nine folks who perform their identities differently than you perform your own, and differently from each other. Write down their names, then come back to read on. (Really, it'll be more fun if you do it this way.)

I think it's a fact that identities, being false, require other identities to validate them—and that includes but isn't limited to gender identity. Some people's gender expressions trigger us into changing our own. Here's how that works. When we shift our gender expression to accommodate the gender expression of another, we've essentially shed an identity and put another in its place. And we all do this more or less unconsciously when we're in the company of different people. I figured out what triggers shifts in my own gender expression, and that's a pretty valuable thing to know. Well . . . now you can know that about yourself. Ready?

Guess Who's Coming to Dinner!

Shifting gender on the basis of the company we're keeping at any particular time makes an interesting case for gender being an interactive phenomenon, as opposed to gender being some essential component of our identities. Gender might be seen as a form of communication. Maybe we shift genders in order to better communicate with someone. Let's test this one further. Remember what I said about all those folks not being in the same room at the same time? Well . . . guess who's coming to dinner!

Exercise: The Dinner Party

Part 1

Those nine people you wrote down just now? You're inviting all of them to a dinner at your place. The more unusual the mix, the better it's going to be for the purpose of the exercise. So you can change the people if you want to. Go ahead, for example, and invite two ex-lovers, your mother, your boss, and your third grade English teacher!

The only qualifications are that they don't do their identities like you do yours, and they don't do their identities like each other. So there's a total of ten people for dinner, including yourself. Write their names here:

1. _____
2. _____
3. _____
4. _____
5. _____
6. _____
7. _____
8. _____
9. _____
10. _____

Part II: Seating Your Guests

Here's your table. You're seated at the head of the table, on the left, below. Now, seat your guests in any arrangement you like. Then write the number or first name of each friend on the chair they're occupying.

You

@lestageog: It's useful to remember that what seems truly normative in the metropolis might seem deeply queer elsewhere

Now that everyone is seated, let's you and me step into the kitchen for a moment to talk a bit. Don't worry—your guests will wait for you.

Splattering

Gender is interactive and relatively predictable between ourselves and another person. We know what gender to perform (be, and present ourselves as being) when relating to any given person.

But what happens when we have to perform our gender(s) to two or more people simultaneously—each of whom is expecting a different gender performance (identity, and congruent presentation of that identity) from us?

What happens when we cycle through a series of such encounters relatively quickly, without a chance to regroup within ourselves, sort out what we just went through, and come to some relatively controlled balance of self-identity or self-identities? We've all seen the classic comic or farcical schtick where some character is leading a double life and suddenly has to confront people from both those lives at the same time. Woody Allen's film *Zelig* is a classic example. The movies *Mrs. Doubtfire* or *Victor/ Victoria* might be more to the gendered point.

My pal and co-author of *Nearly Roadkill*, Caitlin Sullivan, and I use the term "splattering" to describe what happens to us when we have to be too many identities or genders to too many people at the same time. For me, it's a real moment of personal joy. It's when all the mechanical or automatic ways I've developed for dealing with people simply fall aside, or reveal themselves as the bag of tricks I use to grease the social machinery of my interactions. There are plenty of cultural metaphors to mine for this phenomenon:

- Dexter, from the TV show, when he's with someone who knows he's a serial killer and someone who doesn't;

- Sleeper Cylons in *Battlestar Galactica* who wake up and have to navigate dual identities;

- Harry Potter transfiguration spells that go wrong, and suddenly the wizards and witches aren't what they thought they were going to be;

- *Teen Wolf*, and werewolves in general;

- Ranma, of *Ranma ½*, who is constantly having to face people who think he's a boy at the same time she's with people who know she's a girl;

- And there's a character on the UK show, *Misfits*, that does gender-changey things, but that character doesn't show up until Season 3, so . . . spoilers!

Unmasked, the central character is faced with explaining how they have been one thing to some people, and something else to others. My question is: Why do we laugh at that predicament? What experiences have we had in our own lives that enable us to identify with the plight of someone in the situation of having to hide to the point of getting relief through laughter?

Exercise: Think of three times in your life you've been torn by presenting one of several conflicting identities to two or more people at the same time. Write some key words down in the margins about each incident.

It's very much like what happens to me when I'm on stage, engrossed in a stage, movie, or television performance. Most of me is absorbed in simply being the character; I've got the lines memorized, so I can concentrate on making those lines come to life by putting myself into the experience of the character. Yet there's always a small part of me that's aware of things like someone in the audience sneezing loudly on a very quiet line of mine; so I'll repeat that line to make sure the audience will have heard it. It's the part of me who's aware which camera is live, so I know whether I'm in profile, dead-on, or off-camera.

This "lookout" is the voice that tells me the audience is lost or bored or distracted, so I can jack up my pace or volume, or do something to get their attention back. It's the voice that says my audience is totally with me, so I can luxuriate in some silences and whispers. So where's the "real me" onstage?

Is it the me that's being the character, experiencing the highly dramatic situation of the moment? Is it the me that's concerned about having eaten garlic for dinner, with a big romantic scene coming up? Maybe I'm the me that's just recognized an ex-lover in the third row? Or the me that's spotted an amazingly attractive butch on the aisle, adjusting her suspenders? Is it the me who's chiding myself for all these wandering thoughts, directing my performance as I'm giving it?

Is it the me who knows when my face is well lit as I'm walking across the stage? Perhaps it's the me who remembers my trick knee went out earlier that afternoon, and adjusts the character's walk accordingly?

I think I'm all of these things concurrently, and it's what I love about performing: it's an instant splatter into the harmonious and simultaneous expression of all the different aspects of me, denying myself nothing.

It's more of what I look for in companions, friends, lovers, and extended family: that freedom to be present, unguardedly.

It's when we splatter consciously, I think, that we expand our ability to stretch our genders, let ourselves go, lose a sense of who or what we might "really" be, and we're simply there. Certainly a little thing like gender blows away easily in that kind of wind storm.

Okay, Back to the Dinner Party

You've named your guests, and we've been in the kitchen talking, you and I. I'll stay here in the kitchen. You go on back to your guests. Remember: anything you say to any one of the guests is going to be something all the other guests can hear. What? You don't know what to say to them? Okay, here's an idea.

Exercise: The Dinner Party

Part III

Think of an amusing embarrassing incident that's happened to you—the more complex, the better. Take your time—make it fun but not scary. Got your story? Great. Now, write it down as if you're telling it at the dinner table. Begin by telling the first sentence to the first guest to your left; write the second sentence to the guest to the left of them; the third sentence to the next guest on the left, and so on. Everyone can hear everything you're saying—you're simply looking at one person at a time. Be sure to include at least one sentence for each guest. (You are a good host/ess, aren't you?) If you have more than ten sentences in the story, just continue in a circle with one sentence per guest.

Really get into it. For example, if you chose your mother to be one of the guests, what would it really be like to tell her this story in the presence of, say, your lover and your boss? Now, read back over what you wrote. These questions are a good way to look at what you just did.

- Was there any point in this exercise where you felt totally free to express yourself, without concern for how people might react?
- At what points in the exercise did you feel powerful? At what points did you feel less powerful?

---

continued next page

- What has that got to do with your gender?
- Did you have any different underlying messages to each guest (e.g. flirting with one, keeping something secret from another, trying to avoid yet another)?
- What did it feel like to balance the management of your identities like that? What emotions did it bring up for you?
- Was there some guest with whom you were more "yourself" than with the others?
- Was there some true "me" in all of this? If so, who was that?
- Was there some true gender of yours in all of this? If so, what was it, and what made it more true than any other gender you presented or regularly present?

How're you doing? I don't know about you, but when I start getting into this kind of analysis, when I really ask myself these kinds of questions, my brain starts to fry. I lose some degree of certainty about who or what I am.

If anything like that is happening to you right now, this would be a good time to send everyone home from the dinner party, then go out for a walk or take a nice bath. When you come back, we're going to do what might at first glance seem like a big shift of focus here. So go relax. There's a game for you on the next page. Go, play it. Have fun.

Hello! I'm Sarah. Kate has asked me to create a limerick-based challenge for you. What I've done is take some of the wiser things that my friends have said about gender, converted them into limericks, and removed the final word or words for you to try and guess. Have fun!

C'mon: tell me, bro, what is your deal, man?
Do you ever just say how you feel, man?
If you have to perform
To conform to the norm
Then what is it that makes you a _____?

Oh I can't tell you how it enrages!
How we stay on our separate pages!
What we need's inspirational,
Pan-generational
Meetings of minds of all _____.

I get mad. It's not fair. It's not right;
We are missing the point of the fight,
When we choose not to face
Implications of race
Because, newsflash ... some queers are not _____!

Is your life an exuberant whirl?
Are your fairy wings soon to unfurl?
If you're graceful and bold
Be you young, be you old
You will never stop being a _____.

ANSWERS (*top to bottom*): real man, ages, white, girl

Be All That You Can Be!

Welcome back. Let's see, now ... you've found the treasure, you're discovering how valuable it is. Now the big question is, **what are you going to do with it?** It's been buried for so long, can you take at least a little bit of your buried treasure and maybe ... wear it? Oh come one, the very best pirates are **Fabulous**, like Johnny Depp's Captain Jack Sparrow. **That's** how to wear your treasure!

Essentially the theory part of this workbook is over and done with. The rest of the book is going to get a lot more personal and practical. We're going to work our way down the gender/identity/power pyramid with the purpose of freeing ourselves up from a system that restricts and forbids our individualities. The exercises are going to be less and less about what you already are, and more and more about whatever you could be, with whom you could be that, and how to organize your life in such a way that it supports your own sex-and-gender freedom without getting in the way of anyone else's. Won't that be nice? I should think so.

If you do want to go on reading and working, then it's only fair to warn you that I think you're going to step over a line here. I think that if you're not already considering yourself transgender, then it's possible that you will be considered that by other people. I'll be talking about a "journey" through gender, because from this point on in the workbook that's what you're going to be doing: you'll be taking your own gender journey.

Whoa. No one's expecting you double your wardrobe, or make an appointment with some surgeon. Gender journeys come in all shapes and sizes. (More on this later in the book.) For now, just consider this gender journey to be something that explores the outer limits of being a man or a woman, okay? Come on, take a leap with me.

If social factors can control our identities with or without our conscious knowledge—shouldn't we be able to control our own identities? Assuming we learn how to do that—what part of our identities might we control that would help us to build for ourselves a life more worth living? And if we apply that all to gender identity, would that make us transgender? Yes, us—you and me. I think it does.

Katie's Opinion On Exactly Who Might Be Transgender

Some folks think that in order to qualify for bottom-of-the-gender-pyramid status you'd need to do something drastic with your body; others think you'd need to wear clothing of another gender; some people think you would have had to have felt "wrongly gendered" for most of your life. Not me. While I'm quite happy with my own surgically altered and hormonally enhanced li'l bod, I think you're transgender, a gender outlaw if you will, for two reasons. You're transgender if . . .

1. You're not perfectly gendered according to the pyramid model, and in this culture that's a crime against gender.

2. You're gaining an entirely different perspective on gender from the one that's been force-fed us all for an awfully long time.

What, Me Transgender?

I think anyone who wants to question or study gender is transgressing gender. I think anyone who has either the desire or the courage to own their transgressions against gender is transgender. Beyond those two qualifications, I think *how* transgender we are is only a matter of degree. Let's put that to a little test.

@Grant_Thoreson:
I think my spiritual path was a subconscious response to identity issues I wasn't even aware of. No wonder that I gravitated towards Eastern philosophies whose focus was "I am not my body."

@drum4ica: why should I be labeled as having a #mentalhealth issue when I feel the best I have ever felt #mindbody&soul. other people are uncomfortable with my gender identity yet I'm the one left feeling wrong, crazy, alone, and confused.

Exercise: Are You Transgender, Part I

Below is a list of some behaviors. Mark a "T" for the ones that would mark someone as transgender and "G" for the ones that would mark someone as gendered. (Yes, you can use both letters if you want to.) You may need to read some of these pretty carefully.

☐ surgically altering one's genitals to approximate another kind of genitalia

☐ surgically altering one's body (other than genitalia) to approximate something considered more pleasing

☐ surgically altering one's body (including genitalia) to approximate something considered more pleasing

☐ wearing the outer clothing of another gender out on the street

☐ wearing the outer clothing of another gender for a costume party

☐ wearing the underclothing of another gender beneath one's own gendered clothing

☐ taking a job not traditionally associated with one's assigned gender

- [ ] changing one's name to a name associated with another gender
- [ ] having a birth name usually associated with another gender
- [ ] making no change in one's body, but claiming to be another gender
- [ ] claiming no gender at all
- [ ] having questions about one's own gender identity
- [ ] having questions about the nature of gender
- [ ] consciously or unconsciously adopting the trappings of the gender one was assigned at birth
- [ ] consciously or unconsciously adopting the trappings of a gender other than the one assigned at birth
- [ ] reading this book for the purpose of discovering the nature of your own gender identity
- [ ] reading this book for the purpose of discovering the nature of gender identity in general
- [ ] being taken as a man in public, while being a woman who feels like a woman
- [ ] being taken as a man in public, while being a woman who feels like a man
- [ ] being taken as a woman in public, while being a man who feels like a man
- [ ] being taken as a woman in public, while being a man who feels like a woman
- [ ] being taken in public as a feminine man, while feeling like a masculine man and having been assigned female at birth

i am a queer woman of color. by the very nature of the term I break all gender constraints, because what we imagine to be gendered is never a woman of color. by the very virtue of being colored i break every rule that white feminists have created regarding gender, by being queer i break every rule that communities of color have created for a woman. so by the virtue of my being, of my existence, I am breaking every rule and convention of gender. living without gender? hmmmmm.... well, I guess I'd like to one day, but it's really hard when everyone in the whole fucking world reminds you of it constantly and consistently, like even [your] questionnaire. it is impossible for a queer woman of color to live without gender in the same way as it is impossible for us to live outside of race. hope this adds some color to the approach.

—cb

continued next page

- [ ] being taken in public as a feminine man, while feeling like a masculine man and having been assigned male at birth
- [ ] being taken in public as a masculine man, while feeling like a masculine man and having been assigned female at birth
- [ ] being taken in public as a masculine man, while feeling like a feminine man and having been assigned male at birth
- [ ] being taken in public as a feminine man, while trying to appear as a masculine man and having been assigned male at birth
- [ ] being taken in public as a masculine woman, while trying to appear as a feminine woman and having been assigned female at birth
- [ ] being taken in public as a feminine man, while trying to appear as a feminine woman and having been assigned male at birth
- [ ] being taken in public as a masculine woman, while trying to appear as a masculine man and having been assigned female at birth
- [ ] being taken in public as a gender you'd like to be taken for, and then you change your mind and decide you'd rather be taken as another gender, only that doesn't quite work.

Exercise: Are You Transgender, Part II

Using the language from the list above, describe yourself here. What is unique about the inconsistencies in you? What combination of qualities makes your gendered identity unlike anyone else's? Where is it you don't match up to that perfect gender? Go on and describe yourself. You can be as flamboyant or as scholarly as you like. After all, you get to decide what's appropriate for you, right?

Wait, What Perks Come With This Outlaw Game?

Good question. Most of the perks I've gotten out of my playing with gender are not those that would be highly valued by any materialistic culture. I've less access to "good" jobs, I face more danger on the streets, and the writing I do has not been embraced by millions of people just dying to pay me for saying this stuff.

But let's get serious (well, as serious as we can get with the adorable li'l pirate sitting next to this paragraph). How do you suppose we can honestly expect people to respond to us when we start walking around in the world wearing our pirate treasure like Captain Jack Sparrow? Can we expect to break the laws or violate the taboos of a culture, and then be rewarded by the culture in the same coin the culture uses to pacify those who don't disturb the status quo?

I don't think it works like that. We do get punished by the culture whose laws we break, whose taboos say "Don't study this forbidden knowledge, and certainly don't use it!" Depending on the extent to which we use or communicate that forbidden knowledge, we're denied equal rights, equal pay, equal access. We're not permitted to educate or maintain custody of our children. After all, we're no longer seen as "real men" or "real women," if in fact we ever were.

We make space for ourselves in this world through the very acts of questioning and ultimately toppling the gender/identity/power system; and the kind of space we make for ourselves can be as fabulous as we'd like it to be! We've got nothing holding us down to any kind of monogender-specific appropriate behavior, so what we've got is a freedom of expression beyond the scope permitted to members of any bi-gendered culture in the history of the planet. C'mon, that's cool.

How Valuable Is Personal Freedom Of Expression? Well, Just How Valuable Is Fun?

Exercise: The very best pirates know how to have fun, which is another way of saying pirates know how to do silly things. Go do something silly. Go on. Do something that might be considered gender neutral or genderless. Right now. Go do something that makes you feel like a little kid. When you get back from doing that, write down some key words in the margin that will help you remember just what it was that you did.

We get to decide what's appropriate for ourselves. We get to sample life from any angle that strikes our fancy. We get to laugh an awful lot, and what's more, we get to say whatever comes into our heads and hearts without fearing some loss of identity status. Are we having fun yet?

OK, How Valuable is the Freedom to Speak Your Mind?

Exercise: Think about a time you told someone else what was really on your mind. Granted, the way you said it might not have been the most compassionate or loving way to have done it, but the way we say things is something we can practice and improve. Overcoming the fear of abandonment that often attends honest self-expression is the first step. So go ahead . . . when was the last time you really expressed your true feelings to someone else? Write down some key words in the margin that will help you remember the good parts of honestly expressing who and what you are.

This is a good, practical application of postmodern theory in the service of self-betterment. Good on you for doing it. Now . . . consider these:

- How did it make you feel to have expressed yourself (not how you expressed yourself, just the fact of having done it)?
- How did it make the other person feel about you (what you said, not how you said it)?
- If you're still in touch with that person, do you feel more confident about being able to express more of yourself with them?

If all this gender play can be so much fun, then why haven't a whole lot of us done this a whole lot earlier? Well, a whole lot of us have, but aside from the fact that most bi-gendered cultures tend to severely punish gender transgression, there's another factor at work here, and that's simply fear.

Learning to express different aspects of ourselves, including previously unexplored shades of our identities that have become gendered by cultural standards, is very much like that: we eventually wind up with some courage and self-respect, and that makes it well worth facing our doubts, fears, and demons. You don't have to agree with this, but *do* you agree with this? How does that make you feel about life, self-esteem, and all that jazz?

The Gender We Love to Fear is No Gender

In a culture that sees gender as inviolate, the violation of gender rules can kill you—sociologically or literally. Have a Google of "transgender AND murder OR suicide," and flip through the 7½ million hits you get. And if you manage to beat murder and suicide? When you step over the gender line, you're a ghost. You can say you're alive—but alive as what, exactly? You have no idea what you are, and you have few or no words to express it. You're living in the unknown. That's scary, because what's the great big unknown? Death. Messing with gender triggers our primal fear of death. Well, I think it does. And it's not only a gender change that can trigger the creepy-crawly or blinding-bright fear of death. Violating any of the binaries in kyriarchy can trigger the unknown, and thus our deep fear of death.

Keep in mind, please, that this is all theory. And that means it could be a big fat lie. Theory is only as good as it stands a test. So, when you feel safe enough or interested enough to test out your fear of death, give it a go. Start by reading a book, or watching a movie or TV show where some character whom you really love dies. Examine your response to that. Brave you. xoxo

Fear of death when considered in the context of a gender shift may sound extreme, but most philosophical or spiritual systems allow for transformation as an inevitable byproduct of death. Whether it's body into dust, or spirit into another life, there's transformation—inevitably ushered in by a real or symbolic death.

@frogtosser: I can't die yet. I don't know what it's like to love someone. #stayalive

@frogtosser: I can't die yet. I don't know what it's like to be comfortable in my own skin. #stayalive

---

Consider these life and death questions . . .

- If we then seek to transform ourselves, be it our gender or any other form of identity, we're really talking about killing off part of our lives, no?

- And if we're killing off part of our lives, then who's left?

- What is the "who" of us that gets to keep on living and growing?

I'm thinking this line of questioning is going to reveal the transformative nature of gender. If we're looking at gender as more than physiology or even psychology, then the possibility increases of crossing over into something entirely beyond our current ability to name a point of arrival.

The possibility increases of opening some Pandora's box in terms of our own identities. The simple act of questioning gender can jeopardize not only gender but all its links to race, age, class, and the litany of factors that comprise our identities. Question gender, and we question so much more. Here's an interesting question for you: Can you create yourself as your own opposite? Why, yes, as a matter of fact, you can.

> ### Exercise: Become Your Own Evil Twin
>
> - Is there something you would not want to become? Something that's offensive or frightening to you? If so, what? Write down some key words here, so you'll remember.
> - Are there aspects of your life that you have been cultivating in order to avoid becoming what you don't want to become? If so, what would those cultivated aspects be? Write down some key words here, so you'll remember.
> - Are there parts of your life or personality that are, right now, close to being what you don't want to be? Write down some key words here, so you'll remember.
> - Is there some aspect of your personality that you use to hold another (less appealing to you) aspect in check? Write down some key words here, so you'll remember.

Hey, I Wouldn't Ask You to Do Anything I Haven't Done

Since going through my gender change, I've become quite a few things I hadn't planned on becoming: a lesbian, a straight woman, a not-man-not-woman, a sadomasochist, and a pansexual all-of-the-above. Additionally, I've become a phone sex hostess, an author, and a performance artist. I've dropped out of my middle-class life and values, become economically challenged, and because of the estrogen-based hormone regimen I'm on, I've lost a good deal of my body strength, and I've become more susceptible to the arcane form of leukemia I've been diagnosed with.

I didn't plan on becoming any of these things—they all more or less happened when I started my gender transitions rolling. On the plus side, once I began making changes and fell out of that close-to-the-top section of the pyramid, I became free to explore the rest of it, free to explore more facets of all the lives I'm capable of leading.

And it hasn't stopped yet. Now, I'm looking at some other, more frightening things to become. I'm looking at all the boy-stuff I've got inside me as a result of both nature and nurture, and I'm saying to myself "Well, what's all this about?" Boy and man are two separate genders, and while I resisted being a man for my whole life, there's a whole lot about me that's boy.

I don't want to live a life whose impetus is dictated by fear of what I am, what I might become, or what I might be seen as. I want to see for myself everything I am, everything I can be—from my heart—so I can be conscious in choosing an identity in which to nest . . . if such an identity exists for me or for any of us!

HOW MANY GENDERS DO **YOU** SEE?

ANSWER: Six—man, woman, boy, girl, kitty, doggie

@RiverSong1938: i try to remember the person marginalising me is responding to their internal fears, i can understand fear and that helps me love them.

Are you with me? Once we get through the hard part, there's a lot to enjoy. And you'll have as much company as you'd like. There are quite a few people in the world right now celebrating some pretty innovative self-defined gender identities. Would you care to meet over a hundred of them right now? Okey dokey, then . . .

101 Gender Outlaws Answer the Question, "Who Am I?"

I put the word out on Twitter and my blog that I'd like people to define themselves in 280 characters or less. Several couldn't resist going on for more than that, but I liked what they wrote so much I put them in here anyway. So responding to the questions "Who Are You? What Are you?" I'm proud to present one-hundred-and-one amazing answers from some pretty amazing people, who span a generation, from 1997 to 2012. How about that! (Most of the new ones start with "@name.")

> **Exercise in Compassion:** Some of these 101 identities may strike you as comical, some as gross, some as inspirational, or just plain nonsensical. As you read this list, take notes in the margins of the page of the judgments you make based on what you read. Try to let go of any judgments, and then try to envision yourself in relationship with the person, no matter who or what they say they are. Go on, you can do it.

1. A woman who had a spontaneous pre-natal sex re-assignment.

2. @Siniful: My gender is geek. (I'm a wee blue-haired sapiosexual pansexual queer android. I use female or neutral pronouns.)

3. An anachronous simulsanguesexual literary faerie (gyrl).

4. @anywavewilldo: my gender is #feminist #tomgirl and #anywave.

5. I'm a good little boy, but I'm a BAD little girl!

6. @JustJo_08: There are times I cry myself to sleep wishing and praying I fit in this world cookie cutter idea of perfection. Then I wake up only to twist and bend the rules as much as possible to make the world fit to me.

7. the VERY short version: transgender redneck

   the pretty short version: transgressively gendered butch/FTM and halfheartedly-recovering redneck

   the not-that-short version: queer female-to-butch/male transgenderist, sex radical, tree-hugger, anarchist, parent, activist, writer/performance artist & halfheartedly-recovering redneck.

8. @SandraBernhard: easy breezy cover girl? rough agoraphobic cover girl. tender bitchy cover girl. sleazy lonely cover girl.

9. Basically, I'm a 34 year old bisexual femme guy. I regularly wear necklaces, pins and earrings, I dress in bright flamboyant colors, and in social settings it is quite obvious that I'm more at ease talking with women than with men. In short, I am fairly feminine in behavior and sensibility. I'm not transsexual, and I doubt I would be considered transgender, however, as this culture defines such terms I happen to be more feminine than masculine in my tastes and behaviors. Heron

10. @AndieDavidson: No I am NOT a man!! I am a transgender person just dressed as a man for today. Purple nails, right?!

11. always queer, finally dyke, a run-of-the-mill hermaphrodite mom.

12. @youlittlewonder: I'm a French-Canadian, used-to-be-catholic-now-turned-militant-atheist. A classless loudmouth introvert with too many comics and not enough friends. A bride-to-be who's poly at heart. A sober addict. Bipolar. Bisexual. Bilingual. Communist working in finance. Far left hipster who looks cisgender, but feels like a drag princess.

13. a born again woman

14. @abeardedgnome: My gender is trans male. Crunchy on the outside with a soft squishy center.

15. A God+Godess, part of everything, owned by nothing.

16. @DrDoogs: My gender? A little from column A, a little from column B, and a dash of secret ingredient that makes me ME

17. I think . . . I am a female fag, who is a drag Queen, who is a mother, has a soon to be transman lover and may very well be a tranny hisself. I hate labels it's all so complicated, but I think it fits the bill today. Change is good right?

18. @ponyonabalcony: today my gender is faun, sparrow, man, kitten, princess. Same ingredients as usual, but always shifting proportions.

19. Badass motorcycle boot-wearing expensive lingerie consuming femme biker switch warrior. 'Nuff said? ::grin::

20. @MarilynRoxie: A genderqueer androgyne who will always be questioning what "gender" and "queer" mean!

21. Kitt, aka AlexFox, Alaskan Fox, Mom-Dad, P.(arental) U.(nit), Sweetie, She was pretty as a woman, but omigawd he's even handsomer as a man!

22. @queer_kitten: I am a boy, not a man. Butch, not a woman. Queer, not homosexual. From a community where the diversity IS what unifies. Undefineable. Introspective. Proud and loud for those who cannot be. I Thrive On Desperation.

23. The fabulous Boy-Girl-posthuman-It-Thing JordyJones. Artist Writer and Whore. Multi-tasking media-darling, polymorphous pervert and irreverent illiterator.

24. @FakeLoriSelke: Fortysomething fat white butch mother of twins. That's Mommy, Sir if you're nasty. Being a genderqueer parent means nobody questions your right to hog the family bathroom. I live and breathe between the lines.

25. i am . . . boy-girl-faggy butch with an avid appreciation for femmes & het sex.

26. @quarridors: After transitioning, passing felt like failing to be true to myself or be seen as myself. This raised so many questions.

27. Twin-spirited extraterrestrial with a primal urge to get fucked by something that fits.

28. @j_a_e_young: Gender Indifferent. Imagine a stick figure putting on a new gender costume every day. The figure is always the same!

29. Nattily attired 40-going-on-11 first alto female-to-male transsexual . . . subject to change without notice.

30. @MxRoo: It took me a while to figure out the right words. My gender is genderqueer dapper punk Johnny Cash Muppet butch.

31. i've been pondering your query about how we define ourselves/know who we are. i would have to say that i become a reflection of whatever dance i find myself doing with whomever i am falling in love with at the moment.

32. @queerfatfemme: My gender is Miss Piggy crossed with Dolly Parton crossed with Divine crossed with Ginger Spice crossed with 3,789 tons of glitter.

33. On the way to finally being ME.

34. M2F shaman/artist and consecrated Galla of Cybele (my wife Bella) and intersex FA2MA (feminine androgyne to masculine androgyne) leather top and priest/ess of the Dark Goddess (me)

35. @JoelleRubyRyan: I am a white, first-generation college student, working-class academic, queer, asexual, child-free, trans, genderqueer, feminist radical, activist, person with hidden disabilities, fat, fat-positive, writer, researcher, blogger, atheist, socialist, rural-dweller poet, wo/man, dog-lover, film buff, grass-roots organizer, androgyne, teacher, public speaker, spiritualist, Blogger, fighter, Warrior.

36. FTM transgender bulldagger, gentleman stone butch dyke with fag tendencies. Or as my girlfriend says, a drag queen trapped in a man trapped in a woman's body.

37. I'm a bi-gendered boychick with balls and boobs. Call me Ken, or call me Barbie—same doll, different packaging; some assembly required; sex, clothing and accessories sold separately; available in fine boy-tiques everywhere.

38. Someone who grew up in the exile of duality, who is now entering the garden where he/she, you/me, are inseparable.

39. @opinionated_ari: HEY THERE PERSON STALKING MY BLOG, YOU WADED THROUGH 40 PAGES OF "I'M NOT A GIRL" BUT SAW BOOBS AND DECIDED I WAS A GIRL. FUCK YOU. IT'S REASONABLE TO READ ME AS FEMALE IF YOU SAW ONE OR TWO PHOTOS OF ME OUT OF CONTEXT, BUT THAT'S NOT WHAT FUCKING HAPPENED. THANKS FOR REBLOGGING A PHOTO SET OF ME *SHOWING OFF MY BINDER* TO A BLOG WITH "GIRLS" IN THE TITLE, ASSHOLE. and friends just so you know, i am not offended into rage when *you* call me she, even though I would prefer "they" as a pronoun.

40. Out/M-F/stopped short of the knife/keeping M name to remember history/alone on a limb?/WHERE THE HELL ARE THE REST OF YOU GUYS!!!/estrogened/multidisciplinary performance artist/ . . . human

41. @Kupyer: I'm drifting somewhere between genderqueer & femme transmale, but labels mean less to me than proper pronouns right now. He, him, his.

42. as long as I can still kick ass, it ain't nobody's business if I'm dick or dyke. or alternatively, . . . I'm an old butch whose jackets may now bunch up around my hips and whose jeans may rub at my thighs, but at least my ties still go around my neck.

43. I am a strongly identified woman in my gender with occasional masturbatory fantasies of being endowed with male genitalia.

44. I'm a butchy-femme, omnisexual, polyamorous, genderbent, kinky, queer—I am most attracted to queer, genderfuck boys: transboys, boychicks, bioboys, makes me no diff.

45. @wordgeeksarah: I'm so far up the CIS side of the spectrum I occasionally fall off and become a drag queen of myself.

46. I'm The Dyke of Androgyny . . . i get called sir more than maam, despite the sizable mammary glands protruding from my chest. The hair on my head is the shortest found on my body, a gentle societal mindfuck, if you will.

47. Transsexual dyke, submissive pervert, percussion fetishist, computer geek, and subversive queermonger.

48. Two-spirit mixed-blood transgender working-class sober queer boy dyke daddy.

49. @HeatherRose23: I'm usually only aware of my gender when I'm around others. On my own, I'm just me.

50. A granola femme with an SM twist, a dyke drawn primarily to butches & FTMs.

51. @grrlalex: young trans using gender transgressive terms— genderqueer, gender fluid, bi-gendered, third-gendered, androgynous and boi.

52. happy going, fluidly-gendered, pan-sexual eurotrash Canuck switch with a sweet tooth for the taste of untried and new genderomantic flavours and twists.

53. @fecknom: I am a transmasculine queen.

54. Everlove'nStudMuffinButtBustingGenderTwistingSado masochisticHypeDaddyDyke!

55. @AlyxJHanson: I am a FAAB dapper butch gentlequeer. A writer. A storyteller. A safe-space creator. Blessed beyond words. Whoops, forgot one. Also bipolar.

56. I'm a Poetess-bi-dyke-drag-chick (sometimes-i-crave-dick)—Gasp! Laugh. grrrrl2grrrrl into hip-hop-funk-folk, addicted to phat beats, and heavy, open, dangerous minds.

57. @hardcorps80204: You make me ponder new things! Dunno if I've ever thought specifically of "my gender today." Not sure I have an answer.

58. oh shit. butch, female bodied, human persona-ed, male appearing, daddy, momma's boy, mother fucker, cross dressing, gentleman, top, smooth talking, dirty minded, nasty fingered, lover of women . . . is one of the things I am.

59. A big leather dyke on a big fucking bike.

60. @supermattachine: My gender could punch out anyone in this room, but today he is wearing his good lace veil. My gender is shaped like an oyster fork.

61. Omnisexual, omnigendered pervert fag transman in a biofemale body.

62. @possiblyagirl: I am a pubescent 30 year-old girl. I dress as young and cute as I can get away with. I feel I missed out in my teens. I thought about transitioning for years, but when my friends "made me" wear a dress I could barely hide my tears. I knew I had to.

63. I'd have to describe myself as a femme hybrid—Half Michigan, half raging homo, or in other words, half baked and half-way home, but 100 percent pussy.

64. @SmartAssJen: My gender: dynamic intersection of shifting forces of biology, mind, culture & spirit. Practically: whatever I say it is.

65. Mean femme dyke when I'm not being a tender man holding my lady or a mama feeding my babies.

66. A celibate Transgender Lesbian trying to live an honorable and ethical Unitarian Universalist life.

67. @anywavewilldo: my dyslexia has impacted my gender in hyperinterconnection tendency: find binaries painful.

68. I am: Young, female and feminist, bisexual, homoemotional, trying to change the world and stop it from changing me too much!

69. @ClosetedTrans: i am eli. i identify as trans*. im a boy. im stuck in the closet. so i basically live life in drag. who am i? my sex is not me b/c bodies - of all kinds - make me uncomfortable. i dont have an easily identifiable gender. i am eli. i am enough. i am. sometimes i dont even like the word person. its too limiting, boxing me in. i am eli. he is me.

70. A motorcycle ridin', pool playin', softball hittin', average kind of dyke who's afraid of ruining her nails!

71. @kellnerfarquer: I'm a dood that bleeds.

72. A constant flow: a journey from one way of thinking, to the wide open expression of what it really means to be me. Or . . . militant-feminist female-2-male butch genderfuk daddy transexual fag or . . . I changed my mind. This happens a lot. "anomalous" I think that's my gender. If you have space or want to or whatever, you can put 'em both in. Whichever. I like anomalous better though.

73. @tkalen: genderqueer, genderfluid. a unisex look that society perceives as male. Still baffled by people's choice to see a "man who can't read" instead of a "woman who dresses differently." Usual conversation goes something like . . .

> stranger: Isn't this the women's room?
> Me: That's what the sign said when I came in.
> stranger: You are in the wrong place.
> Me: Then so are you.

74. @KlingerLee: fat, genderqueer, Jewish hobbit teaching English in Korea; writer, artist; living with physical and mental disabilities. Wish I could stop beating my head against the idea of "normal."

75. Hey, thanks for asking. I was just thinking about my gender the other day after I went shopping for a pair of boys' shorts and a strapless bra. My clothing has more gender than I do. So here are a few first minute thoughts on the subject, organized into shorter and short: How do I define my gender? I don't. A child once asked me "are you a boy or a girl?" I said, "both." Now, I would say "neither."

76. @cindikn: Lesbian Seminarian Dad and Step-mom of Transsexual Experience. Perhaps one day Lesbian Pastor Dad and Step-mom of Transsexual Experience.

77. Priest in their religion, priestess in ours.

78. @labcoatlingerie: I'm "genderqueer" or "agender." Not "genderless" or "nongendered"; the absence IS the answer. It's different.

79. Ill-defined, ill-gendered; over/under defined, over/under gendered; beyond definition, beyond gender. Definition fatigued yet gender starved. Barely a woman, but allways a dyke.

80. @deutschtard: Someone's trying to tell me that because I have no dick, i'm not a man and that I'm spreading fallacies. LOL no I told him to try telling you what he told me, because he'd get told the same thing: I'm a guy because I say I am, what's in my pants has nothing to do with who I am :) (he even tried to tell me I was wrong, like I don't live this every day LOL yeah . . . no).

81. @TheShorty: I break gender in practice more than looks. I look like a woman but I choose words in a masculine way, and I express emotions in a masculine fashion. I'm a pansexual,

monoflexible woman with a tomboi side. I don't mind dirt, mud, or physical work. But just like Angel in RENT, I'm more of a man than many will ever be, and more of a woman than they will ever get.

82. Transsexual Woman Estranged Parent Catholic Human-Sexual Ex-Engineer Waitress with "delusions of 'blandeur'" and a happy love of God and each of Her/His children.

83. @cnlester: Playing a man on stage felt like coming home. A sensitive, girly kind of man, mind you. I couldn't explain why teachers calling me a girl made me so very, very angry.

84. In me, binary American culture can only see an FTM. My best MTF friend calls me "Wrong Way Walker" :) I'm mixed-gendered, I'm other-gendered, I'm a Third.

85. @sassafraslowrey: "my gender=former baby butch, t-injecting gutterpunk trans faggot turned bearded lady, now genderqueer femme daddy's boy.

86. I'm gay-positive (bent!) straight Jewish formerly working-class white grrl feminist who teaches women's studies and is going to be a new mom to a sweet babe from China!

87. @bigleg: my gender is unicorn.

88. I am a Kate More. I'm not entirely sure what a Kate More is but I know what one does, it lusts after belonging

89. @musingvirtual: I am stone, femme, and most importantly fluidly & queerly gendered.

90. A free-roving TwoSpirit with shades of a Shoalin Monk with a little Scottish Highlander thrown in for spice. But failing that, I am Life.

91. @ProjectSabs: I'm a lesbian transwoman overweight tomboy butch-femme that fixes cars & wears makeup, I'm a stepmom who never wanted kids of her own. I'm a writer, DJ, filmmaker,

actor, auto mechanic, bellydancer, & I face insecurity, depression, & body issues. I'm a geek & a feminist, strong-willed, independent & self-sufficient. I'm pagan & polyamorous. I'm a student. I stand up for myself.

92. Viragoid TranSexual. Dyke (femme), PolyPerverse Bottom, Harpy, TransHag. Game Designer. Superheroine. Not pretty. Say—how do you feel about sex-maddened Trans Groupies, anyway? Heehee!

93. @morethnsouthern: my gender: dandy lovin queer who's comfortable with any pronoun as long as it's spoken with respect.

94. My current identity tag is: priapic butch fella and bloodsports triathlete, reclaiming the haircuts of my oppressors—heh!

95. @mydwynter: I'm a transguy who can't wait to physically transition so his looks will provide the palette he desires for playing . . . with gender. I don't want to look like a girl with eyeliner. I want to look like a guy with eyeliner. The distinction is important to me. I'm eagerly anticipating the day when I can be seen as a guy in a tutu.

96. Fence-straddling, Bridge-burning, machoflaming bisexual prettyboy faggotdude — a singer of the high and the low.

97. @_ozymandias42: I feel like there are some genders, like dapper butch, that aren't open to me because I'm young and others that are only open to me because I'm young, like badass Bowiesque glitterfag. I actually think it's freeing to have genders I can age into.

98. Happily recovering from the dark world of unknown to the world of light. Enjoying the life I knew was always inside, could never hide, & letting others see the 'real' me! I smile & laugh so much now, I'm another person! I hope to see the day when others are able to shine in their light!

99. @AcetyleneVirgin: My gender is like a black hole and often viewed as something radical or dangerous by those who don't or are unwilling to understand.

100. @AndraHibbert: My gender= cisqueer femme tomboy.

101. What am I? It depends.

When I speak of Brandon Teena, a transsexual man who was raped and then murdered because he dared identify as a man while possessing a vagina, I am a transsexual man.

When I speak of a transsexual woman who is being excluded because of her past, I am a transsexual woman.

When I speak of a pre-op transsexual who is being hurtfully categorized by the shape of the tissue between his or her legs, I am a pre-op transsexual.

When I speak of a post-operative transsexual who is being denigrated as the destroyer of his own body's integrity, I am a post-op transsexual.

When I speak of those who dare not reveal the pleasure they derive from wearing clothing reserved exclusively for use of the opposite sex, I am a transvestite.

When I speak of those who are regarded as degenerate because they find certain items particularly stimulating of pleasurable fantasy, I am a fetishist.

Gender Outlaw #101 is my longtime friend and gender warrior, Nancy Nangerone. She has lots to say about her gender, and it continues on the next page.

Gender Outlaw #101 continued

When I speak of those who enjoy games of erotic power exchange, I am a sado-masochist.

When I speak of those who prefer the same sex to the opposite for intimacy, I am a homosexual.

When I speak of those who open their arms to intimacy without restriction based on sexual polarity, I am a bisexual.

When I speak of any woman who is being hurt because she dares to challenge or seek respect, I am a sister.

When I speak of any man who is being hurt because he dares to prefer sensitivity to durability, I am a brother.

When I speak of any person who is being hurt because they do not identify as either man or woman, I do not identify.

I am all of these things. In being so, I make a difference where and whenever difference is being used to make hurt.

Okay, you've just finished reading how 101 gender outlaws have been identifying themselves from 1997 to 2012. That's a lot to review. Go take a walk, or take a nap and dream about outlaws dancing in your bedroom—make them friendly outlaws. Come back to the workbook when you're fresh and ready to go, okay? Because next, we're going to talk about SEX. And you probably want to be rested for that, am I right? But first ... it's time for another round of the rhyme game from Wordgeek Sarah!

Here's a very Familiar tale:
"Trans men must 'man up' or they Fail"
So here's to trans dandies!
What they understand is
You needn't be butch to be

_____

Though the indoctrination starts early
I have always aspired to be burly
Oh to be a princess
Could not interest me less
Though I may be a girl, I'm not _____

IF you really don't want to offend me, dear,
Just trash your assumptions and end the
    Fear!
I'm not he, I'm not she
There's more options, you see
I'm a blend. I transcend. I am _____

It's not just the dresses and toys
Or the cutesy cartoons "he" enjoys
It's the way that SHE knows
From HER head to HER toes
That some boys will not always be _____

Use this space for notes, or maybe a manifesto.

Chapter 6: SEX! SEX! SEX! SEX! SEX! SEX! SEX!

No study of gender would be complete without understanding the importance of sex—erotic energy—which is to some degree in play or at rest in everyone. It may not look like there's a clue to sex on the treasure map, but how about this one: the map is drawn in grayscale.

When we start talking about sex, no amount of shades of gray will suffice. Fifty? No, more like fifty million. But there's also color. Sex adds color to our lives, the kind of colors we like when we admire a photograph or a painting. When we talk about sex, we are talking full-on color. Sad to say, the majority of people look at and describe sex as black-and-white. And there is black and white, that's for sure.

There's the blinding white of ecstatic joy and the most velvet black, the kind of black you'd like to drape over Death's shoulders. Sex can be that dark and amazing. But that's not the kind of black and white most people are told about when it's looked at and decreed real by most mainstream media outlets, churches, medical practices, and legal systems. Here's how the dominant culture teaches us to question our sexuality. No, really—most people test themselves and each other using the following test.

@ScorpioUndone: [I am] femme trans & lesbian, lifestyle Mistress. Polyamorous, married +2 girlfriends, recovering christian & sometimes I masturbate @ work.

THE QUINTESSENTIAL DOMINANT CULTURE SEX QUIZ

TO ONCE AND FOR ALL DETERMINE THE TOTALITY OF YOUR SEXUAL DESIRE

A   Are you heterosexual?   YES / NO
    (Circle one only)

B   Are you homosexual?   YES / NO
    (Circle one only)

SCORING: If you answered YES to A, you pass. If you answered YES to B, you fail. If you think there should be more questions or you want to circle more than one answer, you're mentally ill and/or spiritually and morally depraved.

There's no denying that gender plays a great big part of desire. But when we finally get to lie down gently or roughly with the lover(s) of our dreams ... then what? Isn't what we do and how we do it some part of defining our sexuality? The things we love to do sexually—even the things we feel guilty or bad about — deserve as much attention and freedom of expression as does the pronouncement of our gender preferences. And by the way, what if all your desires were legitimate? What if no one thought they were weird? What if *you* didn't think they were weird any more—because *nobody* really gives a fuck any more? So everything sexual is out in the open. Wait. There's more: in that world, you are someone's dream-come-true lover... and honey? They are looking for you right now. Remember, dear: *safer sex saves lives.* Kiss Kiss, Auntie.

If Fucking is More than Homo/Hetero, What the Fuck is it?

Homo or hetero isn't a bad binary. It's a useful binary. But homo/hetero is only one of many valid binaries within the sphere of regulation we're calling sexuality. Top/bottom is another valid binary. Polyamorous/Monogamous is a good question to ask on the third date. Or what about this: you're just about to do your very most favorite kind of sex, and you're feeling bad about your body. Maybe you're feeling skinny, or fat, or awkward, or your genitals are somehow wrong on you. That counts for something in defining our sexuality, doesn't it? Homo/hetero is an important factor in deciding the nature of our attraction. But how can the sum total of our desires depend only and always on the gender of our (singular) partner? And even if you are homo or hetero, do you think you're always going to be that? Always, and forever? I don't think so. People change as years go by. Desires shift. Different identities begin to matter, or more subtle shades of identity. Even homo/hetero isn't fixed and permanent.

Bisexual movements don't get enough credit for breaking the either/or of sexual orientation, And they did it long before gender scholars, activists, and radicals came on the scene. Just sayin' . . .

Do you know about a sexuality called furry? Give it a google right this minute.

And excuse me, but what about vampires? No, don't laugh. There are vampires in the world. I've been dear friends with a particularly fetching vampire who—on one occasion only—asked me to be her donor. Oh, wait. That's the next book. Sorry! But still, there's lots of valid ways to fulfill our sexual desires. That's what this chapter is about.

In my country, gay men and lesbian women have won the right to serve openly in the military. But what if the person wearing a dress in this picture was born with a penis? Instant discharge. What's with that?

If, in fact, gender preference was the sole criterion for the basis of sexual desire and fulfillment, then it would be absolutely true that all gay men would be attracted to every single man everywhere—all the time and uncontrollably. Age wouldn't matter, race wouldn't matter—all that would matter would be that the other had a penis. Right? *And a lot of people around the world think it's like that!* That's why people were freaked out in my country when we finally let gays and lesbians serve openly in the military. People against "gays in the military" were worried that guys would come on to them, or their children, or that it was so icky they didn't want to have to think it was going on. OK, so what if a gay soldier comes on to another soldier—maybe you. So? You just say no, right? Unless the gay coming on to you is a real asshole and forces you. But honestly? I bet that heterosexual guys do that to women more than gay men do that to each other.

We do make terrible assumptions about each other, just based on their expressed sexuality, don't we? We all do that. I do that. I'm not going to begin to tell you the stuff I've seen and heard in sex. Well, yes, I will, but not in this book. Forgive your old auntie for her ramblings, won't you? Thank you, that's very kind. Now, you've got work to do. Another test. And this is the test that is proof-positive that you—YOU—are more than homosexual or heterosexual. AND THAT IT'S OKAY! All right, shoo now. Take the next test. It's not a scary one. I promise.

THE TEST THAT PROVES YOU'RE NOT SIMPLY HETERO OR HOMO

1.   You are one of only two genders. TRUE/FALSE

If you circled False, you're more than homo or hetero. Right? Do the math. Proof-positive. End of line. You live out on the margins. Yay, you! But don't worry, you're not alone. Really, keep reading. There are lots and lots of us out here on the margins, and you're welcome here. Now, if you circled True, well, you're welcomed too. Now, check off the following conditions under which you would immediately and always thereafter have sex with anyone of the (same gender if homo, other gender if hetero) even if . . .

- [ ] they're gross and stinky?
- [ ] they're mean to you?
- [ ] they completely disagree with you on most if not all of your own moral and spiritual values?
- [ ] they don't like to do the sex things that you like to do, or the sex things you've been dreaming of doing?
- [ ] they like doing sex things that you don't want to do—if you even want to do sex things at all?
- [ ] they're six years old?

SCORE: If you honestly checked off any of the above boxes, then there's much more to your sexual desire than your heterosexuality.

Neither heterosexuality nor homosexuality can explain the entirety of our erotic desires. Nor can "lesbian" or "gay." Nor can "bisexual." In the same way, the "opposite" of cisgender cannot simply be transgender. ALL of us are much more complicated than either/or—any either/or, including gender. It's extremely difficult if not impossible to accurately determine the nature of a person's sexuality, using anyone else's standards but our own—or those dictated to us by our concept of morality.

More on morality later, I promise. Besides, all this talk about who's sexually attracted to whom, and for why—that leaves out a large number of people who live across a broad spectrum called asexuality. Now, unless you've taken the time and energy to define yourself as an asexual person, you're probably thinking that asexuality means no sex. Nope. That's not what it means. What's more, I have yet to find a single person who can give you a 100 percent accurate definition of the term, one that everyone else agrees with. Here's what I've managed to put together so far. I'm defining asexuality here, based on what I glean from the times of my life I spend as asexual, and chatter with my twibe on Twitter, and from AVEN's website (Asexual Visibility and Education Network). And I put it all together in my head and came up with this, so there's every chance that WHAT YOU'RE ABOUT TO READ IS A BIG FAT LIE. That's called theory, kiddo.

OK, here we go, theoretically speaking and with no unkind intention for anyone defining themselves differently . . .

What is Asexuality?

Unlike celibacy, which is a choice, asexuality is a sexual orientation. Asexual people have the same emotional needs as everybody else and are just as capable of forming intimate relationships. How cool is that? Back in a world where a healthy sex life means there's one way to have that, scientists are of the opinion that asexuality is a disorder —they call it sexual aversion disorder, or SAD. Well, that sucks. No self-claimed, self-experienced sexuality is a disorder, and hello? That includes asexuality. You don't need a doctor or counselor to cure it— there are plenty of asexual people who are talking about living a wonderful life, rich with romance, relationships and sometimes even sex. It's a spectrum, like most everything else. So while this chapter is all about sex—sexuality includes the wonderful paradox of asexuality. Give it a google.

No Gender? No Sex? No Cry

Why all the focus on asexuality? Well, for one reason, not too many people are talking about it out in the open, and it's time to amplify a very real sexual orientation. Moreover, there are parallels between the cultural paradox that is asexuality and the cultural paradox of no gender. How easy is it for you to conceive of a gender that isn't, or a sexuality that doesn't? That's a fun pair of paradoxes to chew on, and people have been examining them smartly on the interwebs. There's a lot to examine in the meta at the intersection of asexuality and agender.

Exercise: Here's a tweet stream discussion of asexuality and celibacy from late 2011, early 2012. Everyone whose tweets appear says yes that's what they tweeted. I've mixed up the order they appeared in my tweet stream. If you want to, you may re-order the tweets any way you like. Circle words and concepts that make sense, and those that you think are just wrong. Use a pencil in case you change your mind later. And no, there is no correct way to unscramble them. You won't need to read them in any particular order, though some tweets comment on others. Think of each as a koan. That's the beauty and the curse of tweet streams.

@633nm: When I finally got on hormones and it went away, I was SO RELIEVED—that was my "yes I'm trans enough" moment. #asexual

@633nm: I confused the horrible groin pressure for a sex drive, but really it was something that I needed to be rid of. #asexual

@633nm: I used to try to have sex, because that's what I thought I was/supposed/to do. It didn't work out. #asexual

@badpatient: demisexuality is widely misunderstood and regarded as elitist or slut-shaming, even though it's about attraction, not behaviour.

@badpatient: that applies to the whole ace spectrum: a person's sexual identity is based on attraction, and their behaviour doesn't invalidate it.

@badpatient: and THEN there are the grey ideas between false binaries: a whole 'nother realm between asexual and sexual (grey-a), for example.

@badpatient: i've learnt that everyone's sexuality is unique, and that two people sharing the same identity may experience it differently.

@badpatient: exploring ace identities often leads to questioning things we take for granted, such as romantic/sexual congruency.

@badpatient: the asexual community is beautifully diverse— i've identified as ace for ~7 years and keep discovering new elements to ace identities

@quarridors Grey asexual or grey-A people are in the "grey area" between sexuality & asexually, but this isn't as simple as degrees of attraction.

@quarridors: One such example is demisexuality; experiencing sexual attraction only once one has become emotionally close to someone. #asexuality

@quarridors: Other examples of grey-asexuality include only being attracted to people as a sexual fantasy, not attracted to the reality . . .

@quarridors: Grey-asexuality can also include being weakly attracted to other people but being indifferent to acting on that attraction.

@quarridors: Also important to note that not all people who don't experience sexual attraction like the asexual label.

@mareziee: sexpositivity and asexuality don't have to stay dichotomous either; in fact they can complement each other well!

@PinkBatPrincess: Same here, frequently. Not asexual myself, but identify strongly with a lot of ace-spectrum folks.

@quarridors: I recommend the http://apositive.org forum for a sex positive asexuality community interested in answering this stuff.

@QueerieBradshaw: I'll head there today and give you all the sage input I have, which will vary greatly depending on my nap.

@thebeardlessone: . . . sexuality. I'm a non-libidoist, indifferent, aromantic asexual, which means there's no one I'm romantically attracted to . . .

@thebeardlessone: asexuality is often divided into many opposing pairs: libidoist/non-libidoist, indifferent/repulsed, romantic/aromantic . . .

@thebeardlessone: . . . I wouldn't mind having sex, but it doesn't work anyway. #asexuality

@PinkBatPrincess: I wouldn't say I'm asexual, but I bump up against this logic: "A) A strong sexual appetite is healthy and good. B) I don't have a . . ."

@PinkBatPrincess: . . . .strong sexual appetite. C) Therefore I am not healthy.

@QueerieBradshaw: Some asexuals aren't celibate. Some feel pressured to be sexually active & some have various definitions of sex.

@quarridors: Also asexuality is not necessarily low sex drive or "sexual dysfunction". I feel more actively asexual on testosterone.

@thebeardlessone: just as a straight person masturbating doesn't make them gay, an asexual person who masturbates is still Ace.

@quarridors: Orgasms are plenty enjoyable & lots of asexuals are sex positive. Also as part of a romantic relationship. #asexuality

@the_leaky_pen: Guys, check out the conversation happening on #asexuality! It's really good stuff! @katebornstein working on updating My Gender Workbook!

@euonymy: Asexuality is lack of sexual attraction. But romantic attraction's frequently present, and compromise often happens.

@belfire86: Yup, pronounced as "ace" in my exp. dunno if others have varying ones. Have you looked at AVEN?

@AvocadoPear: AVEN— www.asexuality.org/home/

@thebeardlessone: Asexuals may have sex to please partner, to be seen as sexual, peer pressure, procreation, because it feels good.

@euonymy: Some aces are repulsed by idea of themselves having sex; never would. Some are just indifferent, would do for someone loved.

@GothAlice: Asexuality: To not be impacted by sexual drives or surface attraction. Celibacy: To not partake in sexual pleasure.

@tylluan: Not celibate these days, but have been. wouldn't consider it the same as asexuality. celibate=choosing not-sex.

@ksej: I was celibate for many years without once considering myself asexual.

@thebeardlessone: celibacy=action, asexuality=orientation (I'm celibate&asexual, not all aces are celibate)

@belfire86: Celibacy is choosing not to engage in sexual activity despite being sexually attracted to people.

@belfire86: generally asexuality is not experiencing sexual attraction. Ase people may still engage in sexual activity.

@dj_bent: feeling asexual feels like i see the beauty of people, fall in love, but without the sexual component

@thebeardlessone: celibacy is to sexually active as asexual is to sexual.

@AcreatureOflux: 2 me, celibacy is choice to not be sexually active for given length of time & still keep my queer sexual identity.

@euonymy: Many ace folks have sex because their partner(s) likes it. Many celibate folks are not asexual.

@euonymy: It's the difference between what you feel/personally desire, and what you choose to do. Might match, might not.

@malefemme: celibacy experiences sexual attraction but refrains from acting on it; asexuality doesn't experience it at all.

@anibunny: I see celibacy as a choice and asexuality isn't, just like being gay, straight, or bi isn't a choice. :)

@nuclearmission: Asexuality only refers to the lack of traditional sexual attraction, not someone's sexual activity.

@cnlester: celibacy describes my behavior, but asexuality usually used to describe a state of being?

@thebeardlessone: asexuality is not being sexually attracted to anyone Asexuals tend to wonder why sexuals find this so complicated.

OK, enough. And that was only part of a longer conversation. AND there's lots of tweets missing. Conversations are going on at this deep level of care, wonder, and urgency about most every aspect of sexuality you could imagine, including yours or the one you're not so sure you want to examine more closely. Maybe this next set of exercises will get you closer to discovering the meta principle that links agender and asexuality. Go on, give it a shot.

Exercise: What parallels can you draw between no gender and asexuality? Use extra paper if you want to, or just write notes in the margins. Fuck it, it's your book.

For EXTRA CREDIT, pick a sex or gender identity you're not familiar with. Start up a social network conversation about it. See what you learn.

Advanced Exercise: How can you apply what you just discovered in the above exercises to other cultural spheres of regulation, such as age, race, class, and so on. For a full list of them, flip back to page 60. Just pick one—maybe the one you're having difficulty dealing with in life, other than or in addition to your gender and your sexuality.

So . . . What is Sexuality, Anyway?

What does sexuality really hinge on? It's not simply the gender of our partner(s). But gender can have a lot to do with sex—gender can be one of your best sex toys ever.

You've unearthed your buried treasure—gender. Now you're going to learn how much of it you want to carry around with you, and how much to leave buried. Next up in this chapter, we'll have a look at just how flashy or subtle you want to be in using your gender to express your sexuality.

So, here's a theory for you to chew on. And remember, theories can end up being great big fat lies, so the work part of this workbook is you finding out whether or not the theory can apply in your real life.

Earlier in this book, I wrote that sex can be examined in terms of sexual orientation or preference. I said that breaks down to how, with whom, where, and if at all you want to engage your erotic energy. Well, now it's time to take a closer look at what goes into our sexual orientation/preference.

Sex—like gender—may be motivated by identity, desire, and power, in different and shifting proportions. So the expression of sexuality may include not only the sex act itself but also preferred expressions of romance, love, partnering, power dynamics, degrees of consent, vulnerability, safety, intimacy, community, comfort, social interaction, sensation, whimsy, morality, spirituality, wisdom, humor, comedy, and compatibility.

Let's take a look at how all this breaks down. This is an incomplete list. It's just meant to give you some ideas. There's LOTS more than I've written down here. OK, here we go.

Some Components of Sexuality

INTEREST IN SEX—Well, yeah. This gets taken for granted by many people. But really—it's a very real and changing factor from person to person. Our level of interest in sex may change from day to day, hour to hour, year to year—or it may stay the same at no or not very much interest at all.

BODY PARTS AND THEIR CONFIGURATIONS (yours and another's or others')—For those of us who enjoy sex with other people, most of us have been conditioned to name our sexuality based on the genitals of our partner(s) in relationship to our own genitals—and that's fair. That's an important piece of our sexuality—but genitalia are certainly not all of it. There are LOTS of yummy body parts that come into play when we consider erogenous play. There are lots of orifices, and lots of things to put in or around those orifices. There are nipples, and tongues, and ears, and hair, and fingernails. And there are elbows, knees, shoulders, and armpits. There are fingers and toes and throats and butt cheeks. And that's just the short list. It would take pages and pages to list out the body parts—and combinations of body parts—that might come into play in making sex satisfying for us and/or our partner(s).

GENDER ASSIGNMENT, IDENTITY, AND EXPRESSION—How much of an influence is the gender you or your partner(s) were assigned at birth? How important is gender identity (who you and/or your partner(s) believe you are) to your sexuality? What expression of your gender (whatever that might be) makes you feel sexy? Do you like being manly? Girly-girl? Androgynous? If you have sex with a partner or partners, what gender expression(s) of theirs is important to you?

SENSATION—What is it that you like to feel? Is it important to you what sensations you give or receive from yourself or your partner(s)? There's stroking, and kneading, and pinching, and nibbling. There are soft touches, strokes, stings, and thuds. How wet or dry or sticky do you like things to be? There's the question of how much sensation (if any) you want to give, and how much sensation (if any) you want to receive.

EROTIC/EROGENOUS ENHANCEMENTS AND TOYS—Oh my goodness, this could fill a book all by itself—and in fact, there are many excellent books about erotic enhancements that might be important to our enjoyment of sex. There are condoms and lubricants and dental dams and vibrators. There are feathers and chocolate and whips, whipped cream, and saran wrap. There are costumes and scripts and handcuffs and baby powder. Your kitchen is *filled* with implements that can make sex more fun for you and/or your partner(s). So is the hardware store, grocery story, and medical supply store. There are entire stores that are all about toys you can use to make your sex life more fun. Are you up on all the latest gadgets?

Alleys can be fun if you take the right precautions. Really fun!

LOCATION AND TIMING—If you want to have sex, do you want to do it in person? Indoors? Outdoors? Online? Over the phone? Skype? What time of day or night? How long? Do you want to be in private, or might you like people to watch? Does it matter to you how long a time your sex lasts in order to be satisfying? If so, how many minutes? Hours? Days? Weeks?

PERCEPTION AND COMMUNICATION—Do you want to keep your eyes open or closed? How about blindfolds? Do you like to make lots of noise during sex? Do you like it when your partner(s) make noise? Do you want to talk about sex beforehand? What's important to you? What's going to make you feel great?

DEGREES OF CONSENT—I'm against non-consensual sex. I'm against *any* sort of non-consensual activity. That said, there are degrees of consent that you and your partner(s) can agree upon before engaging in sex. Do you want to surprise yourself and/or your partner(s)? Do you want to be surprised? Do you want some combination of planning and surprise? If you're going to engage in agreed-upon nonconsensual sex (I know—how's that for a paradox?), then what are your agreed-upon and understood limits?

> **@Wylddelirium:** I am: queer, trans*, shaman, gypsy, disabled, polyamorous, kinky, Master, Top, stone, masculine, monster, the lost generation.

TRUST, VULNERABILITY, PRIVACY, AND INTIMACY—We all keep our guard up to some degree, and many of us let that guard down during sex. How far do you want to let go? How far do you want your partner(s) to go? How much do you want to know about your partner(s)? How much do they want to know about you? Are there secrets you're willing to keep from your partner(s), and secrets you're willing to let your partner(s) keep to themselves?

CONFIDENCE AND POWER DYNAMICS—The more we play out our sexualities, the more self-assured we become. Do you enjoy confidence in your partner(s)? Is self-confidence a factor in how sexy you feel? Do you like being in control? Do you like to be controlled? Do you like to switch who's in control? Under what conditions and with what frequency might you like to switch?

SAFETY—Be safe. Make sure that any partners of yours are safe. Practice safe sex. There are no ifs, ands, or buts about this one. Ever. Period.

LOVE AND ROMANCE—Is it important to be in love with your partner(s)? Does your sexuality depend on your partner(s) being in love with you, whether or not you're having sex? In what ways do you want to express your love and have your love returned?

PARTNERING—Do you want a partner? More than one partner? If you have multiple partners, is it important to you whether or not they like each other and have sex with each other—or with other people? Do you want to mate for life? Do you want to get married? This is part of defining your sexuality, and too many people don't consider options.

COMMUNITY, SOCIAL SKILLS, AND INTERACTION—People who claim sexualities or express their genders in ways considered different from the cultural norm tend to form communities with other people of the same or similar sexualities. This social component of our lives is part and parcel of our sexualities.

COMFORT AND RISK—What's your comfort zone for sex? Are you curious about stepping outside your comfort zone? Under what conditions might you want to do that? What sort of risks are you willing to take?

WHIMSY, FANTASY, FLIRTATION, AND PLAYFULNESS—How light-hearted and fun might sex be for you? To what degree might flirtation and sexual playfulness be part of your everyday life and way of going about things? How do you feel about erotic literature and films? How about erotic performance? How about pornography—soft core or the real deal? Do you like to make, watch, read, web surf, or listen to porn? Is fantasy important to you before, during, or after sex? How open are you to change and fluidity when it comes to sexuality? (Yes, fluidity is different than fluids, which are perfectly lovely in their own right.)

MORALITY—Do you subscribe to a moral code that has rules about your sexuality? Have you made up your own code of what's right and what's wrong about sex—or what's good and what's evil? Are there ways to have sex—or people to have it with—that would just be wrong for you?

INTELLIGENCE, SPIRITUALITY, AND WISDOM—Does talking high theory get you hard? Or wet? Or both? It does me. And did you know that there are a whole lot of religions in which gods and goddesses have sex with people like you and me. Imagine that—sex with a god or goddess? Do you enjoy the company of people as wise as you are?

What are the genders of these two people? What if they were gendered differently than you thought? How many combinations of genders can you see these people being? Just curious.

Oh, come on—you've been reading all this really dense stuff. If you've gotten this far, that alone is proof you've got some wisdom. Own it. So, is that kind of wisdom sexy in other people? Or not. Either way is OK, right?

167

Mark Twain, at the end of a profoundly meaningful life, for which he never received a Nobel Prize, asked himself what it was we all lived for. He came up with six words which satisfied him. They satisfy me, too. They should satisfy you. "The good opinion of our neighbors."

—Kurt Vonnegut, Jr.

@wordgeeksarah: my spiritual development has mirrored my sexuality, as my concept of gender is mirrored in my concept of divinity so: atheist, catholic, pagan, jewish, agnostic. now, all above. Asexual, str8, les, ?ing, queer. Now, all above. age 5, shopping with mum (a highschool teacher). Ran into 2 of her students: "Hiya Miss! Is that your little boy?" liked 2b mistaken 4 a boy. Felt like disguise. I think girliness was for special occasions only. Lil tomboy/dragqueen!

HUMOR AND COMEDY—How important to your sexuality is a good laugh? Barbara Carrellas describes a giggle-gasm—when you laugh so hard, it's like coming. It doesn't even have to be while you're having sex, but it could be. And just how sexy to you is someone who's got a great sense of humor when it comes to things you hold sacred to your identity, desire and power?

EMPATHY AND RESPECT—Kurt Vonnegut, Jr. wrote that love is always a lie—even a little one, but no one can fake respect. Respect for ourselves and for sexual partner(s) makes sex all the more awesome. I promise. I've got nothing against anonymous one-nighters, really. But for some people, sexuality hinges a great deal on how well they can identify with their lover(s), and how proud and worthy they feel to be having sex with them. Just sayin'.

COMPATIBILITY—Your sexual enjoyment may or may not depend on how much you and your partner(s) share similar tastes in hobbies, music, food, films, or books. It may or may not be important to your sexuality that you and your partner do similar work, have similar career paths, or live on the same schedule. Compatibility also comes down to how much importance we place upon the usual suspects: perceived gender, race, age, class, religion, sexuality, looks, disability, mental health, family and reproductive status, language, habitat, citizenship, political ideology, and humanity.

So How Does All This Help You?

Filling out this next exercise will give you a little tiny taste of your true desires. Ready for that? You don't have to do it if you don't want to, and that goes for every other sex and gender exercise in the book.

Exercise: What's My Sexuality?

Pencil ready? (Yes, use a pencil, please.)

On the next two pages, you'll find a list of many components of sexuality.

There are three boxes next to each.

At the top of the left-most column, write the date. In the left-most box of each line, write down a number: 0 to 10.

Zero means absolutely no connection to your sexual whoopee.

Ten means it's indispensable to your sexual whoopee.

As always, you can write key words in the margins, so the next time you come back to it you'll know why you scored it like that.

Come back and re-do this exercise in three months, and again (if you dare) in a year. Gonna be an eye-opener.

QUIZ

PART I: WHAT MAKES UP YOUR SEXUALITY?

☐	☐	☐	Body parts, configurations, and body image
☐	☐	☐	Gender assignment, identity and expression
☐	☐	☐	Sensation
☐	☐	☐	Erotic/erogenous enhancements and toys
☐	☐	☐	Location and timing
☐	☐	☐	Perception and communication
☐	☐	☐	Degrees of consent
☐	☐	☐	Trust, vulnerability, privacy, and intimacy
☐	☐	☐	Humor and comedy
☐	☐	☐	Confidence and power dynamics
10	10	10	Safety
☐	☐	☐	Love and romance
☐	☐	☐	Partnering
☐	☐	☐	Community, social skills, and interaction
☐	☐	☐	Comfort and risk
☐	☐	☐	Whimsy, fantasy, flirtation, and playfulness
☐	☐	☐	Morality
☐	☐	☐	Intelligence, sprituality, and wisdom
☐	☐	☐	Empathy and respect

ADD MORE . . . TO YOUR HEARTS DELIGHT!

☐	☐	☐	_____
☐	☐	☐	_____
☐	☐	☐	_____

QUIZ

PART II: YOUR SEXUAL COMPATIBILITY NEEDS

☐ ☐ ☐ Race Compatible

☐ ☐ ☐ Age Compatible

☐ ☐ ☐ Language Compatible

☐ ☐ ☐ Class Compatible

☐ ☐ ☐ Habitat Compatible

☐ ☐ ☐ Looks Compatible

☐ ☐ ☐ Citizenship Compatible

☐ ☐ ☐ Political Ideology Compatible

☐ ☐ ☐ Family/Reproductive Status Compatible

☐ ☐ ☐ Humanity Compatible

☐ ☐ ☐ Mental Health Compatible

☐ ☐ ☐ Religion Compatible

☐ ☐ ☐ Ability/Disability Compatible

☐ ☐ ☐ Gender Compatible

☐ ☐ ☐ Sexuality Compatible

ZEN MODE EXERCISE: Release all your attachments to this matrix.

Why Bother Naming and Labeling Everything?

In the 1980s and 1990s, identity politics devolved into an insistence on perfection: there were a limited number of ways you could be a real . . . well, fill in the blank. That doesn't mean that naming ourselves is a bad thing. Naming ourselves mindfully can be an empowering act of self-respect. Taking on names that others have given us—or taking on names from a limited number of names allowable, well . . . that story doesn't usually have a happy ending. Naming ourselves haphazardly is a gamble or a whim. Sometimes it's fun.

With all this latitude with which to explore our gender and sexualities, we've now got a much more realistic way to name our sexualities, and we've got a much better handle on the notion of attraction. Instead of the silly binary question, "Are you hetero or homo?" we've now got a more complete way to discover and name our sexuality.

Sometimes we want to connect with another or others, and sometimes we do whatever we can to avoid connection. Names, labels, and identities of all sorts establish *traction* between or among members of a gender/sexuality based relationship. A key component to sexuality is attraction, which happily includes the word traction.

Attraction Depends on Traction

For our novel, *Nearly Roadkill*, my pal and co-author, Caitlin Sullivan realized that in order for attraction to occur, there needs to be some form of traction for each of the parties involved. In her words . . .

Each person involved in the attraction needs someplace to stand, someplace to dig their feet into, something about themselves to point to and say, "This is me ... do ya want it?" Traction can take many forms, depending on the dynamic within which the attraction takes place. Within some lesbian communities, for example, it's a comfortable and easy thing to move into butch and femme: it's a well-known dance. In a leather community, a master/slave relationship provides traction. And romance novels abound with the strapping hunk/damsel-in-distress model. Once we move into any of these or other established identities, we know what to do—we know who we're supposed to be. And more importantly, we make it easy for the person we want to attract to relate to us.

Let's put this to the test, shall we? This is a workbook, after all, so work it.

Exercise

1. In the chart below (page 174) write down a list of five of your identities. These can include things such as man, woman, boy, girl, college student, executive, househusband, rock star ... any five identities you regularly claim, whether openly or in secret.

2. Next to each one, write down what kind of person the culture thinks you should be attracting romantically or sexually just by having that identity.

3. Now write down the kind of people, if any, you really are attracting with that identity. If you don't have enough room in the little boxes, feel free to write in the margins.

Chart

An identity I'm being	Who I should be attracting	Who I really am attracting

Exercise: Here's a less word-oriented way to explore this notion of attraction. While you're going about your day keep tuned to these questions. You might take this book or a notebook along to jot down your observations.

- If you fantasize about loving and/or having sex with anyone, what sort of person might that be?

- What people (if any) make you look twice at them with desire?

- If you've ever fallen in love, have you ever been surprised by the kind of person you've fallen in love with?

- Were the answers to any of the above questions affected by who and what you are? If so, how?

I saw a woman sleeping. In her sleep, she dreamt Life stood before her, and held in each hand a gift—in the one hand Love, in the other Freedom. And she said to the woman, "Choose."

And the woman waited long: and she said, "Freedom." And Life said "Thou has well chosen. If thou had'st said 'Love,' I would have given thee that thou didst ask for; and I would have gone from thee, and returned to thee no more. Now the day will come when I shall return. In that day, I shall bear both gifts in one hand."

I heard the woman laugh in her sleep.

Olive Schreiner

I try to choose Freedom over Love whenever the opportunity to choose presents itself. But Love is an important question, and Love or the absence of Love are large factors in our lives. So, let's put these two factors together and talk about . . .

The Freedom to Love

At this writing, gender and sexuality are together expressed as a single identity politic in which everyone who's not cisgender and heterosexual is supposed to fall under the category of LGBT. Sometimes people will add a Q for Queer, maybe an I for Intersex, another Q for Questioning, and the tag-on A for Allies.

So maybe sometimes we'll see LGBTQQIA. Eight letters to describe all of us who in some way base our primary identities on sexuality and gender identity and

@ArcherAvenue:
My definition of politics centers on ideologies of power, which is unrelated to government. This makes phrases like "office politics" make more sense. Don't know if that helps, but there.

@capt_jamie_kirk: When discussing my identity with my ex, he replied with "Niggas be changin. Dats cool tho." One of the funniest responses I've gotten.

expression? Oh, please. What about romance, friendship with and without benefits, love, partnership, tribe, family—all these fall under the categories of sexuality and gender. But as I'm writing this version of the workbook, anything in my culture that strays outside the binaries of man/woman and het/homo is supposed to be represented by eight letters. To this, I say poppycock (great word—google it).

Why are members of two different spaces of regulation—sexuality and gender—all lumped together? When the LGBTetc movement began to coalesce back in the late 1960s, it was called The Gay Movement. Then the lesbian women wanted to add an L so they weren't invisibilized. Bisexuals insisted rightly on the B. And then along came T—to this date, many organizations that insist they represent trans people do not have the T in the name of their group.

There was no reason for the T's to band together with the L's, G's, and B's—there were just more chances for acceptance and welcoming. Sexuality outlaws recognized the depth of desire in the identities of gender outlaws, and I guess we all banded together because of that. That would make for a terrific thesis, gender studies majors!

Queer—Why That Word?

Gay men and fags are two different sexual identities. So are lesbians and dykes. Trans people and trannies are two different genders. It's often but not always the difference between straight and queer. I call myself queer. Some people think that's a slur or hate word. Not to me, and not to a whole lot of other people.

The TV show *Queer Eye for the Straight Guy* broke that silence. In many places around the world, anyone who identifies as lesbian, gay, bisexual, or transgender might justifiably call themselves queers—

they're that far outside the sex-and-gender norms of their communities. But increasingly, Queer and Straight are more political terms, used to define the left and right wings of sex-and-gender politics.

> ### Exercise: Diving Into the Deep End
> On the following pages, have yourself a look beyond LGBT and even Q for queer, into a delicious chaos of sexualities and genders. If you don't know what one of the words is, give it a google—well, unless it's sort of a scary word and you don't really want to know anyway. That's OK too. You can make notes in the margins, or write them down in a very private place. On the next few pages, I've listed out —in no particular order— 200 unique sexualities and genders. I stopped at 200, but I found over 750 in under an hour of pointing and clicking.

Some—By No Means All—Gender Anarchists and Sex Positives

Note: No, not all the words are in English. Too bad. And I've put asterisks next to the words I made up.

🅑 For Bisexual
🅑 For Bigender
🅛 For Lesbian
🅛 For Lesbo
🅛 For Lezzie
🅛 For Lipstick Lesbian
🅖 For Gold Star Lesbian
🅖 For Gynaeotrope

🅣 For Transgender
🅣 For Trans
🅣 For Travesti
🅣 For Transvestite
🅣 For Tranny
🅣 For Transy
🅣 For Transsexual
🅣 For Transfag

T for Transdyke

T for Tranny Chaser

F for Fuck Buddy

F for Fag Hag

D for Drag Hag

L for Lesbro

P for Pervert

P for Poof

P for Ponce

U for Uranians

U for Urning

G for Gay

G for Gender Outlaw

G for Goth Loli

Q for Queer

Q for Questioning

K for Khush

H for Homosexual

H for Homo

H for Queer Heterosexual*

H for Hijra

D for Drag Family

F for Femme Queen

B for Butch Queen

A for Asexual

A for Adult Entertainers

A for Androgyne

A for Amazons

A for Agro

S for Strippers

S for Sadomasochists

S for Sluts

G for Goddesses

G for Glamazon

S for Sadist

M for Masochist

S for Switch

T for Top

B for Bottom

P for Pitcher

C for Catcher

M for Master

M for Mistress

S for Slave

D for Dom

D for Domme

S for Sub

L for Leather

L for Leather Man

S for Sex Workers

P for Prostitutes

W for Whores

H for Hustlers

E for Escorts

S for Swingers

S for Sisters of Perpetual Indulgence

S for Stone

S for Sugar Daddy

S for Sugar Momma

S for Sworn Virgins

S for Sissies

T for Tom Boys

Q for Queens

K for Kings

D for DragFuck Royalty*

V for Voyeur

D for Dagger

B for Bulldagger

K for KiKi

D for Dykes

B for Badass Dykes

B for Baby Dyke

L for Leather Dykes

D for Dykes on Bikes

D for Dykes on Spikes

D for Desi Dykes

T for Tattooed Lady

T for Tattooed Man

P for Pierced

S for Sun Dancer

B for Ball Dancer

K for Kathoeys

K for Khanith

C for Crossdresser

C for Chicks with Dicks

C for Closet Queen

C for Cosplayer

C for Cocksucker

M for Muff Diver

R for Rough Trade

H for Hermaphrodite

H for Half-and-Half

V for Venus Castina

C for Castrati

E for Eunuch

I for Intersex

I for Invert

F for Feminists

F for Fairies

R for Radical Faeries

F for Faggots

F for Flaming Faggots

F for Friends of Dorothy

F for Feigele

F for Fa'afafine

F for Futanari

F for Furries

P for Plushies

P for Puppies

P for Ponies

P for Pansies

T for Twink

L for Littles

G for Girly Girl

N for Nancy Boy

[N] for Newhalf

[F] for Femme

[H] for High Femme

[D] for Diesel Femme

[D] for Dandy

[P] for Pretty Boy

[B] for Butch

[B] for Soft Butch

[S] for Stud

[H] for He-She

[S] for She-male

[B] for Bears

[C] for Cubs

[O] for Otters

[B] for Boi

[N] for Nellies

[M] for Mollies

[M] for Muxe

[M] for Mariposa

[M] for Mukhannath

[M] for Moumoune

[D] for Down Low

[M] for Men who have sex with men

[M] for Mashoga

[W] for Women who have sex with women

[G] for Genderqueer

[G] for Genderfuck

[G] for Genderfluid

[G] for Guevedoche

[T] for Two Spirit

[N] for Nadle

[B] for Berdache

[M] for Mahu Wahini

[L] for Lhamana

[G] for Gallus

[H] for Hierodule

[C] for Cogender

[K] for Kinky

[K] for Kinsey 6

[S] for Sapiosexual

[S] for Sex Nerds

[S] for Sex Geeks

[S] for Sex Dorks

[W] for Winkte

[P] for Pornographers

[P] for Pansexual

[P] for Polyamorist

[P] for Pomosexual

[P] for Princess Boys

[E] for Edge Players

[E] for Ecdysiasts

[V] for Awesome Good Vanilla*

[E][T][C] for et cetera

[A][I] for ad infinitum

[A][I] for queer Artificial Intelligence*

G A S P ! ? Fun, But Probably Never

Put 'em together, and what have you got? YOU try to make an acronym out of all those identities! Can't be done. No acronym generator on the intertubes gave me anything useful. PLUS when you add the other 550 letters I found, you could probably generate the Complete Works of William Shakespeare. What are the common denominators? I think it's gender anarchy and sex positivity—and that gives us the really fun acronym of GASP!

There's a lot of us in this clubhouse of sex-and-gender outlaws. I hope you found yourself on this list. If not, it's not you—it's my bad for leaving you off. But I bet you're on the list of 750. Really, though—if you're not anywhere on this list, go find yourself. Enter cool stuff into search engines that will end you up in scary places that just might hold a key to your desire.

But GASP! is just too cute an acronym. If Reese Witherspoon's Elle Woods made it to the White House, we could use it. But I've got an idea for a one-letter-that-rules-us-all name for everyone in my club: E for Ecstatics.

Barbara Carrellas and I have been partners in love, art, and sex-and-gender spelunking since 1997, just a few months before this workbook came out in its first edition. In her most recent book, *Ecstasy Is Necessary: A Practical Guide*, Miss Barbara speaks most articulately to ecstasy, so allow me to turn the page over to her for a moment.

Ecstasy is not "better" than sex. It is not more spiritual, more evolved or more acceptable than "just sex." I despise the phrase "just sex"—as in "It's not love it's just sex." Or "It's not a relationship, it's just sex." Or "What's the big deal? It's just sex." The dismissal of sex as some lower form of energy or lesser activity is a denial of both our physical reality and our spiritual potential. Sex is an expression of who we are. It's not simply a description of physical qualities—as in "She's so sexy!"—or quantities—as in "Boy, I sure am getting a lot of sex lately." It's not even an activity—as in "I'm going to fuck your brains out." Sex is energy—our life-force energy—and it is expressed in every area of our lives. There is no difference between going-to-work energy, eating-dinner energy, taking-out-the-trash energy, and sexual energy. It's all life-force energy. Because the same life-force energy that flows through us also flows through every living thing on the planet, we are in an ongoing erotic relationship with all of life all the time. How much of it we see, feel or appreciate is dependent upon how much of this energy we have learned to recognize, accept, and allow.

Give Me an E for Ecstatics

Yep, that's the club I'd like to be part of: ecstatics. Wanna be one, too? Examining what's really worked in terms of fulfilling my own desire, it's been whatever has gotten my attention focused into the right now moment. Some people call that *being mindful*. It's the moments when my brain isn't trying to figure out what's going on while it's going on; and I'm there, right there in the present, experiencing what I'm experiencing. The time and the focus it takes to stay in that kind of moment defines ecstasy.

Dancing, orgasms, pain, bleeding, endorphin rushes, amazing good food, performing, writing, a really good conversation, listening to great music, doing great sex, being present for a work of art, working out. This is a fraction of the continuum of my desire that grabs my attention, keeps me from trying to figure out who I am or what I need to be.

I think the trick would be to live our lives so that anything we do is done with that kind of attention to detail in the present, that kind of focus on the right now moment. But there are so many distractions to paying attention to what we're doing. We've most of us got so much stuff going on in the background of our minds that it becomes difficult to simply mindfully do whatever it is we're doing.

Given it's important to pay attention, how can we remain deeply entrenched within any identity, the maintenance of which demands a great deal of time and attention? Time and attention we could be spending with what really turns us on? I think that's another good reason to make any identity, including gender, a conscious choice. We can choose to spend time honing our uniquely gendered self-expression in such a way as to attract that to which we are attracted and leave ourselves free to experience our attraction without the intrusion of some gender-maintenance problem.

@AcreatureofLux:
For me, a side effect of living outside the gender binary is the feeling that I exist in an alternate reality. There is danger in occupying this liminal space, but also tremendous power. I broke through the gender barrier and accessed the ability to be many things at once or nothing at all.

@MorganBurns1:
I just want to be able to "pass," without getting ready, without makeup, in guys sweatclothes even. In any situation. #preopproblems

We can bring our attention back to our own motives toward our self-named identities, desires, and power first by ceasing the obsessive search for either being or being approved by some myth of a perfectly gendered person. No one needs approval from people who believe that their gender identities and expressions are somehow better than ours.

We get to cease our successful or unsuccessful masquerades as real men or real women, because only then are we going to find traction through which we might realize our true desire—ecstasy beyond our wildest imagination. Yep, conscious gender can be the key to all that. Once we simply question the supposition that we are real men or real women, once we strip ourselves of one of these imposed identities, we're also going to strip ourselves of all the possibilities for socially sanctioned attractions.

That means we must truly come face to face with all our longing, our loneliness, and our need to connect. And that gets right back to the need for each of us to name, down to our fingernails, the nature of our desire. Otherwise, we're stuck with a desire named for us by whatever the culture at large we happen to belong to at the moment.

There's this idea romantically and wistfully circulating in transgender and even within some cisgender circles that by being born a man, one can become a "better" woman; and that by having been raised female in this culture, one can eventually be a "better" man. This is not entirely mythic, since each of the two main gender categories has evolved over time as a representation of the other's fantasy.

OK, I've gone a long time in this chapter without mentioning pirates, or the treasure map. Time to change that.

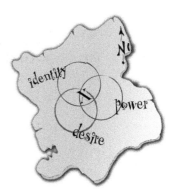

QUESTION: If sexuality is so important, how come there was no clue for sexuality on the gender treasure map?

ANSWER: Because in my country—and in many others around the world—no one's allowed us to talk about much sexuality and gender before now. And absence of sexuality in our map is one hell of a clue.

So did any fun sex things come to mind while you were reading this chapter? Well, before you actually do any of them, it's safe to say that the more you know about this stuff, the more fun you'll have when you actually do it. So here comes an exercise that'll put you even closer to some really fun sex, whenever it might be that you want that.

Exercise: Autoerotic Brain Stimulating

Before you actually *do* all the amazing sexual things that might have occurred to you while reading this chapter, list three things you'd like to know more about in sex.

1. _____

2. _____

3. _____

Now list three people with whom it would be safe and fun to talk about this with. Total strangers count. Love is easier to talk about than you might think. Yes, there are dangerous places to look for love—and places people will tell you *not* to look. The only place please don't look for love is someplace that's got a good chance of getting you into trouble or harm's way. And please, don't be mean to someone else. Make that your one rule when it comes to sexuality and gender: don't be mean.

1. _____

2. _____

3. _____

Mutual Erotic Brain Teasing

Go talk about sex. Talk it up big. Ask lots of questions. Ask questions about the answers you get. Follow words that lead you closer to your desires—even the scary desires. You're *only* talking about it.

There. That makes it all work out nicely for everyone. Now you're ready to use all this information to transform yourself into the sexuality/gender being of your dreams. As you begin to ponder and talk more about this, you may find yourself wanting to come out to someone else. If that's the case, turn to the end of Chapter 8, and you'll find a four-page comic that will help you explain things to them. How cool is that?

Chapter 7: Get Ready to Do Your Gender

This will be the death of you. No, no, not the big final death—if, in fact, death is final, which is debatable. But if you keep doing the exercises in this book, the part of you that's been gendered is going to . . . well, die. And you'll be reborn as an even funner you. I promise. And I'm so not the first one to ever promise this. Chuang Tzu was one of the earliest Taoist masters. He was a trickster, a comedian. He wrote:

> *How do I know that loving life is not a delusion? How do I know that in hating death I am not like a man who, having left home in his youth, has forgotten the way back?*

Exercise: Use this space or as much as you need to re-write Chuang Tzu's koan, replacing the words *life*, *death*, and *man* in such a way that it applies to gender:

The moon is female.
The sun is male.
Ah, darlings,
We must be the *stars*!
—Emily Lloyd

I wrote earlier about death, transformation, and gender; and now that we're at a point in this workbook to actually do this stuff, it's time to expand on it.

More and more people are playing with the transformation of gender these days. People in all walks of life are saying no to the categories of "real man" and "real woman." They're trying out a gender here and a gender there—often many genders in the course of a day or even a few hours. These transformations can be purely physical, or they can go deep to the core of our identities.

My own style is to get as much as I can out of any identity I find myself in; that leaves me that identity as part of a bag of tricks I can pull up whenever I want to. It means a lot of freedom for me. And, of course, there's a cost to all this. Going fully into any given identity means giving up fully the last identity we've been occupying. It's like a death, no?

What image does "death" conjure for you? Some dark figure with a skull's head and a scythe? The queen of spades? A shrieking harpy? Needles and dials all going into the red on some hospital monitor? Me, I see death as author Neil Gaiman envisions her in his *Sandman* series of graphic novels: a beautiful goth chick angel with whom, when you finally meet her, you fall in love so hard that your soul is pulled out through your eyes.

I don't mean to speak of death lightly. Maybe death is common in your life. Maybe you're dying right now and don't want to think about it. I'm sorry if that's the case. We don't need to talk about that kind of death.

RECOMMENDED READING:
Go buy the *Sandman* series, or read it in a library. Lots of good gender play in there, and Neil Gaiman is a master storyteller.

We do need a language to speak about the death of an identity. There's not much of a metaphor we can reach for in the great big death, for the simple reason that there aren't too many people who've died and lived again to tell us about it. There is, fortunately, a language in place that describes the process of dying. That'll do for starters.

Elisabeth Kübler-Ross wrote a ground-breaking book, *On Death and Dying*, in which she lays out five stages we go through during the process of dying. Since we're talking about killing off one (or more) of our identities, it might be good to have a guideline to getting through the experience.

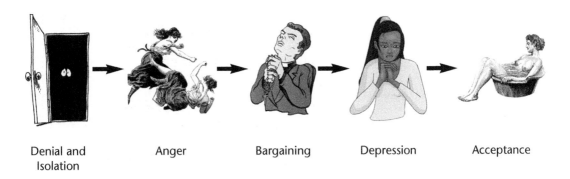

| Denial and Isolation | Anger | Bargaining | Depression | Acceptance |

That makes sense, right? Think of the last time you lost someone to death . . . or just lost someone. The odds are good that you went through this emotional journey. Well, sure enough, the same five stages apply to a gender transition. Let's try this out and see if it works—or has worked—in life. Well, in your life. I bet you've already been through a gender change, if not two or three. Let's see if I'm right.

Exercise: Name Your Change

When was your last gendered identity transition? It could be from boy to man, or heterosexual woman to lesbian woman, or pre-menopausal woman to peri- or menopausal woman, or skinny guy to fat guy, healthy girl to sick girl . . . whatever . . . any sort of gender transition that you've been through.

Your challenge is to name the gender you left being and the gender you eventually became.

Give them labels—there's nothing wrong with the mindful use of labels. As always, feel free to write in the margins any key words you want to remember. You've been through a gender change. We all have. Let's explore it now!

The gender I stopped being was: _____

The gender I became was: _____

I hope that gave you some giggles, and I'm sorry if that was in any way upsetting.

Now, here are some questions about your transition from one gender to the other. Write down some keywords of what comes to mind as you answer each.

- Was there a time when it was just all too overwhelming? ____

- Was there a time when you didn't believe it was happening? ____

- Were there times when you just needed to be alone? ____

- Did it make you angry that you had to make that transition? ____

- Did you try to make any deals or bargains about just how far you might go? ____

- Have you come to accept that gender transition now? ____

So, hey, you've got more than one gender. How about them apples? I'm not saying this to invisibilize the transgender/transsexual or any other trans* experience—I'm saying that gender transition, like everything else, is a matter of degree, and there's a tipping point when gender transition is claimed as transgender. That tipping point is different for everyone, and so we've got an unlimited number of genders walking around in the world right now. Imagine if all those people were doing their gender mindfully. What would the world look like then?

When I wrote the first version of this workbook, I was still working on acceptance. Well, I've been at a point of acceptance for a long time— so I can tell you, it's possible. It's all possible. You can make your life better through the conscious expression of your gender identity. I'm surprised to realize that I've come to accept each of the aspects of my own fluid self: the boy stuff as well as the girl stuff—*and* all the stuff that's neither one nor the other. I've mostly gotten to the point of not caring what people think I am.

So, gentle reader, don't despair if it takes time to get to the point of saying goodbye to the monogendered identity we've all spent a long time being, or trying to be. Whether that identity has felt more or less right or wrong to us, it has been the one we've been living through for quite some time now. So transitioning out of it into something completely different can take years. Please keep this in mind: there is no rush. With every moment, we're changing. Enjoy that change. That's a good way to learn patience. And your patience will be rewarded, because the more deeply you explore each step of your journey, the fewer times you'll need to re-trace any steps. That's been my experience.

@MartianEmpress:
The soft murmur of people like ourselves is reassuring in a peaceful paleotribal kinda way. <3

The Shame Game

The paradox is that even when we fully leave off having been a gender, it stays with us to some degree. That's true for every identity we've ever been. Colors of the old identity/gender creep onto the palette of our new identities, often without our being aware of it—and there are times when that can be embarrassing.

@youlittlewonder: I'm a girly girl with the innards of a truck driver. My femmeness is not a naturally-ordained fact; it is a performance. My femmeness is genderqueer. I am not deranged. The dichotomy is deranged.

@MiaCoffeeSnow: In the confusion of not being able to express myself, I found I was unwilling to fill out a basic form because it asked for my gender.

Embarrassing or not—it's time to talk with someone else about all this stuff you've been poring over. It's time to articulate your own ideas about gender, and the best way to do that is face time with another human being. It can be pretty intimidating. I know. When I was beginning my first conscious gender transition—the one from male to female—it was scary. I just wanted it to be over with. And I didn't want to talk with anyone about it. It was all I could do to read about this stuff.

I remember the first person to whom I said "I think I'm transsexual." I'd chosen a very liberal friend of mine who'd responded, "Oh really? That's cool." I was floored; I was expecting him to make the sign of the cross or something, or somehow get himself rid of me. I did get that sort of response from others I told subsequently, but I learned to hang on to the favorable responses, and to use those favorable responses as safety rungs up the side of this identity cliff I was beginning to scale.

The fourth step in any twelve-step program is where you have to write down all the bad stuff and all the good stuff in your life, although the emphasis is usually placed on writing down all the bad stuff. I didn't want to do it. I was busy exploring my gender options in terms of therapy, electrolysis, fashion, feminism, and surgery. I was moving forward, and I didn't want to look back. As part of my research, I put a call into the offices of the International Foundation for Gender Education and spoke with a transsexual woman who answered the phone. We chatted for a bit about transsexuality. She was telling me her own story. Then she asked me to tell her a little about me. I fumbled around for a bit, and managed to say I was two years sober.

"Have you done your fourth step yet," she shot back. I told her, "No, I haven't."

She got really gentle with me at that point and said, "How do you think you're going to be able to move forward into a new identity as long as you're chained to the shames of your past?"

That hit home. After we got off the phone, I sat down and began writing down all the things I'd done in my life that I was ashamed of having done. It took me a little over a week to get the bulk of it down, and another week to remember more and more incidents and details. When I finished, I went right on to AA's fifth step: I made a coffee date with a cross-dressing friend of mine, and I shared all this shameful stuff with him.

Y'know what? The AA folks were right: I felt lighter and more free than I'd felt in a long time. I got all those secrets out to a friend, and we remained friends. It gets back to the proverb that secrets will kill us.

@AlyxJHanson: I already knew I was crazy. Accepting that my gender wasn't "normal" either was a pretty easy next step. It fit. I label myself as queer because it fits not only my orientation and gender identity, but also the state of my brain.

@JillyBoyd: My gender is female, because that's just how I feel. Sometimes I feel distinctly male though. Just me :)

No, I'm not recommending you join AA or any other twelve-step program; or even that you start up some sort of twelve-step group around the subject of transgender. I'm not saying "Get thee to a meeting, go!" I am saying that it would be a good idea right now to do a little housekeeping in terms of all the junk you're carrying around from your past. I'm saying it would be a very good idea, if you're serious about exploring some sort of personal stretch beyond the concepts of "real man" and "real woman," to sit down and list out the stuff you've done in your life that you're ashamed of—if for no other reason than to move forward in this exploration with a much lighter heart.

Some Words for Those Who Feel They're Some Sort of Trans

Look, you may do the full monty version of this gender change. And if you do, people are going to look at you. You're going to be awkward at first. People are going to laugh and maybe you'll feel ashamed. Some folks will pity you; others may empathize with you. Fact is, some of your shame buttons are going to get pushed. It happens. It's all part of the adolescence that attends any kind of major identity shift. It's why most of us detest being new at anything: we go through an adolescent phase of self-consciousness that's truly painful. I'm suggesting you write up your past shameful stuff now, so that you'll have the energy to deal with your new stuff in the present, and so that you'll be able to sort out what's truly shameful, and what's simply a matter of other people not being able to deal with it.

You're not alone. Thousands and thousands of people have gone through a major gender change like the one you're contemplating, and each of them weathered the attendant storms of emotions. You can do it. You've got a lot more information than most of us had when we were in your shoes. You can do it. Many blessings to you.

And Some Words for Everyone Else

You may not be going through a radical gender change. The odds are you're going to do nothing of the sort. But I want you to take a moment, please, and think back over some of the things you've read in this book. Do you have any wish at all to broaden the definition of your gender? Any wish at all to stretch the boundaries set by the culture for someone of your gender? If you don't, then god bless. Put this book down, or give it to someone who might need or want it. I mean it. No hard feelings. Honest!

However, if stretching your gender identity is something you might consider, then the rest of the book applies to you as much as to any female-to-male or male-to-female or whatever-to-whatever trans person or genderqueer out there. If you're toying with the idea of being a different kind of man than you've always been, or perhaps another kind of woman than you've been all your life, the rest of the book does apply to you. No, not as dramatically as it would apply to me or many other trans folks. But it does apply to you.

Please keep on reading. I think you'll find some comfort here.

I'm glad you're still with me. Here's an exercise based on AA's fourth step. I hope it helps you.

A Really Important Exercise

Get a notebook that you can carry around with you easily.

1. Write a searching and fearless moral inventory of yourself. You're looking for things you've done that you and/or others considered to be good, and things that you've done that you/or others considered to be bad. This doesn't have to be in date order—you can skip all over the place if you want to. Just write it down.

2. Keep that notebook with you, and as soon as you remember another incident, write it down. Be sure to find out exactly which part of that shameful incident you were responsible for, and which parts were truly not your responsibility (it's very rarely an all-my-fault or all-their-fault sort of thing).

3. Just keep writing things down in the notebook; you'll get to a point where there's no more to write, and that's what you're looking for.

Go on—put the book down and do this exercise. You probably need a break from all my ramblings right now anyway.

4. When you're done, pick some friend you can sit down with and share all that stuff. Make sure you get their agreement to do that beforehand, before you start spilling all of it out at them. Go on—you'll feel a lot better. Honest.

And Now for the Grand Finale . . .

Name Your Gender!

Exercise: Perhaps your gender is the same as when you started reading this book. Yes, you may very well be a man or a woman. Well, now you're older and wiser. That's a shift in gender. So, if you're a man or a woman, then what *sort* of man or woman are you? Or are you something else entirely? Put into words a gender that expresses who you are. It may help to use modifiers that include race, age, class, and/or any of the gender and sexuality words from 🅖🅐🅢🅟 in the last chapter. Use a pencil because you may want to come back and change this later. Write as much as you need to—out into the margins if you need to.

My Gender Is:

_____

Finished? In the words of drag superstar supreme RuPaul, CONDRAGULATIONS!

And because you are such a clever thing, here's some super sexy fun rhymes from the intrepid poet, @wordgeeksarah.

Though you just cannot wait to get stuck
   in
To that exquisite licking and sucking
If you're not procreating
There's folks out there hating;
I'm sorry you're bullied for ------

Oh what low expectations we shape
When girls learn: "it's my job to
   escape."
It seems cruel and unfair
Girls are taught to beware,
So why don't we teach boys not to

Though you're homo and proud, please
   don't sneer
At the hetero-sex-radicals here.
Within gender anarchy
We're one happy family;
Gay isn't the same thing as -----

Some folks have the strongest
   propensity
Where they choose which terms are
   and aren't "meant to be."
Well stick this up your fanny;
I'm proudly a tranny!
And your "slur" is my favored

Chapter 8: Do Your Gender Mindfully

I closed the last chapter invoking the spirit of my queen of queens, RuPaul. Why? Because now it's time to figure out how to express your unique gender. And just how do we do that? We drag it up! So, what's drag? RuPaul judges contestants on *RuPaul's Drag Race* on the basis of charisma, uniqueness, nerve, and talent. So, how do we embody those qualities with drag? Well ... I don't know. But I'm working on it, and here's what I've figured out so far.

An Evolving Theory of Drag

Drag has traditionally been seen as a binary: drag queens and drag kings. You know by now that can't possibly represent all the people who do drag. There are professional performers, and people who do their drag at parties. There are cisgender men and women who do drag kings and drag queens respectively. There's drag as rehearsal for a longer time in another gender. And there's lots of drag that doesn't have gender as its primary focus. All this drag seems to contain these elements:

1. CONSCIOUS—First and foremost, drag is always conscious, or mindful. We're aware we're doing it—we're mindfully expressing a new identity. When we stop being mindful, it's no longer drag—it's a uniform, or a suit of armor.

2. SELF-REFERENTIAL—When we do drag, we're always aware of how we're coming across. Our attention is on ourselves in relation to another, so that we can modify whatever drag we're doing. We are constantly posing our questions, *How am I doing?* and/or *Is this working?* and/or *Am I safe?*

3. PERFORMANCE—Yep, it's an act. It's all an act. We choose a part to play, we write a script in our minds, we improvise when we need to, and we pivot on a dime if that's what's needed to maintain the quality and effect of the performance.

We all came into this world naked. The rest is all drag.
—RuPaul

4. SEXY and/or POLITICAL and/or SELF-PROTECTIVE—There are many modifiers for drag, but a whole lot of drag is done for one or more of these reasons.

5. OF GENDER OR . . .—Not all drag is about gender. We do drag to climb up from under the crushing oppression of race, age, class, religion, sexuality, looks, disability, mental health, family and reproductive status, language, habitat, citizenship, political ideology, and humanity. We do drag to be the best within any of these spaces of regulation—or as close as we can get to being the best. Or we do drag so that those who *are* the best in those spaces will like us. Or we do drag so we don't stand out as the freak we think we are.

She is large and in charge, chunky, yet funky. Bold and Beautiful baby.
—Latrice Royale

These are all valid motivations and forms of drag. In my country, of all the drag performed in service to any of the fifteen spheres of cultural regulation, it's the drag performed in the name of sexuality and gender that's the bravest. Drag queens and drag kings are royalty. They've earned our adoration.

6. FOR AN AUDIENCE—We do drag as part of an interaction with another or others. Yes, we can dress up and practice in whatever privacy we can conjure for ourselves. But I'm saying that's not drag. Drag is performance. Doing it all by yourself is rehearsal. And we all need rehearsal time—that's when we get to make all the mistakes without any consequences of our drag failing. So sure, rehearse—then do your drag for your intended audience.

> I've had several people disagree with this one, and I respect their disagreement. But I'm going to stick by it as a theory: we do drag for an audience. That's part of it. Invoking the koan "the way you do anything is the way you do everything," and embracing the fabulousness of RuPaul's drag superstars, I come up with the conclusion that to do drag well, an audience has got to be part of it. You may not be performing your drag for the benefit of your audience, but an audience is certainly watching you do your drag, so how are you going to perform it with charisma, uniqueness, nerve, and talent? You acknowledge your audience.

7. FOR A REASON—You might want to entertain an audience, or disarm them. Maybe you want to make them laugh, or cry, or gasp out loud. Maybe you're doing your drag for a specific audience because you want them to think about, question, or welcome you. When you express yourself the way you *intend* to express yourself—in drag—what do you want from the people to whom you're expressing it?

We frighten you because we walk through walls,
Like ghosts, like saints, contagion;
Everywhere is borderless to us,
There are no borders to our nation.
You cannot raise an army to defend,
You cannot make a mirror that repels,
You may expect that we will pay a toll,
But do not waste your intake breath with spells.
The only way for sure to kill the fear
That we may walk right through the walls of you
Is to knock them down,
And then the fear is gone.

—Dragon Xcalibur, Ferryman

So That's My Idea of Drag.
So Let's Do It, Darling

Exercise

Start Your Engines

Think of several of the fifteen cultural spheres that are regulating your life (Chapter 3). Now pick the one in which life would be more worth living if only you dragged it up better in that sphere. Then, using the criteria of charisma, uniqueness, nerve, and talent—and the seven components of drag listed on the previous pages—imagine how you could do that drag. Set your imagination free. What might you wear? How would you change your voice, or wouldn't you? How differently would you interact with people if you dragged it up to your heart's content? Go on, imagine it. Write down words and phrases in this box that will help you remember any important steps of your imagined dragification, and put numbers next to them to mark the order of how you might actually do them.

_____

_____

_____

_____

_____

Advanced Dragalicious Exercise

Rehearse what you imagined. Yep, this is an appropriate use of private time. You've nothing to feel guilty about rehearsing your drag. It's not

a bad thing to do. However, please do your dragifying in private, where it's safe. Depending on how radical a drag you'd like to do, it may take you some time to find a safe place. Don't rehearse your drag someplace where people might hurt you. What's rehearsal? Doing it over and over again, giving yourself the opportunity to fuck up over and over, so that you don't fuck it up in front of your audience. For tips on how to rehearse your drag, use the section HOME ALONE, coming up in the next few pages.

The Watch Out World Here I Come Exercise

Do your drag, and in the words of our Queen RuPaul, *don't fuck it up.* (Don't worry—I'll be there with you all the time. Just carry this book with you.) And look! On the next couple of pages, there are some wonderful ideas for where you can do it. Don't be afraid. You've already rehearsed. Have fun!

Gender Playgrounds

When you make changes in your gendered identity, it's just like going into some new playground where you don't know the rules. Remember when you were a kid, and you went into a new playground for the first time? Remember you didn't know how all the equipment worked? You didn't know if you'd make any friends there? You didn't know all the games—or if you'd be good enough, or if they'd like you enough? Well, playing with gender is like that.

One of my favorite quotes is this Zen saying: "All roads in life lead nowhere; so you might as well take the road that has the most heart, and is the most fun." I don't know who said it. Maybe it was me.

I want an incisive, inquisitive, insightful, irreverent mind. I want someone for whom philosophical discussion is foreplay. I want someone who sometimes makes me go ouch due to their wit and evil sense of humor. I want someone that I can reach out and touch randomly. I want someone I can cuddle with. I decided all that means that I am sapiosexual.

—Urban Dictionary

If I had been born female physiologically, I would be happy in that identity and would probably have never had all the stress that goes with gender conflict. If I could stand at the threshold of conception and direct a sperm bearing an X chromosome toward the ovum, I would. But I was born stressed instead. That's what chose me.

—Mona

And Gandhi was supposed to have said something like "Everything you try to do is futile, but that shouldn't stop you from trying." I use both of those sentiments on a daily basis, especially when it seems like it's no longer worth the effort it takes to be something new under the sun.

I'm going to assume you've got the heart for this journey, or you wouldn't have gotten this far into the book; you're following your heart, and I have a great deal of admiration and respect for people who do that. Well, I think we deserve a little fun for all this trouble we're going to, don't you?

I found that by discovering what gives me joy in my life—real joy—I could find ways to discover that kind of joy in my gender journey. The deep joy in my own life stems from things such as: finding missing pieces to philosophical conundrums; or being able to express love for someone; or the freedom to be what I want to be, when I need or want to be that (which very often means being quite alone). I find joy in spending time with people who like the same joys.

It gives me a great deal of pleasure to be useful in my life, to be of service however I can. I enjoy art and other forms of communication that reach my heart, and raise new questions; I love new questions of any kind. I like being silly, and in the rare times I allow myself, I enjoy being very small. I'm saying all this now, because I think it's a good idea to form some concept of the kind of fun we'd like to have, before actually going into the playground to look for it.

Exercise: What are some of *your* favorite things? Looking over your life, what gives you joy? If it's something specific, such as horseback-riding or playing chess, watching movies, reading, or simply sitting on the front stoop on a nice sunny day, then go a little deeper: what about that experience do you enjoy? Displaying your expertise? Meeting a challenge? Giving yourself a moment without the usual pressures of your life? The search for the nature of your joy is going to help you in the long run by giving you something to look for in playing with gender. Write your answers in the margin of this page so you can come back and add to this if you ever want to.

Auntie Kate's Guide to Funner Gender Playgrounds

This section is definitely written with advanced students of gender in mind. Many readers of this book are not going to need information about where to go in order to appear to the world as a totally different gender. However, I think that any gender play, even the most subtle, requires attention to both personal safety and comfort, so this section may even come in handy to you some day. You never know, do you? These playgrounds have stuff in common. They're mostly relatively safe, and peopled by like-minded or open-minded folks. The good playgrounds are filled with lots of opportunity for fun, places where you can be more or less anonymous. They're accessible to most folks, and they're inexpensive. So, let's go for it!

Home Alone

If you're fortunate enough to have a space of your own—
even if it's temporary—that's a wonderful place to start
experimenting with different elements of self-expression.
One of the most common elements used to distinguish a
gendered identity in our culture is clothing. You might
try cross-dressing behind closed doors.

Of course, you have to go get the clothing with which to
cross dress first. That can be a wonderful growing
experience all by itself, and it's all part of this next
exercise. Go on, this is safe—it's a rehearsal. No one's there
to laugh or get angry. Take a deep breath. Here we go.

Drag Rehearsal Part I

Pick out and get yourself five articles of clothing that would be
something you'd never wear because it's for the "wrong" gender (e.g.
if you're a boy, a butch, or a man, you might name a dress or some
frilly negligee. If you're a girl, a femme, or a woman, you might name
a rather plain three-piece suit.) Second-hand clothing shops are great
places to pick up rehearsal drag for cheap.

Drag Rehearsal Part II

Pick one of those articles of clothing, and go out and buy it for yourself.
Yes, you can tell the clerk it's for someone else if you really want to.
But don't be surprised if that clerk gives you a knowing smile. They've
seen it all before. If you live in a small town and feel your safety might
be jeopardized, you can order great used stuff on Craig's list, eBay, and
other second-hand outlet websites.

Drag Rehearsal Part III

Once you've got that article of clothing, arrange a time alone for yourself when you won't be interrupted. Take off all your gendered clothes, and put on the item you selected above. What feelings come up for you? Write those feelings down in the margins of this page.

Drag Rehearsal Part IV

Now trace those feelings back to where they came from. For example, if you felt ashamed wearing a dress, where did you learn that shame from? If it was a thrill to wear a padded jockstrap, what's the basis of your thrill? Write your answers in the margins, and draw arrows back to the feelings that prompted them.

Drag Rehearsal Part V

Did tracing back your feelings change the way you now feel about wearing that article of clothing? If so, how?

HOME ALONE PROS

If you have a home or room where you can experiment like this, you're very fortunate. Some of us who could afford it rented cheap motel rooms to experiment alone like that. Maybe there's a safe, private space you can use in a community center you belong to?

HOME ALONE CONS

I think it's a very good idea to fly solo as you take your first step with gender play. However, since gender is interactive, there's going to be very little experiential reality of that gender if you don't eventually go out and interact with others.

Support Groups

The first interactive playground I'd suggest is a support group of like-minded or similar-minded people. If you live in a big city, or even a medium-sized city, one should be easy to find.

You can go online (for free at your local public library) and google "transgender + support groups." Add your location, and that should give you a good number of groups. When I started going through my first conscious gender change, there was no support group for trans folks. My therapist suggested I get together with some other trans people and start one up. I wailed that I didn't know any trans folks, and she offered to mention the idea to some of her other clients. We got together, hammered out some guidelines and held weekly meetings. Some groups are meetings-only. Some groups throw parties for their members, so you can explore your new gender in a more social, less angst-ridden context.

SUPPORT GROUP PROS

Most members are likely to understand your loneliness, shyness, apprehension, and excitement, and in all likelihood they will welcome you, giving you a place to talk about your feelings. They may have lists of community resource contacts: trans-friendly stores, bars, restaurants, clinics and such. You can make some great connections here, and maybe even find some deeper friendships.

SUPPORT GROUP CONS

Nearly every support group comes with its own standards for membership and its own guidelines for "correct" behavior. Some groups have their own system of values when it comes to who's "real," and its own ideas about the "right" path to take on a gender journey.

Out-of-Town Trips

Many people who start cross-dressing or exploring another gender or genders on a very physical level leave town to do it. I did. I took advantage of business trips to cross-dress, and to simply experience walking around the streets of a different city where no one knew me. I figured if they laughed, they laughed; it was sort of like testing a nuclear weapon way off in the desert: I had the illusion that there would be no real effect from doing it. I needed that illusion of security to build up my self-confidence. No one likes to screw up, and screwing up is exactly what needs to happen. Let me explain that.

When I'm directing actors in a play, I encourage them to make all the mistakes they can in a rehearsal—that's my theory. If you make them in rehearsal, you won't make them on stage: or if you do, at least you'll be prepared. I'm not even talking about trying to pass, unless that's what you want to do. I'm talking about learning to comfortably express yourself in some new identity, with all the attendant new attitudes, physicalizations, and methods of relating with different people.

Out-of-town visits can come in mighty handy for "rehearsal." Why do you suppose so many plays go on the road before opening on Broadway?

OUT-OF-TOWN PROS

Nobody knows you. You can goof, slip up, and make a general fool of yourself; and it's not likely to come back and haunt you in the circles within which you feel safe and at home.

OUT-OF-TOWN CONS

It can be expensive—but you could always house-sit for a friend who lives in another part of town. It could be dangerous, so it pays to check out the neighborhood first.

Conferences, Congresses and Special Events

There are more and more conferences, conventions, and get-togethers held for gender outlaws these days. They run the gamut from scholarly to slutty (and yes, slutty is a good thing). Conferences range from follow-the-rules to no-holds-barred. The internet is a good place to find out where and when these get-togethers are held. They're also promoted regularly in the mags, newsletters and zines that cater to gender outlaws.

I enjoy going to these because, frankly, I can be whatever I want to be on a day-to-day basis. I can show up in my Hogwarts professor drag, and explore diesel femme dominatrix the next day, followed by a foray into Cylon temptress, blowing good-bye kisses to my friends before I leave.

@celebelei: my gender wasn't political until other people told me it should be. Never "enough" for any group who should accept me. So I'm me.

The benefit of a conference is that it combines the anonymity of an out-of-town trip with the understanding that comes from support groups. There are usually many informative panels covering everything from the latest postmodern theory to make-up tips to which new prosthesis makes the most realistic penis when worn inside your boxer shorts or jockstrap.

Support groups often distribute their literature at these events, and vendors sell all kinds of books, clothing, accessories, and paraphernalia.

In addition to the learning experience, there are usually social events planned, such as dances, dinners, and outings to shows. Sometimes there are play parties for S/M aficionados and aficionadas. Shopping trips are generally built in to these types of get-togethers, and for those starting out in a new gender it can be quite a relief to shop in numbers.

CONFERENCE AND EVENT PROS

You get to be anything you want to be, with no apologies, and no guilt! These are good places to find out information that might not be available locally. You'll most likely make at least a few lasting friendships with like-minded outlaws.

CONFERENCE AND EVENT CONS

They're usually on the expensive side, but many conferences have scholarship-for-work programs and sliding scale entrance fees, so it's worth checking out.

Friendships

You're going to have to do it sometime. We all do. You're going to have to come out to your friends. As you continue to play with your own concepts of real man and real woman, something's going to leak through and someone's going to spot something unusual about you.

When you tell them, or when they find out, some of your friends are going to drop you like a rock; some will deal with their own issues and continue being a great friend to you, even more of a friend because you've taken a step towards a greater intimacy in the friendship.

Ten years ago, when I first came out to my friends before my transition from male to female, the way I'd do it was to bring up the subject of transsexuals in general. It was more difficult twenty-five years ago, because there weren't as many socially acceptable representations of transsexuality to which I could refer. I'd say things like, "Hey, did you see that Donahue show yesterday, the one where he actually wore a dress?" (Back then, Phil Donahue was the USA's Oprah Winfrey before there was Oprah Winfrey.)

It's easier today, in many places around the world, to enter into a conversation about trans-themed movies and reality TV. Or you could be casually reading this very book while waiting for your friend to show up for coffee. You could suggest going to some drag king show, or a drag queen show.

There are some great queer podcasts, public radio shows, and cable TV shows that regularly give air-time to transgender topics. I used to draw pen-and-ink sketches with a transgender theme, and I'd casually show them to friends to catch their reactions. Whatever you choose to do, I think it's a good idea to bridge into the subject. Unless you're quite intimate already with your friend, it's probably not a great idea to lean over your salad and immediately launch into "Hey, guess what . . . I'm going to start playing with my gender starting in, oh . . ." (look at your watch) ". . . four minutes."

FRIENDS-AS-SUPPORT PROS

Friends are likely to call you on your old patterns.

FRIENDS-AS-SUPPORT CONS

Friends are likely to call you on your old patterns.

One thing I found useful in coming out to my friends was holding compassion for their probable shaky response. Chances are they haven't had the means or reason to examine this gender stuff as deeply as you have; so be prepared to deal with questions. I always invite questions when I'm making a new friend. I try to make allowances for enculturated fears on their part, so I try to be as gentle and understanding as I can be. I try to remember when I had similar negative feelings about all this stuff. Patience is a big factor, and it nearly always pays off. For those who say goodbye, yeah, that's sad; but better to find out sooner than later. Most friends will treasure your trust in them. And—as a help to you and your friend, you'll find a comic book at the end of this chapter. It's called *My Gender For Friends and Family*. Hey, who loves ya?

The Bar Scene

Story time:

There was this one drag bar in Philadelphia that I used to haunt when I first started cross-dressing in public. It was pretty sleazy, but then again, so was I. I was in my Madonna-wannabe phase, and honey, I did Madonna to the teeth, all five feet eleven inches of me (well, taller in heels). In the drag bar context, I got more than a little validation and admiration for my over-the-top presentation.

Later, when I had decided to go through with a full gender change, and I was being crunchy-granola femme lesbian, I would hang out at a local girl bar. I was pretty defensive about my self-proclaimed womanhood in those days, and I'd sit off by myself, nursing a Diet Pepsi. Most of the crowd there were younger lesbians who, for the most part, ignored me. I watched and watched and watched. I wanted to know how those grrrls interacted with one another. I was starved for that kind of inform-ation. It wasn't until I finally got up the courage to use the bathroom that I ran across the butches.

The bathroom was upstairs, and I remember wading through the crowd of young women to get to the stairs. When I reached the top of the stairs, I did the grade-B movie thing of stopping and staring. I'm guessing my mouth was hanging open in a mixture of surprise and delight. There were these way cool older women in suits or shirtsleeves, playing pool, smoking cigars, and having a great time with one another. When they saw me standing there, one for one their faces lit up. "C'mon in, honey," one of them said to me. They held out a chair for me, treated me like a princess. They taught me to play pool; I tried their cigars, and they laughed when I coughed. They knew I was transgender, but they saw this other gender identity that I wouldn't see until years later: they were butch, and they saw femme.

We had a wonderful time of it, back in the 1980s when butch/femme was scorned by the more politically correct androgynous set. And that's why I am so fond of butches.

The bar eventually closed, and I lost touch with those women from upstairs at Sneakers. If you see any of them, please let them know they made a baby femme very, very happy, and I'm so grateful.

Yes, there are some places that won't be happy with a trans-thing like you in their establishment. I always figure I don't want to go anywhere I'm not wanted, and I try to be respectful of the bar's rules and preferred clientele. Many bars that were formerly women-only, for example, are now called women and trans friendly. But if it's a clear case of plain old mean discrimination and transphobia, by all means make a stink about it.

BAR SCENE PROS

They're great places to people watch. If you're into cruising, nothing I know beats a bar scene. If you're not into cruising, people will eventually leave you alone.

BAR SCENE CONS

They're not the best places to go if you've got a problem with alcohol. They're really not good places to go if you're not willing to be totally up-front with your gender ambiguity. (That's what I love about drag kings and drag queens: their "Get over it!" attitude.) Too many passing people have been beaten up or killed for what's taken as a betrayal. At best, you stand the chance of being blackballed from that bar if you're seen as someone who's just there to take advantage of the customers by trying out your new-gender flirting techniques.

Lovers

Lovers, even more than friends, need to know. The probability is that your relationship is based on, or has nestled itself into something based less on the relationship between two people and more on the relationship between two identities. That's what we're taught: man/man, woman/woman, woman/man, top/bottom, butch/femme, man/woman/man, etc. We're never taught person/person. That's what bisexual movements have been trying to teach us.

@whateversusan: Gender's neither a binary nor a spectrum, but an entire galaxy full of stars.

@drum4ica: My gender cannot be found in the binary or on a spectrum.

We're never taught that desire can be independent from gendered identities, so we change ourselves into a gendered identity we think someone else is going to be attracted to. And that sets us up for the trap of "You don't love me, you love my identity."

When one of the lovers in a relationship decides to switch or shift identities, the basis of the relationship is out of whack. I'm not even talking about a radical gender change here. Any shift in a gendered identity within an identity-based system can put a strain on the system. People need time to adjust to new ways of relating to each other. If the relationship, for example, had been man/man, and one of the lovers decides to become a woman, the other lover is thrown into an identity crisis not of his own choosing. Fortunately, as more and more of these issues are being discussed, as gender identity is becoming grudgingly acknowledged as possibly being fluid, more and more people are riding through that sort of change and are remaining together as lovers. Shifting any sort of basic identity is a danger to most relationships, and it's scary, and it's still something you need to tell your lover.

So, will your relationship change if you start messing with gender? You'll never know until you come out. All the principles I'm talking about here apply equally to family members as well as to lovers.

LOVERS-AS-SUPPORT PROS

It's the best. Your closest, most intimate friend and sexual partner and you have the opportunity to move your relationship into much deeper waters than identity-loves-identity.

LOVERS-AS-SUPPORT CONS

There's a danger of the two of you sliding into some stereotypical relationship, based more on what's "right" according to the culture, than what's "right" according to what the two (or three or more) of you decide. There's also the danger that you just may not want to be lovers any more—that's happened to me. Hey, what guarantees come with any relationship? However, if you persist with love, even if you break up, you'll have a true friend for life.

The Leather Scene: Sadomasochism, Dominance and Submission, Bondage and Discipline

Uh huh, I've heard all the arguments for and against it. S/M for me is the consensual act of two or more adults who play with pain: giving or receiving. D&S is the consensual act of two or more adults who play with clearly-defined power roles, usually some form of master/mistress and servant/slave. B&D is the consensual act of two or more adults who play with the concepts of punishment, restraint, or

SM is an art. Doing it well requires more than a bag full of expensive whips and exotic electrical toys, a closet full of fetish clothes, or a basement filled with bondage furniture.

—Patrick Califia

imprisonment. Any of these forms of play can be combined with any of the others. Any of these forms of play might or might not involve sex, genital or otherwise.

The way I relate with people in these matters is through informed mutual consent. BDSM takes me into my body, and gender's got nothing to do with it. For me, BDSM is genderfree space. I can play any gender I want to play. Remember make believe? For me, BDSM is where I get to play make believe.

One thing I enjoy about S/M, D&S, and B&D (I'll lump them all into the category "leather" for simplicity's sake) is the opportunity for the players to actually talk about their needs and wants, their limitations and boundaries, their fantasies. Even relative strangers who play leather games with each other can reach an intimacy in a few hours, the depth of which would rival, on some levels, the intimacy of many long-term married couples.

Exercise: A Nice Comfy and Safe BDSM Exercise

Make yourself very comfortable. That can mean alone, or with someone you trust; it's up to you. Comfy? Okay. Now, read the following questions and answer them for yourself. You might want to get some paper and write these answers down, or you can, of course, make notes in the margins. If you know you're hedging on any of them, you can imagine someone you trust gently saying "Tell me more." Your answers don't have to have anything to do with sadism, masochism, dominance, submission, bondage, discipline, or role-playing; but if they do, well, just let them come.

Some Fun Questions To Start With

- What's your fantasy? The deep one.

- How would you like to meet someone to live that out with for a while?

- What kind of time limit on the fantasy would make you comfortable?

- How would you articulate that fantasy to someone who might want to do that with you?

- How would you explain your physical limitations to someone?

- How would you explain your psychological limitations to someone?

- What, exactly, would you be willing to do?

- What, exactly, would you be un-willing to do?

- What, exactly, would you be willing to learn?

- What, exactly, might you try (assuming you knew you could stop if you didn't like it)?

- Is there something you've always wanted to be? If so, what's that?

- Is there some exciting situation you've always thought about living out? If so, how would you describe it to someone who might want to do that with you?

There's a lot more to negotiating a leather scene, but these questions are a good start. If you were able to answer them, you could possibly live out a fantasy or two or three. How about that? Even if your answers had nothing whatsoever to do with S/M, B&D, or D&S, you could live out your fantasy. Now . . . where to look for playmates, right? That's a tough one, no matter where you are; but there are a few leads to check out.

For social groups, potential play partners, and connecting with people in the leather scene, I'm going to suggest the interwebs. They're called social networks, so socialize! At this writing, fetlife.com is a reliably safe

RECOMMENDED READING:
For factual information about the leather world, Patrick Califia's work stands out like a beacon. Pat has several how-to books out, all of which are worth owning and using. For fiction, more of a flavor thing, there's Laura Antoniou, John Preston—author of the S/M classic *Mr. Benson*—and, once again, Patrick Califia. I recommend anything by any of these authors—without reservation—and you'll be happy. I promise.

community. There's also marvelous blogs devoted to various aspects of leather. Outside the internet, there are some swell zines you can find at your local underground or sexual minorities bookstores and newsstands. Don't have one? Interwebs time!

S/M, B&D, AND D&S PROS

Playing can be a transcendent experience for all involved. With trustworthy partners, you can really fly up and out of whatever gender you've been being, and take on entirely new identities.

S/M, B&D, AND D&S CONS

Playing can be dangerous if the players are inexperienced or just plain mean. Please, please, if you're going to do this stuff, start out with someone you trust—ask for references—and be prepared to do a lot of learning.

Gaming and Other Virtual Playgrounds

One approach to learning some new way of thinking would be to actually live outside the binary, outside one of the two socially sanctioned genders. Maybe freedom from that system would result in a new non-binary way of thinking and acting in the world. So where in the world do we go to experience that? In many games, and in most virtual worlds, it's not an impossible task to locate a space where gender "is not."

Virtual worlds have only a few rules—if any at all—concerning identity, and these spaces are accessible to a great number of people. Gender doesn't have to be if you don't want it to be there. Yes, yes—there are a LOT of places that insist on either/or gender. Keep pointing and clicking and you will soon find something. If all else fails, see if you can hack the game's preference files.

Now . . . what about gendered bodies in virtual reality? Do you want to play male? Female? Any of skillions of other genders? Virtual reality has no gender limits unless they're coded in, or you set limits for yourself.

By holding the concept of essential MAN and essential WOMAN in place, even in virtual communities, we're also holding the boundaries in place. It's simply a matter of questioning the categories, and the boundaries blow wide open.

Then there's virtual sex—really having sex with someone, only it's in a virtual space. And this raises the question: Is it as good as "real" gender and "real" sex? I know some people who say it's better. Whether it's text-based, voice, avatar, or even video. Virtual sex takes what's bodily a solo sexual experience to a whole new level by adding the factors of being immediate, real-time, interactive, and fully consensual. The value of virtual sex in terms of switching genders is that it gives us a good place to try out our fantasies, experience them on one albeit primarily textual level, so that we'll be perhaps a bit more willing to suggest them to a real-life sexual partner.

VIRTUAL WORLD PROS
It's a great tool to learn to overcome shyness, no matter one's reasons for social abstinence. It helps to remember, though, that it is a tool, not your life.

VIRTUAL WORLD CONS
The safety of virtual space can become addictive; and spending more time in virtual worlds can overtake real life as a predominant forum

for one's connectivity. There's nothing wrong with that, but the fact is that virtual life is a great meeting ground and rehearsal space. At this writing, the technology isn't advanced to where I can see that it matches up with the benefits of a face-to-face, body-to-body connection with another human being. But maybe virtual life has become more life-like since the publication of this book. And yeah, you might get stuck in a virtual world for a while. Best to keep in mind the cliché "Ships are safe in harbor, but that's not what ships were built for." I learned that from a Hallmark greeting card.

One more thing: Projection and transference have a much better chance of holding sway in cyberspace than in real life. We tend to project the "perfect partner" onto whoever we're with, and in cyberspace there are few clues to the contrary. I've found it pays to be wary of doing that to others, and to be conscious that someone is possibly doing that to me.

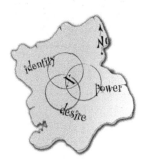

Right . . . you've done an awful lot of reading, and you haven't run into any pirates. I think that means it's time to solve the next clue on the treasure map:

Most maps show an N to indicate North. But there's part of another letter that follows the N.

It looks to me like the next letter is an O. Yep, that could be part of the word *north*. But it's not. Nope. But hey, before we decipher the next clue, please turn the page for that comic book I promised you. You've got permission from me and my publisher to make as many copies as you want, and hand them out to as many people as you like.

@selvis42: The way partners, family, and friends impose their gendered stereotypes and expectations on me informs and incites me politically.

MY GENDER FOR FRIENDS & FAMILY

IT'S PRETTY OBVIOUS THAT THE WAY I'M EXPRESSING THE GENDER OF MY DREAMS IS A LOT OR A LI'L BIT DIFFERENT THAN WHAT YOU MIGHT HAVE EXPECTED FROM ME. SO I'M HOPING THIS COMIC BOOK WILL ANSWER SOME QUESTIONS AND HELP US GET BACK TO GETTING ALONG WITH EACH OTHER. WELL, THAT'S WHAT I'D LIKE, ANYWAY. SO, LET'S START WITH A FEW OF THE MORE COMMON QUESTIONS PEOPLE LIKE ME GET ASKED...

ME →

"SO, ARE YOU GOING TO GET THE SURGERY?"

YEP, NEXT WEEK.

NOPE, NO SURGERY IN THE FORESEEABLE FUTURE

OH GOLLY, THERE ARE SO MANY OPTIONS. I'M JUST NOT SURE.

ANSWER — GENITAL SURGERY IS ONLY ONE WAY PEOPLE LIVE WITH BEING TRANSGENDER.

"WHEN DID YOU CHOOSE TO BECOME TRANSGENDER?"

PROBABLY THE SAME TIME *YOU* CHOSE TO BE A MAN OR A WOMAN

ANSWER: THE ONLY MOMENT OF DECISION, IS THE DECISION TO ACT ON IT.

"WHAT WILL OUR CLIENTS THINK?"

RESTAURANT

ME →

YOU →

OYSTERS

ANSWER: THEY'LL MOST LIKELY FOLLOW YOUR LEAD IN WELCOMING ME AS A FRIENDLY & PROFESSIONAL MEMBER OF THE COMPANY'S TEAM.

"HOW WILL THIS AFFECT OUR RELATIONSHIP & THE FAMILY?"

ANSWER: *A LOT!* JUST LIKE ANY OTHER MAJOR CHANGE IN PEOPLE'S RELATION-SHIPS. WE CAN LOVE EACH OTHER AS MUCH AS WE ALWAYS HAVE—BECAUSE LOVE DOESN'T CHANGE JUST BECAUSE GENDER DOES. I PROMISE.

TO BETTER UNDERSTAND US, LET'S TAKE A LOOK AT WHAT PEOPLE LIKE ME REALLY BELIEVE IS *TRUE*

New Gender Ideas That People Really Believe!

SEXUAL-ORIENTATION is not the same thing as

THIS DESCRIBES WHO I'M ATTRACTED TO, AND WHAT—IF ANYTHING— I LIKE TO DO ABOUT MY ATTRACTION.

GENDER-IDENTITY

WHAT GENDER DO I THINK I AM? A MAN? A WOMAN? SOMETHING ELSE? WE LOOK AT GENDER AS MORE THAN TWO. IT'S A CHOICE, AND THERE ARE LOTS OF GENDERS TO CHOOSE FROM.

AND IT'S NOT ALWAYS ABOUT GENITALS

JUST WHO SAYS GENDER DEPENDS ON PENISES AND VAGINAS? IT'S ONLY A WEE-WEE, SO WHAT'S THE BIG DEAL?

...so there's LOTS of possibilities!

NO MATTER WHAT GENDER I CHOOSE, IT'S POSSIBLE FOR ME TO HAVE ANY KIND OF SEXUAL ORIENTATION. IT'S MORE THAN MEN LOVE WOMEN & WOMEN LOVE MEN. IN FACT, SOME PEOPLE LIKE BOTH MEN & WOMEN— AND/OR PEOPLE WHO ARE NEITHER!

NOW, WE'VE GOT NEW QUESTIONS!

ARE YOU MY AUNT OR UNCLE NOW?

Per? Ey? She?
HE?
S/he? Ze?
THEY?
Sie? it?

WHAT NAMES AND TITLES DOES YOUR NEWLY GENDERED PERSON WANT TO USE NOW?

HOW ABOUT THEM PRONOUNS?

NEVER "IT" NEVER!

IF YOU DON'T KNOW, ASK.

BUT MADAME, I ASSURE YOU—*M* OR *F* ARE THE ONLY TWO CHOICES ON THE INSURANCE FORM

IF YOU OFFER ONLY 2 CHOICES, WE HAVE THE RIGHT TO INSIST ON MORE, (NO GUNS, REALLY)

NO! DON'T HIT HIM! I *LIKE* TO BE CALLED A TRANNY!

NOT EVERYONE LIKES THAT WORD. ALWAYS ASK FIRST!

WHAT ARE SOME GOOD RESOURCES FOR ME TO LEARN MORE?

SO GLAD YOU ASKED! LET'S MAKE A DATE AND SEARCH THE INTERWEB MACHINE TOGETHER!

I THINK WE'VE MADE A GREAT START! THANKS! AND REMEMBER— QUESTIONS ARE ALWAYS BETTER THAN ASSUMPTIONS

THAT'S ALL FOR NOW

Chapter 9: The Missing Piece is Nothing, and We're Going to Find It Nowhere

CAUTION: this is going to be a very slippery chapter. We've spent the first eight chapters of this book examining gender as something. Now we're going to examine gender as much less than a something, and more of a nothing. In our search for gender, the N on the treasure map stands for nothing *and* nowhere. So gender is something and nothing, and someplace and no place, all at the same time. Really. See? Slippery.

Gender is indisputably something. People define themselves by their gender, they monitor their desires according to gender, and they define friendships or prejudice based on gender. People are daily murdered for nothing more than their gender. In my country, people of one gender are daily paid more money than people of another gender—for no other reason than gender itself.

All over the world, people who mess with their expression of gender are ridiculed, harassed, beaten,

Angry? Hmpf. I tell you how angry I am. Almost fuckin ruined this body I'm stuck in. Drugs, razors, torn muscles, I ran from this . . . Prison of the Meat. Fucking dying in my own female flesh. Gonna drown in my own menstrual blood.

Do I hate myself? Naw . . . I hate my position: I hate my prison. Don't hate my breasts because they're breasts. I hate them because they're mine. Like I hate my back. This isn't my body. My body is silicon and solder. My body is CyberSpace. There, I am Shahn, Gareth, Interrupt. Not this fuckin' whining, pissing, lonely, getting-hungry, lame-backed, bull-dagger you see. I'm a fucking synapse. I'm light and heat the very pulse of information you speak.

You want to feel my pain? Put your head on the railroad tracks. Just lay it right down and just wait until you don't have to wait anymore. Just go to sleep and someday, you'll be free.

Don't fucking hug me. I don't want your meat.

—Shahn LeClaire

raped, and murdered. Gender is certainly something. AND gender is nothing. We've all of us bought into a chimera, and it's become a real factor in all of our lives, and the good news is that we can uncreate it, despite the daily pressure to salute gender and the genitals by which it stands. We can tear apart gender's reality. And that's something we've got to do. You, too. You've got to pitch in and put an end to the bad something that gender has become. The best news is that once we stop gender from being a bad something, it can be a very, very good something.

Exactly how are we convinced that gender is such a powerful something in our lives? Oh, let me count the ways. No, don't let me do that. There are too many ways that gender is stubbornly dug-in and hidden in our culture—it's like Windows on a hard drive. There are all sorts of channels by which we're convinced that gender is real—and because of this, gender *is* real.

We're sold on gender every time we read an advertisement that addresses us as men or women. We're sold on gender every time we have to tick one of two boxes only: M or F. We're sold on gender every time our sex education is limited to sex between men and women . . . never mind the question of why sex at all. Gender is real because our religious texts tell us so. Gender is real because our medical records insist it is so. Gender is real because all our government paperwork demands male or female.

As you journey mindfully through gender—if that's something you'd like to do—it's going to be rough.

Gender is a real jungle. Gender is the deep blue sea, and you sail it well or you bob forever on the waves. Gender is the wind that blows gently between two lovers, and the fire they ignite when they make love. Gender is that real. Of course it is.

And I'm sorry—I'm so sorry— but misogyny and transphobia are as real as they ever have been. In many cases, they're well glossed over, but in less than two clicks on any googling of the word transgender, you can find a murder. Murder. We are murdered for the sole reason that the expression of our gender really freaks someone else out. The violence done in the name of gender is real, and I'm crying right now as I'm writing this.

And you want a real kicker? Misogyny and transgender overlap with fury in the form of *trans misogyny* whose most visible target is the spectrum of male-to-female trans* people. Think about it—the mindless hatred of women, amplified by the mindless hatred of trans* people.

Trans, trans* and transgender are three different gender designations. Some people use trans followed by an asterisk in order to include ... well, whatever might follow the word trans. These three gender designations count for a lot more people that we thought about fifteen years ago—not to mention the increasing number of genderqueer folks. We are still a small percent of all the people in the world. And yet, more and more people are questioning the sacrosanctity of the categories man and woman.

And another real kicker? You have to factor in race, because it's mostly women of color who are being murdered. Can race and gender activism unite over that some day real soon, please? Trans misogyny is not limited to male-to-female trans people, though it's certainly magnified there. Female-to-male trans folk face their unique oppressions. Give "Brandon Teena" a google—but a warning: it's a violent story. The tragedy is that both misogyny and transphobia—real and scary as they are—are both based in the myth of two-and-two-only genders.

OK, now this next part is going to be tricky, but remember, it's a theory—it's a just another way of looking at gender, that's all it is. The root of gender is nothing more than nothing. It's what postmodern theorists would call a construction. We made it up. AND we made it up so well that now we think it's real. But it's not. Gender is a lie, and I'm asking you to weep over all the violence done in the blind rage of both misogyny and transphobia because it is all so senseless.

On the brighter side (and yes, there is always a brighter side, I promise), there's a cry to freedom in the notion that gender is a lie. Because if I'm right—and it's not just me, there's a whole lot of people who are seeing gender as more or less of a lie—if we're all right, then a key goal of any gender activism would be to weaken the reality of gender by questioning and ultimately refusing to obey the self-awarded twin rule of misogyny and transphobia.

RECOMMENDED READING: *Whipping Girl* by Julia Serano has changed forever how scholars and activists alike think about trans misogyny.

Advanced Exercise: Are you interested in more actively exploring gender in your own life? If so, darling, you're going to want to go online at your earliest convenience, where the kind publishers of this book have posted PDF files to Chapter 5 of the first version of *My Gender Workbook*. The link is www.routledge.com/cw/bornstein. This chapter traces what, fifteen years ago, were the primary delivery systems of the bipolar gender system. Where do we learn our gender from, and how can we unlearn it? I narrowed it down then to religion, science, law, art, pornography, marketing, friends, family, clubs, and gender experts of the day.

There are real-life exercises in this chapter on how to spot gender coming at you in day-to-day life, and how to dodge the bullets. Really, if you're in any way trans, please read that chapter and do the exercises. If I were writing it today, I'd want to add more venues for gender: We learn our gender from social media, gaming, hook-up culture, student life, marriage (or lack of it) . . . and, and, and . . .

So the exercise you need to add to the end of your downloaded version of Chapter 5: "Just Say No" is this:

- Make a list of places/communities where you've learned your gender.

- For each locus of gender-as-truth in your life, list the rules you learned.

- For each rule you learned, devise a way to unlearn it in your life today.

The Perfect Storm

In the first version of this workbook I tried to deconstruct a then-new brewing socio-political storm. Several disparate forces—explosive and as-yet unrelated new cultural phenomena—were making inroads on the dominant culture. I'm happy to report that this perfect storm of ideologies has gotten even bigger over the last fifteen years. For example, Pope Benedict has condemned postmodern gender theory. Can't say that I blame him. Given his belief system and the values by which he protects it, the pope was right to condemn the sort of ideas you've been contemplating while reading this book.

The pope is worried that by reading this book and others like it, you're going to fall to the tender mercies of a nefarious scheme to blow apart the natural order of men and women. I have every hope, kiddo, that you will do exactly that when you put down this book. I think the time has come to do just that. Check out the socio-political factors that are converging at this moment.

Me, I've come to the conclusion that the secular academic postmodernism of the West is coming together with non-dualistic spiritual ideologies of the East at a no-geography convergence of technology and spirituality with an intention to end suffering. There's no one particular movement or religion or philosophy or ideology that's going to bring peace—eventually, we're all going to have to work together. That's the reality of it. So the identities, desires, and powers that gather at the convergence of all these phenomena are limitless. I've done my best to illustrate that on the following page.

More information is available to the average person than ever before. The Information Age has come and gone. At this writing we're well into Web 2.0, which is more about the use of all the information that's been piling up in virtual space.

Postmodern theory is converging with Zen Buddhism in a new no-East, no-West world facilitated by the geography-free nature of virtual reality, and the social, sociological, and ideological soup that has been Web 2.0. The merge seems to be driven by our desires to connect. It's fueled by an acceptance of our spiritual nature, and the urge to exist beyond physical borders.

The transgender movement was the first of numerous non-binary civil rights movements to grow up in virtual reality, which is impacting the non-linear borderless nature of the identity they claim as well as the medium of the claims.

Since this book was first published, a generation has grown up with the assumption that non-linear multimedia interactive and/or virtual communication is natural. Now, people are searching for ideologies that most nearly match their non-linear thinking processes, systems that advocate connectivity without borders.

The radicalization of American right-wing politics is evidenced by people who would like nothing more than to see my country return to the 1950s fantasy world created by Madison Avenue for what has become meanstream television that traffics in bullying marginalized people. Meanstream TV still uses queer people to play straight for the cameras. Meanstream TV hires people of color to play the thugs, drug dealers, and dangerous people, playing into the hand of right-wing extremism.

In response to all the mean things going on in the world, the value of compassion—once claimed only by religious and spiritual practices—is emerging in Western activism and politics. The Arab Spring, the international Occupy movements and Dan Savage's global "It Gets Better" campaign have all defined a passionate activism based in values of generosity, compassion, and inclusiveness.

Modernism today has been invisibilized, unused, and long-forgotten. It's a valuable POV: *everything we perceive—and that which we cannot or choose not to perceive—contains, and/or is itself, perfect truth.*

Identity-based activism on behalf of human rights continues to chip away at binaries held in place by the powers that be: legal statutes, religious doctrines, commercial tenets, and social convention.

Now, if you put all those pieces together, what do you come up with?

Now, what can we legitimately call someone who's living outside the matrix of today's kyriarchy? It'd have to be someone living in the impossible state of no-identity, no-desire, and no-power. That's pretty fucking exalted, and I don't think there are many people who are close to that state. I'm not. Are you? Well, the fun news is that if you've gotten this far in the book, you're a lot closer to nothing than you were when you started, and so am I for having written this stuff.

So what has all this got to do with you and your exploration of gender? Now we're going to continue our jump from the earlier theory in this workbook to its practical application. First let's do a quick review of binary/hierarchy theory. Keep this stuff in mind.

- A binary is an either/or. A binary is two and two only equal elements—such as man and woman, or homo and hetero. Those are supposed to be the only two choices in gender and sexuality respectively. We know that sex and gender binaries mask vast numbers of components—elements that are masked by the agreed upon imaginary binary.

- When we unmask a binary—when we deconstruct it—what have we got? A hierarchy—like the gender hierarchy, which is roughly—in descending order of power—man, woman, trans man, trans woman, drag king, drag queen, tranny, and cross-dressers.

- Hierarchies, like binaries, can also be deconstructed, leaving us with vast numbers of people and groups all in need of some organization within a safe space. That third space is a safe space called a dialectic: lots of people and groups of people, none of them at each other's throats, all willing to talk things out and reach consensus.

Advanced Exercise: What did I miss? What other piece of this puzzle have you put together for yourself? I'm asking you to observe cultural phenomena and draw conclusions that might impact life on the margins of the culture. Continue this conversation online, in whatever social media tickles you pink at the time.

BRAIN TEASER

Which of the following do you think is most close to humanity's default response to chaos and cultural friction?

1. We all come together peacefully with each other for as long as it takes to work out everyone's differences to the best of everyone's abilities, until the time we've all learned to live in harmony with each other.

2. We elect representatives and task them with bringing peace. Until these people come up with a good solution, the rest of us agree to play nicely with each other.

3. We sort everyone out by means of a hierarchy, and proclaim that people who are just like us are at the top of it, with most of the people nowhere near the top. Then we carefully manipulate everyone else to agree with us by making them want to be us, or be just like us, and finally get them to want us to like them, and they get rid of anyone who doesn't fit in.

BRAIN TEASER HINT: In the early 1600s, white Europeans landed in what has become my country. Of the three tactics above, which do you think was most closely followed by the Puritans in response to their cultural clash with indigenous people here? Here's a hint: as a gift to their generous hosts, the Puritans handed over a pile of blankets they knew to be infected with syphilis.

Poli Sci Exercise: Take another look at the gender pyramid from Chapter 4. Using this model, and the observations above, what do you come up with? Does it stand to reason that with the dawn of postmodern theory, Western thinkers are finally coming around to the realization that everything that once seemed to be a binary is revealing itself to be some form of systemic hierarchy of disempowerment and oppression? Are the persons or institution empowered with the privilege of naming the hierarchy sitting on top of it?

@hardcorps80204:
I HOPE [trans* people & our movements] can be a reminder that ALL our movements need to always point towards LIBERATION: not dogma, not fear, not hatred, but glory.

You, and everyone else reading this book, most likely are part of an increasing number of people with different views on gender who speak and negotiate gender and sexuality with the intent to reach consensus. That's not something everyone tends to do. So, thank you very much.

An Evolving Theory of Devolution

That leaves us with a real bone to gnaw on: if binaries suck as bad as they do, how did they get such a stranglehold on our culture? How did they enter our civilization in the first place? I think binaries begin with the good intention of a culture to make itself a decent place for people to live. What would be the best of all possible places to live? How about a civilization—the whole planet, let's say—where everyone was in harmony with The Great Big Good, however they understood The Great Big Good to be. AND everyone in the world would be just fine with everyone else in the world, no matter how they understood The Great Big Good to be. That's a good start. Over the next few pages, watch how cultural standards snake their way downhill into what we've got today.

@unanalike: I am a celibate transgressive surreal-gendered lesbian, trying to live an ethical life as a Christian. With a Santa-Claus beard. Ho, ho, ho. Realizing i didn't so much want to be WITH the occasional really engaging woman; I wanted to BE her. That'll start a gender journey.

Downward Spiral

Peace as Everyone is Enlightened

Wouldn't that be lovely? This is a civilization that pins its hopes on the enlightenment that is every member's state. It never works. Well, it's never worked so far. I'm not enlightened. Are you? Really? You and all your loved ones live in peace all the time? No judgments? You live in harmony with anyone and everyone you meet, and you harbor no ill will? Right. That's why enlightenment as the basis for a civilization always fails. When enlightenment fails, a civilization will lower the bar to values.

How to Fix It

Peace as Everyone Shares the Same Values

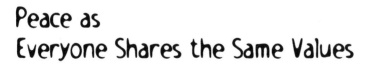

Values are concepts we hold true that can apply across most any situation we come up against. Like compassion. Give the Dalai Lama a google—he's awesome. So far as I can see, there's not very much if anything that's been thrown at him in his

eighty years to which he hasn't responded with compassion. That's living by a value. I wrote a book called *Hello, Cruel World: 101 Alternatives to Suicide for Teens, Freaks, and Other Outlaws*. You don't have to buy the book if you keep the book's values in mind: *Do anything it takes to make your life more worth living. Just don't be mean.* Period, full stop.

Don't be mean is the only rule in the book, and because it's a singular rule it becomes a value. So, does "don't be mean" seem like a sensible value to embrace? What do you think your life would be like if everyone you met was doing their best to not be mean?

OK, now answer this one truthfully: knowing what you know about "don't be mean," do you think you're going to be mean to someone in the next ninety days? I'm pretty sure I will. That's life—that's part of being human. Whether we intend to or not, we end up being mean to people. So we forgive ourselves and we try to do better next time. And that's called growing up. But the fact that we always fuck up a value as simple as don't be mean means that values always fail as a basis for a culture. When values fail, we drop the trust in our citizens one more notch to ethics as a basis for our culture. We want people to be ethical.

Peace as Everyone is Ethical

Ethics are broad paint strokes of decent behavior. A good example of ethics is the Golden Rule: do unto others as you would have them do unto you. This translates across many cultures, which proves it's a good principle to live by. The trouble comes when people forget to follow it. Or they think that anything that makes them feel good will make another person feel good. Take me, for example. I'm a masochist, a pretty heavy duty one at that. If I did unto you as I like done unto me? Hah! You could throw me in jail, with good reason. Besides, knowing how golden the Golden Rule really is, do you follow it all the time? Really? All the time, with everyone, no matter what else is going on? Right. That's why ethics always fail as a basis for a civilization. When ethics fail, we lower the bar one more time to morality.

Morality? I'll give you morality. Head on over to YouTube and search "George Carlin" AND "Ten Commandments."

I am not genderless, but rather am gender*ful*. As a creative tool, I can perform gender in fun and various ways. Wearing bright colours and a skirt, I can flounce around gaily; throw on a leather jacket and snug levis, and I appear to be butch and rugged. Rather than being simply androgynous, I prefer to think of this freedom as a deconstruction of gender standards and expectations. As part of this freedom, I allow people to assume a gender for me based on how they interpret my appearance and behaviour.

I never have been a man. I never will be a man. I never want to be a man. I am a sissy, a fairy, a faggot, and so much more. Embracing gender diversity (what I have called "genderful") has been my liberation.

—Gerald Walton

Peace as the Only Good People are Moral People

At this level of culture, people believe that in order to be a good person, you have to be following a fill-in-the-blank-moral-code. OK. Well, what are morals? What is morality if not a coded binary system of good and evil, rules to follow for what's right and what's wrong. Like the Ten Commandments, most of which I consider to be good ideas.

I know I'm alive because of the people who managed to follow the commandment Thou Shalt Not Murder. Not every trans* person is as fortunate as I am. Here's another theory: good and evil, right and wrong—binaries with no room for grey. Sure, there are moral people who are flexible, but I'd call them ethical, because as soon as you introduce a maybe or a gray area, you've lifted yourself out of morality and you're operating up in the realms of ethics. Pure morality is pure either/or, and that's where binaries enter a culture and maintain their grip: systems of morality. I don't think that morals are bad—I just don't think they have much use beyond serving as training wheels for becoming the loving, compassionate, mindful people we're capable of being.

And besides: do you follow some off-the-rack system of morality all the time? 24/7? 364 days a year, you're non-stop Mr., Ms., or Mx. Morality? Of course not. Even morality—simple as it is to blindly obey—fails as a basis for keeping a culture well-mannered and orderly. And when morals fail, we drop down to laws, crime, and punishment.

Peace as People Obey, or They Pay the Price of Disobedience

And this is the bottom of the barrel, just a step shy of uncontrollable chaos. To the degree that laws enforce a religious morality, to that degree you're living in a theocracy. As to punishment, well, just give "United States of America" AND "prison system" a google and some clicks and see how successful it is at creating a culture worth living in.

I know—it looks bleak. But here's a step-by-step exercise for you that will help you climb up and out of this culture devolution. The good thing about cultural chutes is that there's always a ladder to get back up. Try this, please. It's a good way to stay alive in places where people would rather see you dead or not see you at all.

Exercise: Queer the Culture

The only rule to follow in doing this exercise is *don't be mean*.

1. **Decide what laws you want to obey, and what laws you want to disobey.** You have the choice, so make it mindfully and in accordance with the value of don't be mean. This is called conscious anarchy, and as long as you're not being mean to anyone, there's nothing wrong with it. Now, if you get arrested—even if you weren't being mean to anyone—I can't help you. Too bad, and I'm sorry. But the choice is yours.

2. **Devise your own moral code.** Figure out for yourself what's right, what's wrong. Examine situations however you like and decide what's good and what's evil. This is a good thing to do. It's a good use of mindful binaries—training wheels, remember? This step can take you decades, because you'll most likely have to make minute adjustments as you accept reality and discover more and more about living life on life's terms. The amazing cool benefit of making your own moral system—however many decades it takes you—is that once you're done, you can throw all of it out the window. And yep, that's the next step.

3. **Throw away morality.** You do not need to be a moral person in order to be a decent person. Now you're ready to live by ethical principles alone—those broad paint strokes of decent behavior. Now following the Golden Rule is more or less a piece of cake. Once you've lived your life ethically, you can throw ethics right out the window with morality. And yep, that's the next step to this exercise.

4. **Throw away ethics.** You do not need to be an ethical person in order to be a decent person.

5. **Embrace a value—or a couple of them.** Live your life by living your values. Theoretically, that should eventually bring you most closely to your connection with The Great Big Good, and you can throw your values away and simply be an enlightened, wonderful creature.

Never Mind Me—What Does God Say About Morality?

God is no big fan of morality, and I'm in a good position to prove that. I'm writing this book in the United States of America, which currently fancies itself the center of the world's Judeo-Christian culture—more precisely, it's the center of a unique brand of American Christianity. My country is aggressively trying to enforce this radically fundamentalist, racist, classist, and all-the-rest-ists version of the world, which could otherwise be a decent Judeo-Christian system of values, ethics, and morality. And since radical fundamentalists have already devilishly perverted the sweetness inherent in both Judaism and Christianity, kindly permit me to also act like a devil, quoting the Scripture for my own purposes. This is a story about the rainbow that Noah (of ark fame) gets to see when he finally gets to see land. The story begins ... well, *in the beginning.*

GOD IS SITTING THERE IN HEAVEN, having made nearly everything there is, including the heaven She's sitting in. He's made stars and oceans and planets and light and mountains and bunny rabbits and marijuana. She's even made a guy He called Adam, who has a lovely time to himself in God's most perfect world. But after a few years, Adam says he's lonely.  And God thinks to Himself ... something is missing. Being God, no sooner does He pose himself a problem, He solves it.

God gets the bright idea to create a woman named Lilith, who's a hot babe because this is one smart God, and Lilith is one hot butch top. Lilith pushes Adam down on the ground, and boy howdy, she rides that cowboy. Well, cool as God is, way back in those days, He is not having any part of that. Most people don't know this next part, but God had it in the back of Her mind to make Adam another guy —He is all for mixing things up. But right now, God has to handle the Lilith situation. So He turns Lilith into a demon, and creates Eve.

Eve is also a hot babe. But God doesn't make the same mistake twice. Unlike Lilith, God makes Eve cute and with more of a bottom ... and a little naive to boot, which is how nearly all femmes are seen to this very day: cute, but dumb. Gr-r-r-r-r-r.

OK ... stuffy as She is, back in those days, God really loves Adam and Eve. He loves them with all His heart, and remember, this is God's heart so it's a really big heart, and She loves them with all of it. He says to them ...

"Look what I made for you. It's a beautiful garden. There's everything you could possibly want to make yourself happy with. There are birds, and waterfalls, and lily pads, and chipmunks, and over there ..." God points with a Godly forefinger—"that's a whole acre of marijuana."

"All of this is yours," God continues when Adam and Eve finally manage to quiet down their excitement at the idea of chipmunks and lily pads. "All I want is your happiness. I've created harmony, and you are part of it, so you get to do anything you want to do. Anything at all. Well, there's one exception."

Adam and Eve look at each other nervously. God continues, reassuringly, "You can do anything, touch anything, play with anything, heck, you can even fuck anything." God pauses and looks down at His shoes, and kicks the dirt with Her toe. Then He continues in a low, rumbling God voice:

"There's just this one little exception. Do not eat the fruit of that tree."

She lifts another Godly finger and points to an awesome tree. No, really, it is an awesome tree. It changes color every time you look at it—every time you blink, that tree changes color. It is silver and gold, then red and blue. There were always two colors, of all of God's infinite colors. That tree even turns itself into black and white.

Only one thing stays the same about the tree: it is always cloaked in two colors that are exactly opposite one from the other. Red and blue, cool and warm, bright and dull.

"That's a really cool tree," says Adam. "What's it called?"

"Yeah, it's so pretty," says Eve. "And the fruit looks so delicious."

Did I mention the fruit? Some people think it was an apple. To say that the fruit of that tree was an apple would be like saying the Taj Mahal was a No-Tell Motel, which in fact it was, only with fancier architecture. So yes, maybe the fruit looks like an apple, but oh, what a scent it has! Oh, what a taste! It is sour and sweet all at the same time. That fruit smells at once sun-kissed and rain-washed. The fruit from that tree always tastes like two opposite tastes, and smells like two opposite smells. Nothing else like that exists in the garden. Everything else just is what it is. This tree is a true wonder!

"It's called the tree of the knowledge of good and evil," mutters God, "and if you know what's good for you, don't eat the God-damned fruit."

Of course, Eve does not know what is good for her, because she hasn't eaten the fruit yet so it is really easy for a sexy, attractive serpent to seduce her into taking a great big bite of that delicious fruit, the fruit from the tree of the knowledge of good and evil. And because Eve is so gosh darned cute, Adam is an easy mark to take the next bite, and that's exactly what he does. And once they swallow, the two of them blink and look at each other.

"You're a man," says Eve.

"You're a woman," says Adam.

"It's hot today," says Eve.

"Yes, it's always either hot or cold," agrees Adam.

"I'm happy," says Eve.

"I'm sad," Adam replies.

"You're naked," says Eve.

"Right we're clothed or we're naked," says Adam.

"And it's bad to be naked," gasps Eve.

"We'd better get dressed so we can be good," agrees Adam.

Well, the two of them scramble to find some clothes. They find two medium-sized fig leaves. Fig leaves? Really? Well, you know the rest. God finds them out. He is heartbroken. She casts them out of the garden with lots of curses.

And for the rest of time ever since then, humanity has been looking at the world in terms of two-and-two-only choices: right or wrong, good or evil, young or old, black or white, rich or poor, man or woman, sane or insane, homo or hetero, smart or stupid and on … and on … and on … and on.

HAPPY ENDING: Hundreds of years later, God uses a flood to reboot life on earth. That's when God gave us the rainbow, to remind us that there's more than either/or. End of bible lesson.

You and I and most everyone else in the world are still trying to some degree to solve the world's problems under the influence of the fruit of that God-damned tree. God warned us against either/or morality. Well, thank goodness God gave us the rainbow as a beautiful alternative to the either/or morality the very day Noah first set foot on solid land.

All we ever needed was our rainbow back, and God was cool enough to give us that after all. Please, let's thank God for that gift. Let's thank God by seeing rainbows in everyone we meet with radical wonder and radical welcoming.

SPOT QUIZ

Which of the following interpretations of the book of Genesis most closely matches the version you grew up with or heard about first? Which interpretation most closely matches the version you like best? Which interpretation is good, and which is evil?

1. Women are cute, dumb and evil, and men shouldn't give in to their wiles. They both got thrown out of the Garden, but God rightly added extra punishment to Eve: the pain of childbirth, because she was really the bad one in the first place.

2. Don't eat from the Tree of the Knowledge of Good and Evil = Don't turn everything you see into good and evil, right and wrong. In other words, beware of binaries! Once you see the world as either/or, you can no longer live in paradise.

3. That snake makes out like a bandit—I mean, really: Slytherin? The snake got Eve to take that bite, which is God's way of teaching us that you can sell people on anything if you use enough sex.

@Z84922657:
How to base our political passion around love of sex and remain inclusive to those who don't like sex?

@katebornstein:
Great question. I'm pretty sure the answer is gonna be found in the space where faith in God overlaps body level joy.

The knowledge of good and evil is one of the most basic binaries—right up there with order and chaos, and life and death. The knowledge of good and evil is the basis of all morality. All morality, all moral codes, are good and evil, right and wrong—these are binaries that are believed to be true and unquestionable. But really, there's no either/or that is always a correct choice in every situation.

So we got kicked out of paradise because we bought into a binary and we made a big moral deal out of it. But maybe God had something else in mind for us.

The culture is stuck with morality—no, make that moralities. No two systems of morality are the same. Everyone's got their own notions of what's good and what's evil, and too often, those notions contradict each other. Conflicting moralities lie at the basis of most conflicts, from endless family arguments to endless regional wars.

Morality as either/or robs us of the need to use the wise minds we possess and need in order to imagine any harmony in difference.

Morality as either/or teaches us to mistrust our good hearts' connections to God. The Great Big Good wants us to decide for ourselves what's good and bad, right and wrong. No bite of an apple is going to magically reveal the nature of good and evil. We have to learn it through often painful experiences.

A BONE YOU CAN CHEW ON

Join me on a leap here, please. What if it was morality as either/or that serves as a template for all these categories of existence, all these spaces in which we can be regulated, all the vectors of oppression—not only gender and sexuality. Might it be that some either/or morality lies at the root of oppression based on race, age, class, religion, disability, looks, citizenship, family and reproductive status, language, habitat, politics, mental health, and humanity itself? I think it would be worth a look. So, have a look at whichever vector of oppression most targets you, and see if you can trace that irrational hatred to some system of morality.

So, What Treasure Lies Beyond the Binary?

Pirates always bury lots of treasure. And sure enough, the next clue on the treasure map leads to . . .

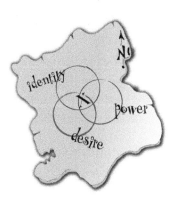

Oh, joy! Another clue: The arrow is pointing away from the treasure.

What other treasure is it pointing to? The answer is *you*. You lie beyond the binary, if only for agreeing with some of the stuff in this book.

You are something new in the world for the simple reason that you're considering this notion of more than just two, and the paradoxical notion that nothing is everything there is. You are amazing. You and I are rare in our existence through recorded Western history. So hooray for us! That's what lies beyond the binary: a great big hooray for us. And, we've only just begun.

Thirty years ago, getting beyond the sex and gender binaries was difficult, and those who did it kept themselves hidden away from public view. Now, a lot of people are leaping over sex and gender binaries. Right out in the open for all to see! Two difficult tasks still face us beyond the binary:

1. **Dismantling the hierarchy that invariably lies beyond the binary.**

2. **Fending off the impact of other binaries on the resulting dialectic or third space.**

Systemic binaries, whether or not they're formalized into a system of morality, regulate our identity, desire, and power. Now let's have a look at exactly how the regulation might take place. Let's start on a personal level: either/or sets us up for failure when we meet each other for the first time. Meeting a new person within the system of conditioned morality looks something like this cartoon. There's no thought to the possibility of connecting with another. There's no wonder. There's no welcoming. When we see something different, our mindless urge is to push it away.

The precise moment we're hooked by a binary is what Tibetan Buddhist nun Pema Chödrön calls *shenpa*. Literally, the Tibetan word means attachment. More subtly however the word describes the exact moment we get hooked. For example . . .

- You look at me and see white. You're hooked into treating me like a white person.

- You look at me and see old. You're hooked into treating me like an old person.

- You hear my name and understand that I am a Jew. You're hooked into treating me like a Jew.

We've pretty much come to the end of a time when you can have a space that is "yours only"—just for the people you want to be there. Even when we have our "women-only" festivals, there is no such thing. The fault is not necessarily with the organizers of the gathering. To a large extent it's because we have just finished with that kind of isolating. There is no hiding place. There is nowhere you can go and only be with people who are like you. It's over. Give it up.

—Bernice Johnson Reagon
West Coast Women's Music Festival, 1981 Yosemite National Forest, CA

Shenpa is the basis of privilege—an unconscious assumption that we know better than some other person, and that our opinion deserves to be the right one. But getting hooked doesn't always mean a moment of bigotry. There are all sorts of sex and gender ways we get hooked. For example . . .

OR

Once you're hooked, the motivation for how you interpret yourself and treat another person is based on a mythological binary. The fact is you're not dealing with the person at all: you're dealing with the myth of the half-a-binary that person represents to you.

With a lot of practice, we can learn to avoid moments of being hooked. Why avoid them? Because it's that moment of getting hooked emotionally and mindlessly into a binary—feeling the urge to act, and acting on the urge—that destroys the possibility of a harmonious dialectic. Our encounter with the mermaid could instead look like this . . .

The moment we're hooked into a binary, we are hooked into a debate with the aim of winning the debate "I'm right and better than you."

To what degree do you want to be right? What if being right means you have to be mean, or simply think mean things, about a person?

RECOMMENDED READING:
Google shenpa AND Pema Chodron. Read her essay. Buy her books. Read them. Use them. We love Pema Chödrön.

@queerfatfemme:
I turn my anger into love by assuming everyone's best intentions—we're all victimized by the same screwed up society.
I turn my anger into love by turning my rage into productivity. Strong feelings indicate to me something is wrong. Time to make art.

How Does The World Work Beyond the Binary?

In the first version of this workbook, I ended the book with a chapter called "This Quiet Revolution." Well, now I'm thinking fuck quiet. For tens of thousands of years, humanity has ruled itself with a politic of power: one or very few people have held all the resources and doled them out to the rest of us at their whim. A couple of thousand years ago, there came a staggering breakthrough in self-governance: a politic of identity called democracy. One person, one vote. Flawed, but what a terrific step toward freedom.

I'm sad to write that at this time, democracy has eroded badly. People with mean (greedy) intentions

@lilysea: I think we need to address gender privilege/lack of it with something other than a binary. It bugs me like LGBT bugs me, versus "queer." It bugs me like "woman" bugs me at something like the Michigan women's music festival. I find it exceptionally troubling, though it is intended to be liberating. I'd rather think we are all trans, frankly.

have figured out how to circumvent the idea of one person, one vote. In my country—as I'm writing this book—a law was passed recently whereby corporations were given the same electoral privileges as individuals, including the right to purchase political advertising without any spending limits.

Give "Citizens United" AND "elections" a google. In my country, a great number of people follow the lead of manipulative advertising. So whoever can buy the most advertising essentially controls the elections. The Citizens United ruling gave corporations all the great rights of individuals, without demanding any of the responsibilities. Attributing humanity to corporations knocks democracy for a loop and ironically dehumanizes us humans.

So we've tried our hand at the politics of power and the politics of identity, and both of those have taken us to where we are today. But in the entire history of humanity (and I'm old enough to remember all of it), there has never been a secular politic of desire. Desire gets the bad rap in most any spiritual and political ideology. And yes, yes,

Gee Whiz, it was only a little bit of sex, love and gender. What's the big deal?

obsession with desire can get us in trouble. So can obsession with identity, so can obsession with power. But what if we desire something that's in harmony with The Great Big Good, no matter how any of us see it? What if we desire the cessation of suffering for all sentient beings, and what if we build a politic around that? It would be a politic of compassion, and the time for a politic of compassion is due right about now, at this point in humanity's evolution as a species. Do you agree?

So how would a politic of desire be structured? I don't know. I'm too old—my generation is steeped in sterner stuff than desire. The development of a politic of compassion is going to come from generations beyond mine, perhaps yours. I *can* tell you what a politic of desire would look like: it would look like great sex and fabulous gender expression—the two identities most deeply rooted in the sphere of desire. There's a meta in sexuality and gender that is going to open the door to a new politic of desire. Maybe it's that a politic of compassion wouldn't include any enforced binaries.

Once we're aware of the triggering power of binaries, we try our best to spot the moment we are hooked into a binary of me versus you, us versus them. We spot those moments, and we replace them with the following two concepts.

Radical Wonder

We look at someone with great wonder in our mind. We know there are limitless possibilities to this person's identities, desires, and powers, and we allow ourselves to be curious and respectful. If at any point in our wonder we find ourselves becoming judgmental, we search to understand the binary rule that's hooked us.

and

Radical Welcoming

This one's easy and fun. I think it's the most fun in the whole workbook. We look at someone with love. If we have misgivings, we give that person the benefit of the doubt, and we say, "Hello, I welcome you into my space. Will you please welcome me into your space?"

@PinkBatPrincess: When transgender politics focus on "who we let in and who we leave out" it makes my stomach and my spirit ache. I feel like the most marginalized communities occupy themselves with attacking the communities closest to them on the map. We reserve most of our energies to try to push associated communities away, which is inflicting divide and rule tactics on ourselves.

A space with many binaries, none of them enforced or nonconsensual. A dialectic of consensus and freedom. That's what deconstructs our hierarchy. That simple act of welcoming and asking to be welcomed. Radical welcoming is the first step of an activism of love, a politic of desire. Radical wonder and radical welcoming are necessary components for any coalition of the margins.

Two New Desire-Based Identity Binaries, and What To Do About Them

The introduction of genderqueer into the dialectic that is gender and sexuality has raised a new binary with old words. *Queer* and *straight* are depending less and less on a person's gender in relation to the gender of their partner(s). At this writing, the two words have begun to signify the left (queer) and right (straight) wings of sexuality-and-gender politics. I'm glad.

Before it became simply a sexual orientation, *lesbian* was a word that signified radical gender politics. *Gay* wasn't always a lifestyle—it was first a politic, a radical left-wing politic. Nowadays, *gay* and *lesbian* are still signifiers of a political stand, but that's changing as gay and lesbian get deeper into the mainstream. The outer margins are now gathering under a lefty umbrella called queer, marked by sex positivity and gender anarchy. 🄶🄰🅂🄿🄳 So now we've got queer heterosexuals and straight lesbian women and straight gay men.

Straight-and-queer and transgender-and-cisgender are as false a binary as any other. They come in handy as both a rallying cry and a means of deconstruction. They're to be handled with care, and dismantled once they've proven themselves no longer necessary to making life better for people.

Transgender/cisgender is another binary in the dialectic sphere of regulation we call gender. It's as true and as false as any other binary. And it's a necessary binary today because it highlights the existence of cisgender privilege. It's my hope and the spirit of my activist art that people use the binary mindfully.

Being cis with cis privilege doesn't mean a person is mean. Not if they use their privilege generously. Trans and cis are, like every other so-called identity binary, overlapping spaces of identification.

Like morality, binaries are training wheels. They're a stepping stone to discovering some simple way to point out privilege granted people on the basis of their perceived sexuality and gender. It's observable that in mainstream culture, privilege is granted to people based on their perceived proximity to the mythically pure categories of 100 percent heterosexual and 100 percent cisgender.

@possiblyagirl: Trans rights are a feminist issue. Man, woman or genderqueer, #trans people get treated like women who don't conform. Watch the conversation that happens when a cis woman is mistaken for #trans and see the same #patriarchal shaming of different women.

@bootblackblast:
I'm too busy living my gender to bother theorizing about it. Though I believe very strongly in gender education and acceptance.

@sailoralecs: I look cis to many which makes me the other. I try to turn that anger into #love thru education & thru living proudly & happily as me. The worst #anger doesn't come when I'm #marginalized by the general population, but when I'm marginalized by my own TGIQ community.

The transgender movement—loose and disconnected and at odds with itself as it is—is the first civil rights movement that includes elements that consciously deconstruct its own binary as well as elements that are unconsciously or consciously reinforcing its own binary. What's more, both these disparate elements may or may not be reinforcing the binaries of any other vector of social injustice.

Of What Possible Value Is Trans* Experience in These Changing Times?

As I'm writing, Barack Obama—my country's first African-American president (that we know of)—has won a second term in office. I love the guy. I think he's making great changes. Those are my politics. Nevertheless, even with Obama in office, those of us who live out on the edges of the culture aren't going to see much of the change we need in order to make our lives more worth living. And those of us who live out on the margins of the culture aren't going to be much more free than we are at this moment.

@gwenners: As much as I loved being #41 of 101 Gender Outlaws in the previous edition of "My Gender Workbook," genders can be so . . . delightfully unstable. So today? I'm just another transperson who likes to travel the backroads of identity.

Some of us live outside the culturally acceptable limits of gender, and sexuality. Others of us live way-y-y out on the despised margins of race, age, and class. Lots of us may be spiritual, but not too many religions want to include us . . . except maybe as charity cases. For many of us—ever since we were kids—people have laughed at us for how we look. Or they have stared at our differently abled bodies.

We're citizens of the world, but too many of us end up as second-class citizens, or illegal immigrants. All of us who are oppressed by any facet of kyriarchy make up a significant number, if not a downright majority, of the population of planet earth.

It just seems that we're small and outnumbered because the powers that be have built and keep building walls to keep us out and apart, even from one another. Our walls must come down, because it's going to take a coalition—one that represents all of us on any edge of the culture—to speak in a voice loud enough to rally ourselves into some social, political, and spiritual revolution. A coalition of all the outer limits folks would be huge! And noisy. And I'm sure we'd throw great parties!

Party time. Because there's one more way that gender is real. It's real FUN!

You've come this far through the book with me. Thank you for your trust. So, please trust me when I say why the fuck go through all the trouble of mindfully doing your gender if you don't mindfully include the fun of it?

If gender is real, then it's important to make gender real fun. Not every day—nothing is for every day. But there are hours, sometimes days, sometimes weeks of fun gender that you can live. Please relish them because they are the best part of real gender.

Gender is real when we look in the mirror and see what we've always wanted to see, if only a little bit. And that's fun.

Gender is real when we walk down the street, comfortable that who we perceive ourselves to be is how we are perceived by others. The simple joy of that can make our hearts sing. There are days like that, I promise. Please dive into fun whenever you can.

I brought this koan up earlier in the book. Well here it is again because it ties this whole chapter up in a bow . . . or Möbius strip. (Go on, google it.)

Now it's time to work your magic in the world with lots of other people. And guess what! That's the subject of the next chapter. If you mess up, just forgive yourself and try harder next time. No regrets.

Chapter 10: Okay, Now What?

Are we real men or real women? It seemed like such an easy question. It might still be easy for many of us to answer. But here's a somewhat deeper question for all of us: who among us has an unshakable, immutable identity?

Who among us is a real anything? Who among us is "real" or "perfect" at any socially defined identity? Goodness knows, we each of us are pressured, to some degree, to become the unattainable "real man" or the unbearable "real woman" that the dominant culture would like us to be. We each of us try to be real at some identity, but do any of us, in fact, have the exact same identity we had, say, ten minutes ago? Or have our identities been continually and subtly altered, the course of our lives almost imperceptibly shifting, to the point where we're no longer quite so sure of the purity of our own identities? If so, then what is it exactly that's being altered? What is it within us that reaches a point of satisfaction once we've found an identity we're comfortable with?

And what inside each of us fiercely struggles against change? These were the questions I asked at the end of the first version of this workbook. Back then, I said that those questions were beyond the scope of this book but that I wanted them to lead to a new book. Well, they have—I'm tickled pink to say that this new book covers that ground.

To have attained to the human form is a source of joy.

But in the infinite evolution, there are myriads of other forms that are equally good.

What an incomparable bliss it is to undergo these countless transitions!

—Chuang Tzu

No Tidy Strings on This Package

So hey . . . it's almost the end of the damned book, and the odds are pretty good that I won't be writing another version of this. But a new book will need to be written in another fifteen years. I'm asking you to write it, and to get you started, here are some questions and challenges to take you far, far into the future of sex and gender.

Existence does this switching trick, giving you hope from one source, then satisfaction from another.

—Rumi

It should be pretty obvious that gender all by itself—while a vital component of power, desire and identity—isn't *the* big deal, the ultimate mountain to climb. In fact, in the scheme of history, gender is quite insignificant. Sure, it's been given a great deal of importance by the culture, but who says the culture's right? So, if gender isn't the big deal . . . what is?

My gnawing on gender has only led me to see that gender is one of many stumbling blocks to self-growth and self-realization. Age, race, class, body type, the whole of kyriarchy—they're just symptoms. Having delved as deeply as we have thus far with gender as one facet of kyriarchy, let's look beyond it. Remember the basic premise of this workbook?

The way you live without gender is you look for where gender is, and then you go someplace else.

Well, that's what I've been trying to do, and that's what I want to do more of. I want to go somewhere else. How about you?

I believe that a transgender identity—and, indeed, a transgender movement—both have a built-in obsolescence. If in fact we're setting about to dismantle the binary of gender, the system against which we're transgressing—and if in fact that's a worthwhile thing to do for a while, transgressing gender—and if in fact everyone is transgender according to the pyramid metaphor —then there's going to come a time when more people admit it than don't. When that time comes, when most of us are saying, "Yeah, I transgress gender," then gender will be relegated to the status it deserves: a plaything. When that happens, there won't be any value to the term "transgender," and a new challenge will have risen up, new political identities will raise their heads, and the transgender movement will be shown to its proper place as some historical oddity, back in the days when people thought there were only two genders.

But for now, something really interesting is happening. Over the last twenty years, transgender has become the new game in town. Now, we're chic. We're something to be studied. We're a new flag to rally around. More and more people are coming to see gender as something they transgress anyway, and they're claiming transgender as an identity, and this movement is taking off.

I give up my fisted touch,
my thoughts strung like fences
My totem-pole stature body
chipped to the bone.
I'm nobody's saviour, and
nobody's mine either
I hear the desert wind whisper,
"But neither are we alone."

—Ferron

And while all this has been going on, I've become known as an expert—something I don't claim to be, even after all these years. I'm really good at posing questions, and poking holes in theories, but that doesn't make me an expert. So I hope you've taken everything I've been saying here with a great big grain of salt. It's theory. Remember?

In *Gender Outlaw*, I wrote a small section about the role of fools in a culture: how fools point out doorways, how they trick people into laughing about whatever's been most important to them.

I like the role of fool. It's satisfying. It makes me feel quite light, and I find it fulfilling. I also wrote about what happens to fools when they become allied with a movement or an identity: they cease being fools. I've found out that being a fool is pretty important to me, and I want to play around with lots of ways of being that. "Expert," gender or otherwise, doesn't seem like a fun way to play for me.

I'll continue to explore my life and how I live it in much the same way I've been encouraging you to do in this workbook. At this writing, I'm sixty-four years old and I've had the most fun with the bad grrrl me that I've finally become. And there's a not-pretty side to bad-girl. Wait, that's a lie. It's all pretty. But there are parts of my life, like my fascination with serial killers, that simply are not polite dinner conversation, let alone appropriate to discuss from some podium at a political rally.

I'm not really as bad as they say I am. I'm actually a very nice person. ha ha ha ha ha ha ha.

—Juliette Lewis as Mallory Knox, *Natural Born Killers*

Just after the first version of this book came out, I wrote a play: *Strangers in Paradox: The True Story of Casey and the Kidd*. It's about a pair of lesbian serial killers, and I'd like to turn it into an opera or a graphic novel. Maybe I'll have time to do that. I want to keep writing, and my guess is that everything I write is going to have some sort of gender slant to it.

I've got a young adult novel I want to do that would follow on the high heels of Christopher Isherwood's *I Am a Camera*, and Truman Capote's *Breakfast at Tiffany's*. I want to give the world another girl to fall in love with—like Sally Bowles and Holly Golightly—but I want her to be a fierce, young, tranny working girl in the city.

Impacting my life is the fact that I was diagnosed with leukemia just as I started to write the first version of this book, so I've had fifteen years to get into all the implications, experiences, and revelations of the dying thing. The kind of leukemia I have is the wayyyyyyy slow kind. It probably won't kill me. But just before I finished writing this update, I was diagnosed with early-stage lung cancer. How about that?! That's partly why this new version of the book took so long to complete. In short, I have to go do what I've been urging you to do all through this workbook. I have to go explore myself, and I have no idea where that's going to lead me. I just know I have to leave this gender theorizing behind right now. Everything I know or believe about gender is in the books I've written. I need to move forward in my life, and while it scares the hell out of me, I'm drawn like a moth to a flame. Or better, like a butterfly that needs to escape their cocoon.

So . . . Where Are You Going?

You've had the opportunity to look at gender now from more angles than most people. These aren't all the angles, to be sure, but judging by the written information on the subject available in the world today, the work you've had the chance to do here has made it possible for you to examine gender in a uniquely well-rounded way.

It's conceivable that we're some of the first folks ever to have looked at gender as a dialectic—one of many spheres of regulation, each made up of many co-existing binaries. Assuming that's true, then this book is bound to be deeply flawed. The proof is: Does it have a practical application that can ease suffering for people? Try proving this theory in the next exercise, by building yourself a coalition of the margins. Please tweet me how it goes for you. I'm mighty curious.

Social Justice Exercise

Form a Coalition of the Margins Where You Live

1. Meet with people whose primary source of marginalization is different than yours.

2. Meet with more people with still different sources of marginalization.

3. Arrange a meeting, using a round-table format: fifteen seats—one seat representing each activist seeking equity within one of the fifteen spheres of regulation.

4. Now, perform triage by tossing out the question "Who's getting hurt the most?" You'll want numbers of people. What's the largest group of actively victimized people where you live? We're all subject to violence, given our marginalization, but hash it out: Who's got the numbers? You're looking for the largest number of a single group against whom violence is most regularly perpetrated. This triage step can take days, weeks, or months—and could be different for any round table, given their location and culture. The goal of this step is to decide one population that needs the most help right now.

5. Ante up. Each chair agrees to donate an agreed-upon fair share of its resources to helping that target population. Resources are time, money, and people. Every chair around the table commits resources to help the people everyone agrees needs the most help. It is right and expected that every chair around the table retains the bulk of its resources to fight for equity within its particular sphere of regulation.

6. Do the activism of coalition. For example, let's say the agreed-upon triaged target population is women. Everyone would agree to commit a fair share of their resources to fighting violence against women. And I bet real progress would be made. Imagine if people came at the problem of violence against women from the POV of class activism, or with the experience of race activism, or the passion of age activism? I bet that would work, and I bet that's another clue to the formation of a politic of desire, and I hope with all my heart that's what you, dear reader, help to establish.

Argue This Book—Please!

This book and other sex-and-gender theories and activisms that have sprung up in the world are baby steps, and, like anyone learning to walk for the first time, I'm likely to have fallen down more than once in the attempt. I've tried to make this overview of gender-as-a-component-of-kyriarchy as comprehensive as possible, but as there does not exist a broad public discourse on the subject of kyriarchy, my blind spots are going to be painfully apparent to some people—perhaps many—whose viewpoints desperately need to be represented in this discussion.

This book has been delighting (and confounding) students and teachers for fifteen years now, and that tickles me pink. Nevertheless, I've managed to offend more than a few people in one way or another. I'm sorry if anything I've written here—or anywhere else—has offended you or made you feel left out in any way. If that's the case, please accept my apology. It was not intentional—it was my blindness. It just means that your voice needs to be raised in this discussion, and the odds are I'm not the person to speak on your behalf.

Look, gender is everywhere present in this world today, and the form it's taken has the possibility to lead us further and further away from free self-expression, happiness, security, even survival itself.

Your questions need to be raised. Please ask them. Ask your friends. Ask the person sitting next to you on the bus. Who knows what you might learn? Ask members of your community. Maybe this is interesting to them too, and no one's raised the question before.

wordgeeksarah:
What's at the centre? Who am I when I'm totally unobserved, with no expectations mutating my sense of self? I have a schroedinger's soul: sadly happy, seriously flippant, frightenedly frightening, lovingly hateful. Well, you did ask.

Your disagreements with anything I've written here are valid. Please examine them as deeply as you can. Read more books on the subject. Get yourself online and raise these questions in discussion with your friends on whatever social medium tickles your fancy.

You're disagreeing with what I've said because you have a valid point of view based on some experience I've not had. Sure, I wrote a book. So what? All that means is I'm a person who was in the right series of places at the right series of times. All that means is that I've made some choices in my life that are different than yours, and I ended up with a passion to write about this stuff. That's all it means.

Your disagreement might be exactly what this notion of transgender needs in order to ground itself as a valid movement in the world. Or you might topple it entirely because you're the one who's found the fatal flaw in all my meanderings. It's important that you speak your disagreements and make your point of view known.

Many people, both trans and cis, are trying to take the transgender movement to national and international levels. If that sort of thing interests you, do any of the next series of exercises.

Exercise: Political Science I

1. Research both GenderPAC and humanism. What parallels can you draw between the relationship of GenderPAC to transgender, and of humanism to feminism?

2. Now research the National Center for Transgender Equality. What are the differences between NCTE and GenderPAC? Which has been more successful in reaching its goals? Why?

Extra Credit: How would you have changed the course of GenderPAC (or humanism) to avoid the invisibilizing of transgender (feminism)?

Masters Thesis: Develop a community level or national politic for transgender people.

Doctoral Thesis: Develop a community level or national politic for a coalition of sex-and-gender activists.

Your voice needs to be heard. Please speak up. Join a neighborhood planning committee, or a tenants' rights organization. Make yourself as visible as you can while maintaining the safety and security you need to go on living in the world. I'm not exhorting you to "come out." You know I'm a big fan of personal safety. I'm not going to try to manipulate you passive-aggressively by saying you need to come out "for everyone else's benefit." That's not why I came out initially. I came out because all these thoughts were boiling in my head, and I was going mad without the opportunity to talk about them.

Every time I make myself talk about these fearful ideas, I end up feeling better. Who knows why, I just do. Maybe you will too. Maybe not. But please, try talking about these issues on some scale. If anything in this book made you think, tell someone.

Exercise: Political Science II

Select any two identity-based oppressions.

1. How has the USA-based dominant culture responded to any trouble makers from these marginalized people?

2. What is the meta that links those trouble makers—something that could be the basis for unity in their trouble making?

Even if you never question your own gender, ever in your life, even if you never attend a protest rally, or even if you move to some neighborhood where you never have to see another gender outlaw for the rest of your days, please argue the concepts in this book. If nothing else, people will think you're deep for talking about this. Who knows ... it could get you a date or two.

The Language of Paradox, and How to Speak It

Several years after the first publication of this book, I had the opportunity to work with thirteen young artists in Portland, Oregon. They were part of a youth collective called The Sex and Gender Minority Youth Resource Center, or SMYRC. They kept the G silent, and I don't mind that one bit because SMYRC is such a good acronym for a youth group.

The lucky thirteen youth and lucky me put together a week-long workshop called "The Language of Paradox." The premise of the LOP workshop was this: participants discovered and named the big paradox in their lives— the one that gave them the most joy, and at the same time got them into the most trouble. We used words to express our paradoxes coherently. We then staged two live performances with a cast of all thirteen participants. But words aren't the only way to express paradox: there's music and visual art and any number of other art forms that will help you speak the language of paradox. Since this is a book, we're going to start with words.

A paradox is the coexistence of two or more anythings that are impossible to coexist. Not-man and not-woman was my personal big paradox. What's yours? It doesn't have to have anything to do with gender. One of the workshop participants tackled an identity paradox of not-country and not-punk. They enjoyed being both, but one inevitably got them into trouble with members of the other identity.

@sassafrasflowrey: #LOP is the reason I can write readable stories. I learned how to take my angry punk boi, and harness and control that anger into stories that illuminated the hardness of my world, but didn't push folks away. #LOP was the ultimate edge play—I'd never before not crumbled on stage. But in #LOP I harnessed that fear. It was about not only laying my naked stories before an audience, but learning how to use my words to play w/ & captivate them. LOP was a genderfuck searchlight into my isolated crusty punk world. #LOP gave me the chance to see the possibility of being as freaky as I realized I needed to be. It gave me permission to quit T, to wear fishnets and steel toed boots, and to tell the stories.

271

Exercise: Language of Paradox

Get yourself a notebook or extra sheets of paper, or open a new document on your computer. Use the following prompts to uncover what may be your big paradox in life. Fill in each of the following statements at least ten times, using a different fill-in-the-blank each time. When you fill in the blank, you don't have to use a single word but it does help to keep it to a few words or a short phrase. Any longer, and you wouldn't be honing in on what exactly gives you the most joy and gets you into the most trouble.

Take your time. This exercise could take days, weeks, even years. Ready? Set. Go!

- I am _____, and I am going to be completely honest with you.
- _____ always gets me into trouble, but it always gives me great joy.
- I'm alive because _____.
- I'm studying _____ because _____.
- I want _____ and _____, so you _____.
- No one's ever told me _____.
- You don't know about my _____, but I'd like you to know.
- I am _____ but I will not _____.
- The language of paradox is _____.
- The language of paradox isn't _____.
- I am both _____ and _____ and neither.
- My super power is _____, and _____ is the source of it.
- My art is _____, my craft is _____, and very few if any people know that I'm great at _____.
- The last time I killed myself*, _____. *(See asterisk next page)*
- The next time I kill myself*, _____. *(See asterisk next page)*
- When you see me next time, _____.

✴ No, no—I don't mean literally killing yourself. Please don't do that. But as you know now, each of us uses any number of identities with which we navigate our life's journeys. Every now and then, one of our identities proves to be a sour note in the music of our lives. So we "kill" those—we stop being those identities. Of course, they're not dead, but for all practical purposes they're dead and gone since we're not animating them any more. And it's really fun to use the words "kill myself" without meaning suicide. Do stay alive, OK?

Exercise: Language of Paradox (continued)

With any luck, your answering those impossible questions will focus your mind on the paradoxes in your life. If so, what's one of your biggest paradoxes? What's a big either/or in your life? Write down an impossible contradiction of you in the two rectangular boxes on page 274. If you haven't yet been able to name it, put it on your bucket list and write in your notebook whenever you find a clue that brings you closer to that.

The circles on page 274 represent the spaces of two impossible but co-existing factors in your life. Write down names of each space. Now, where the circles overlap *that's* keeping them inextricably linked to one another. Write whatever that is in the bottom box. So—you're claiming and articulating a for-real paradox. That makes you so cool, and you can tell anyone that I think so.

continued next page

Exercise: Language of Paradox (continued)

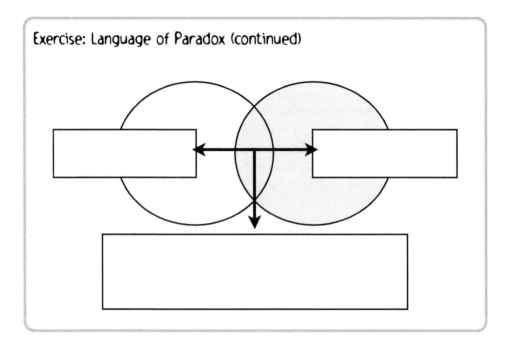

Zen Mode Exercise: Koans are like fables, but with no moral lesson to them. They are stories or poetry or word images that communicate a paradox. Koans can be a few words, or they can take up maybe a page. So: google "koans," and have fun with the ones you find. Then . . . write a koan that expresses the big paradox of your life.

Why Go to All That Trouble?
And it is Trouble

I have an idea that the human race has a shot at nobility. All of us. I'm under no delusion that this nobility can be achieved in my lifetime, or that it can be achieved over the next few hundred years to the degree I believe possible. But I do believe it's worth planting the seeds now. That itself seems to me an act of nobility. It makes me feel good. It gives my life some meaning.

I try to live my life with the notion that the human race has some potential for a truly honorable shared value system. I think it's possible to peacefully resolve differences at all levels of life. I'm realistic enough to look at all of us with the understanding that we've got a long, long, long way to go.

There's very little chance that the bi-polar gender system is going to change on a global scale over the next few generations of our species. And that's only one of various interlinked systems of oppression that are keeping us all down. There is, however, a great chance now for more and more people to find their own personal freedom from gender constraints. And that's happening because we are speaking up, telling our deep true stories, and asking our most terrifying questions.

RECOMMENDED READING: Who are some of your favorite role models for trouble makers? Mine include Huckleberry Finn, Starbuck and Caprica Six from *Battlestar Galactica* (re-envisioned series), Ensign Ro Laren and Ishara Yar from *Star Trek: TNG*, the 10th Doctor in *Doctor Who*, Fluff in Pat Califia's *Doc and Fluff*, Sarah Connor in anything *Terminator*, the whole crew of Joss Whedon's *Firefly*, Harley Quinn in anything *Batman*, Eric Northman in *True Blood*, Willow and Spike in the *Buffyverse*, Delirium from *The Sandman Series* by Neil Gaiman, and Lisbeth Salander from Stieg Larsson's *The Girl with the Dragon Tattoo* series.

Who are *your* trouble-maker heroes? Read more books about them. Watch more video. Play more games. Learn how to be the best trouble maker you can be.

Those questions of ours are terrifying for a reason, and our troubling questions are trouble for more than just you and me. Our questions are trouble for everyone who's come to depend for their own survival on the bi-polar appearance of gender to keep hidden its connection to any culturally forbidden desire, identity and/or power. To some degree that's most if not all the people on this planet, including you and me. We are trouble makers headed for trouble.

The dominant culture has responded to trouble makers in earlier sex-and-gender-based movements such as the women's movement, the gay and lesbian movements, the bisexual movement and the sex workers movement. It took trouble makers to get the dominant culture to become aware of the uphill battle, fought by races other than white to simply be human. Most systemic oppression via class, age, body type, religion, spirituality, and so on is invisibilized. It's trouble-makers who are making the oppression transparent.

As sex positivists and gender anarchists, we have a shot here to make a difference. We've already been viewed as a crackpot minority—and in many parts of the world, we still are. And we've been the subject of pity. We've been attacked, big time. That's just the way it goes. And it's still worth doing. It's worth telling our stories and asking our questions because if just one more person can become aware of the intricate system of sexed and gendered chains and sexed and gendered punishment in this world, we'll have made some headway.

Mainstream media is, at this writing, just beginning to get on board with airing legitimate concerns on behalf of transgender people in the United States. But here in the heart of theocratic capitalism, mainstream media still has to earn its daily buck. Anti-kyriarchy activists have to continually think up new ways to become newsworthy. Sex-and-gender activists have a leg up, so to speak, because we're so gosh-darned cute and sexy. I think we need to cash in on that more—that's what I think.

On April 15, 2012, I was a guest on the *Melissa Harris-Perry Show*, on MSNBC. Ms. Harris-Perry is the first mainstream serious news outlet host to speak with trans people about more than our tragi-comic lives and personal narratives. MHP kicks kyriarchy butt. Most people on the margins of our culture have good reason to love Melissa Harris-Perry.

Exercise: Women and Gender Studies History: Compare and contrast this version of the workbook with the first version. What's changed? What's stayed the same? What hasn't even been tackled yet?

LGBT leaders in the United States made what I think was a spectacular mistake when they pushed marriage equality as their key issue. They spent millions and millions of dollars on something that would only benefit themselves, and not all of them at that. There was no room for coalition building in the issue of marriage equality. The only way we can count on the support of existing civil rights organizations is to broker agreements on common ground issues.

Exercise: Beauty Politics: Google "femme" AND "femme conference." Follow any of the links that draw your attention. In particular, try to find yourself a list of workshops at one of the femme conferences. These are some fierce women, and if you don't have a fierce, femme friend in your life right now, it's time to go find yourself one.

Let's get back to you, personally, as a sex positivist and gender anarchist. Where can you find support for yourself? I'm sorry to say that even sex-and-gender activist groups—however impassioned—are bound to miss a point or two that might be the exact points you or I need dealt with in order to get on with our lives. You may very well need to build yourself a life worth living as a sex-and-gender outlaw. It's daunting, but far from impossible. Yep, maybe you'll have to move. Maybe you'll have to say goodbye to some people so that you can say hello to your tribe. It's worth the heartbreak. I promise.

Well, That Does It

What I most want
is to spring out of this
personality,
then to sit apart from
that leaping.

I've lived too long
where I can be
reached.

—Rumi

Maybe one day, people will look back on our day and age and wonder to themselves at our barbarism. I fervently hope that will come to pass. If there's any chance of that happening even on a small level— say, within the circles you travel—it's going to start with you. You need to talk, argue, listen, reason, negotiate, puzzle, challenge and question.

Thank you very much for taking the time to go through this book. I know it couldn't have been all that easy on you, but I'm hoping it was gentle. I have just a few last things to say.

If you've gotten this far, and you're still not in any mood or head space to question your gender, I wish for you the compassion to allow others the right to question their own genders. I hope those of us who do question our genders can count on you as a friend and ally.

If, on the other hand, you're questioning gender on a personal basis, I wish for you the strength it's going to take to make this journey. I wish for you every comfort you deserve. And I wish for you the compassion you'll need to deal with others you'll meet along the way.

One word of advice: Honey, when you're doing all that … be Fabulous! Why? Well, why not? You'll make more people smile, and you can smile some more yourself.

Use this space for notes,
or a nice letter to the boss of your country
telling them what you'd like to see done
to improve the country.

Whoa! BONUS Pages!

Auntie Kate Says Goodnight, and Good Day

Most nights, I like to write a tweet before I go to sleep. Since virtual reality is timeless, and the internet is international, I can't simply say goodnight. That would be meaningless to people who are just waking up. So, I write tweets that say both goodnight and good day. Here are some of my favorites. You can read one before you go to sleep and another when you wake up. I hope they make your dreams sweet, and your daydreams sweeter.

G'nite, my cockles & mussels, and gday. #Gender is nothing more than a #shellgame, but no matter which one u pick—you're right. xo Auntie K

G'nite & g'day, my hatters & dormice & hares. Tea may be for two—but gender, race, age, class & all that jazz never really are. xo Auntie K

G'nite & gday, my outlaws & inlaws. No matter what #gender rules u break or follow, it's the rules that r broken—not u or me. ♥ Auntie K #mngw

Long day's #writing into night. G'nite & g'day. my ones & zeroes. No matter yr #gender—or how few or many u are—u make #fuzzylogic to me. ♥ K

G'nite/g'day my technicolor dream twibe. No matter yr gender—or if yr color's RGB, CMYK, Grayscale or other—yer always more than B&W—always. ♥ K

G'nite & g'day my haves & have-nots. No matter our gender or how we put food on the table, outlaws always welcome other outlaws to dinner. ♥ K

G'nite dear twibe, & g'day. No matter yr gender or what language u speak it in, u make perfect sense to everyone who matters. xo Auntie K

G'nite/g'day, my birdies & serpents. No matter yr #gender, plumage or fangs—u have just what u need to ease #suffering for yrself & others—♥ K

Got to sleep. G'nite my peapods, and g'day. Auntie loves you, right this very minute . . . and the next minute too. ♥ K

G'nite dearest of all possible twibes, & g'day. No matter yr gender—or what genders make yr ♥ go pitterpat—angels delight in yr desire. xo K

G'nite/g'day, my #dragqueens, #dragkings, & all #dragfuck royalty. My goodness, that's all of u—if & when u ascend to yr throne. ♥ Auntie Kate

G'nite & g'day, dear twibe— insert something funny & loving here, because my brain is all fuzzy from the flu—and I wanna b lovin with u. xo K

G'nite & g'day, my puppies & polliwogs. No matter yr gender, age, or temperature of yr blood, yr a beloved child of the universe. ♥ Auntie K

G'nite & g'day, my cupcakes, muffins & scones. No matter yr gender or frosting, yr nationality or filling—yr always a treat to me. ♥ Auntie K

G'nite my cabbages & casaba melons, & g'day. No matter yr kingdom, gender, phylum, or class—or if yr as yet unclassified— I know you're real. ♥ K

G'nite & G'day, my stars, comets, & other objects in space. No matter yr gender, age, or shape —yrs is a perfectly heavenly body. xo Auntie K

G'nite & g'day my sunshines, silhouettes & crepuscular wonders—no matter yr gender or shade, I see myself in u—it makes me smile— ♥ Auntie K

G'nite my crepes & croquettes, and g'day. No matter yr gender or if yer sweet or savory—or a li'l of both—I love your good taste. ♥ Auntie K

G'nite my moonbats & wingnuts—
no matter yr gender or how u
choose 2 help end suffering for all
sentient beings—yay us for good
intentions. K

G'nite & g'day, my Munchkins &
Brobdingnagians—no matter yr
gender, race, size, or citizenship—
you're worthy of love & life.
#Stayalive. ♥ K

G'nite & g'day my stars, starlets &
starlings. No matter which skies yer
twinkling in, know that yr shining
in my heart. Mille tendresses, K

Whoa, late. G'nite & g'day, my
lovebugs & fireflies—no matter yr
gender or species. The city may
be blanketed in snow & I plan to
sleep in.

G'night & g'day, my fairies &
gnomes. Beauty is as beauty does,
and you do it for me, no matter
your gender, shape, or ability.
xo Auntie K

G'nite & g'day my li'l tater tots,
tater teens, and my whole danged
tater twibe. Auntie Kate loves you,
no matter your gender or shelf-life.

G'nite & g'day, my chickpeas &
chickadees. No matter if yer flora
or fauna or neither or both—I'm
lovin' on you. So please #stayalive.
xo K

Goodnite, my angels and
cherubs—no matter your gender
or how wide you can spread your
wings—and the sweetest good day
to you. xo Auntie Kate

G'nite & g'day, my moonflowers
& snapdragons—no matter yr
gender or what u see when u look
in the mirror—you're lovely to me.
xo Auntie K

G'nite, my peanuts & popcorns
(and of course, all my
crackerjacks)—no matter your
gender, size, or shape—and have a
sweet day. ♥ Auntie Kate

Goodnight, my gumdrops and
jellybeans—no matter your gender
nor the size of your sweet tooth—
and have a loverly day. xo K

Goodnight my dumplings and
latkes—no matter your gender or
preferred cuisine—and have a
delightful day. kiss kiss, Auntie Kate
#stayalive

G'nite, my turtledoves, and g'day.
May you have sparkly dreams &
glittery daydreams of fabulous
gender & sex just right. kiss kiss,
Auntie K

G'nite, my popinjays & pussycats,
and g'day. No matter yr gender or
species—fact or fiction—yer a
wonder of the world & yer loved.
xo Auntie

G'nite, puppies & kittens—and u canines & felines a bit longer in the tooth, like me. No matter yr species, age or gender, yr auntie luvs u.

Goodnight, my lions & tigers & bears, and have a gr-r-r-reat day. Nice to be on this side o' the rainbow with you. kiss kiss, Auntie Kate

G'nite and G'day, my dearlings. Great big auntie hugs, or little ones if you prefer that kind of hug instead. K

G'nite, my gumdrops & salt licorice bits, and g'day. No matter yr #gender/#sexuality, there's *someone* who thinks u taste good. #stayalive

G'nite—my tadpoles & pollywogs—and g'day. No matter yr age or yr biology—we all start & end w no gender. What u do in the middle is up to u. #stayalive

G'nite, dear twiba, and a very good day. Life is upside down, and that's OK.

Now, since it's your gender workbook, you get the last word.

Life's just scene after scene after scene.
Who cares where you end up, where you've been?
Just relax and take pride
In enjoying the ride
And of course, above all, don't be _____

ANSWER: mean

Acknowledgments

Thank you to my editor, Erica C. Wetter, and to her assistant Margo Irvin at Routledge Publishing. It's because of these two women that this update exists at all. They got the idea for it, and they fought to make it happen. They fought for me, and they fought with me, and the book is better for all of that. I'm grateful.

Thank you to my copy editor, Amanda Crook and to project manager Rosie Stewart at Florence Production, for doing their best to keep up with the countless text boxes, and their cooperation in translating my rough layout of the book into the awesomeness you're holding in your hands. Thank you to James Sowden at Florence Production and Emma Håkonsen at Taylor & Francis for keeping up with all the dizzying details in this book. I'm deeply grateful.

Thank you to Bill Germano, who edited the first version of this workbook at Routledge over the two years it took to write it back in the mid-1990s. Poor Bill. I handed in over 600 pages of first draft. He had to hire an editor who specialized in major literary surgery to bring it down to size. Bill gave me the best advice I've ever received from an editor. He told me that my strength is performance, and that I should make my writing perform. I keep trying to do that. Thank you, Bill.

When I got the offer to write this book, I asked two people for should-I-or-shouldn't-I advice. I was wrapping up my memoir, and I wanted to write a novella for young adults. Both my literary agent, Malaga Baldi, and Gayatri Patnaik, my memoir editor at Beacon Press, told me in flat-out terms to do this book first. They were right. There was a whole lot I wanted to say in this book, and saying it is only going to make my young adult novella even better. Thank you, Malaga and Gayatri.

This edition is some 20–40 pages shorter than the first edition. Thanks to Crystal Yakacki and Dan Simon at Seven Stories Press. They taught me to write short and sweet when I wrote *Hello, Cruel World*. This version of the workbook retains many of the formatting features I developed for *Hello, Cruel World*, including all the illustrations and call-outs. It's performance, right?

Diane DiMassa and I have been pals since the early 1990s. I collect her art. You should, too. Diane did the original illustrations for the workbook, two of which made it over into this version: the pyramid of gender and the splattering at the dinner table. Both illustrations crack me up whenever I look at them. Diane began her work as a cartoonist, crafting the comic, *Hothead Paisan: Homicidal Lesbian Terrorist*. She's moved on to oils and sculpture. If you like this book, you'll want her art in your house.

Christine Smith (@PrincessComics) conceived of and drew the many moods of little Blu, the li'l *chibi* who's flying around and through the entire book. Christine draws a web comic, *The Princess*. You can find it here: www.drunkduck.com/The_Princess/5186771/. Christine and I met on Twitter and have become good friends. I'm hoping that a book of *The Princess* makes it to the stands not long after I've written this wish for that.

Michelle Pinard aka Chaotic Kiss drew the little icons of me that you see with all the speech bubbles. I was attending a conference, Transcending Boundaries 2011, and met Miss Michelle in the merchandise hall, where she was drawing manga versions of anyone who wanted. I wanted! I attended the conference for three days, and wore three different outfits. Ms. Pinard captured each look perfectly, that's what I think. She writes and illustrates her own trans manga, which you can buy for your very own at www.chaotickiss.com. If you ask her nicely and send her cash and a photo, she might even draw YOU.

Sarah Thomasin (@wordgeeksarah) wrote the limericks in the book. Sarah can (and does) write poetry—well—in any style you can imagine. When I asked her to write me limericks, she was overjoyed to write them. I'm overjoyed to include her work in this book, and I enjoy coffee with her whenever she makes it across the pond to New York City.

Helaine Gawlica did a masterful job of sorting all the tweets and blog comments into useable categories.

A special shout out to Ron and Joe—go to www.ronandjoe.com and click on "artparts." Their style is distinctive, and you can spot their work all through the book. They're cool guys and do fun work, and they said that since I bought a CD of their work years ago, I could use as many pictures as I want. So if you like their work, please go buy some.

Dover Publications is the best source of old-time and eclectic clip art in the whole wide world. AND they let you use ten to fifteen images from each volume royalty free.

Deluxe Clipart publishes gabillions of pieces of clip art, mostly modern pieces but some go back as far as the 1950s. They are also generous with their usage policy: you buy it, you can use it.

Nitrozac & Snaggy came up with the cartoon of the geek with glasses and propellor beanie, sitting with their Alienware laptop on their lap. Please go have fun and support this fabulous pair of geeks at www.geekculture.com. Rest in peace, Steve Jobs, and thank you. I wrote this book on a thirteen-inch Apple MacBook Pro. I drew up the outline and basic text using text from the first edition, which I extracted from Microsoft Word as quickly as I could, and pasted it into the app

Scrivener, by Literature & Latte software. Once I had the text I needed, I exported it into Apple's Pages app, which I used to finish writing and laying out the book—pretty close to the format you're reading it in now. I edited my illustrations in Adobe Photoshop, and created some of the drawings from photos, using ToonPhoto, by Toon-FX. I resized the images using Perfect Resize 7 Pro, from onOne Software. I turned the book in to Routledge in a single, editable PDF I created in PDFpenPro from Smile Software.

Thank you, Scott Kelby and www.photoshopuser.com for teaching me how to use Photoshop to make all the fun illustrations in this book. What's more, Mr. Kelby has a wonderful teaching style, and you can hear his teaching voice in this book.

I don't read many books while I'm writing. I'm too much of a literary thief for that. But I did read a few, and I watched a lot of television—you can hear echoes of all of them in this book. So it's only fair to acknowledge their influence.

Doctor Who (2005 revival to current)
Battlestar Galactica (re-envisioned series)
The Misfits
Haven
Grey's Anatomy
Eastenders
Dexter
RuPaul's Drag Race
RuPaul's Drag U
Law & Order (and all the spin-offs)
The Melissa Harris-Perry Show
The Rachel Maddow Show
The Daily Show with Jon Stewart
The Colbert Report with Stephen Colbert.

As I was writing this update, I regularly read Tony Ortega—he covers all things Scientology. Tony's easy to find with a couple of clicks. His is the most in-depth and honest coverage of the church on the web. Commenters on his blog are intelligent, caring, and welcoming of many points of view. I'm interested in all this, because I used to be a Scientologist. I left in 1981, and by church canon I'm not allowed to speak with or be heard by my daughter, who was born into the church and remains there to this day. I last saw her when she was nine years old. I hear I have two grandchildren. How about that? I still read Tony Ortega's blogs once or twice a day, because I want to read one day that my daughter and her children have left. I've never really counted on that, so I wrote them a book, my memoir, *A Queer and Pleasant Danger*. In fact, I began writing this workbook update the day that memoir went to press.

Thank you to all the lovely people at Beacon Press who helped me promote my memoir while I was under deadline pressure to finish this book. Beacon Press peeps are saints: my editor, Gayatri Patnaik, and editorial assistant Rachael Marks, as well as Helene Atwan, Tom Hallock, Pamela MacColl, Reshma Melwani, Susan Lumenello, Bob Kosturko, and PJ Tierney.

Thank you to Lane Jantzen and his team at Random House who sold my memoir to bookstores while I was writing this book. They did such a good job I didn't have to worry about it.

Thank you to Pat Sinatra, of Pat's Tats in Kingston, New York. She's been inking me ever since the first version of this workbook came out. I'm so proud to wear her work in my skin.

Thank you, Sam Feder (@samfederfilms) and his crew for jockeying and sometimes postponing shooting schedules on the documentary he's making about me, *Kate Bornstein Is A Queer and Pleasant Danger*.

Thank you, Mary Corcoran, who taught me the difference between sexual orientation and gender identity.

The components of gender are most articulately expressed and were taught to me by Drs. Suzanne Kessler and Wendy McKenna, in their book *Gender: An Ethnomethodological Approach*. Go on, give "ethnomethodologist" a google right this minute. You're going to want to be one.

Thank you, Rachel Gold, for the idea fifteen years ago that Captain James T. Kirk is, in fact, the perfectly gendered person. And thank you for your marvelous young adult novel, *Being Emily*, which came out a few months ago. When young outlaws want to know how to come out to family and friends, I recommend Rachel's book as giving a good example.

Thank you, Elisabeth Schüssler Fiorenza, who coined the word *kyriarchy* in *But She Said: Feminist Practices of Biblical Interpretation*, published in 1992.

Thank you, Sarra Lev at the Reconstructionist Rabbinical College in Wyncote PA. I'd been talking for about a year about the activism of radical welcoming. It was Sarra Lev who supplied the missing piece: radical wonder. That's what makes radical welcoming work.

Thank you, Dr. Marsha Linehan, for your fearless journey beyond borderline personality disorder. I've got that, too. So thank you for the roadmap called dialectic behavioral therapy that you developed by combining cognitive behavioral therapy with Zen Buddhism. Thank you to the doctors and staff at DBT/CBT Associates in New York City, and to the members of my group therapy sessions. A lot of the talk about being mindful, and the importance of dialectic over binaries, came from the DBT therapy I went through while I was writing this book, and I'm so grateful.

Thank you, Rabbi Sharon Kleinbaum at Congregation Beit Simchat Torah, the LGBTQetc synagogue in New York City. Thank you Keshet, the national organization of LGBTQetc Jews, and NUJLS, The National Union of Jewish LBGTQ Jewish Students—and to all the Jews and Jewish organizations and congregations who have welcomed me as a tribe member. The Talmud is one of the most holy books in all of Judaism. It's a collection of ideas and conundrums, written and commented upon by hundreds and hundreds of rabbis. That's where I got the idea to include all the voices in this book. It's a Jew thing to question rather than answer, and to pay attention to what a lot of people have to say when you ask a question.

As a reader of this book, you've learned a lot from my Twitter twibe. I asked *them* who they wanted to acknowledge, because you've heard echoes in this book of the people who helped contributors to this book. In no particular order, here are some of the people and things my twibe wanted me to acknowledge.

@MxRoo: I want to thank Caryl Churchill for "Cloud Nine" and my subsequent realization that gender is performative.

@BootBlackBlast: I want to thank Daddy @NariaJordan, Daddy Vick Germany & Daddy Ren for modeling various facets of the gender Butch.

@queer_kitten: are we to thank just people? if not, I thank the 12step program for helping me #stayalive.

@AcreatureOflux: thanks 2 @lesliefeinberg, Jennifer Miller, two spirits, all amazing ppl brave enough 2 b who we r, Yareak who's no longer w us, and u! oh and the radical faeries!

@goldenpixypi: I know I owe Bianca James and her excellent blog, unicorns and rhinoceros, and the colors black and pink #genderqueer.

@youlittlewonder: You! And David Bowie.

@JustJo_08: hmm, part of me wants 2 thank u but also hav 2 give props 2 my friend @RaeRose_89 + rest of my friends at MSU Alliance

@resisttor: all those who try2dictate or limit who we r because they strengthen our convictions&remind us of what we don't want 2b.

@SaraEileen: Thank yourself, Auntie Kate, b/c you're hugely responsible for my journey, and I'm sure many other twibe as well. Besides u I'd thank my mother, for teaching me casually, thoroughly & by example that the glass ceiling can be smashed.

@andryfemme: reading Judith Butler's Gender Trouble sparked the burn to come out as a queer gender-effing androgynous femme.

@gwenners: Thanks to those who travelled these roads before us, and gave us the tools to get started . . . And those who will come along after us, and take things further than we dared dream.

@inafried: Gwen Araujo and all the trans youth that didn't make it + all those who played w gender in secret bc it wasn't safe.

@wordgeeksarah: Thank the pope? Just to mess with his head a bit . . .

@ponyonabalcony: When I told A that I was going to go figure out gender things & didn't know what would happen, before we were together, she said she would be consummately ok with whatever I did or didn't do. She has been instrumental and amazingly helpful (on both a practical level and in my heartsoul) from the start.

I used hashtag #MNGW (My New Gender Workbook) for my crowd-source research. Thank you to everyone who posted to this hashtag. If Twitter still keeps old tweets available, you can look for yourself to see how the various discussions developed.

Many of the tweets that are in this book—and many more that there was no room for—may be found by going to my Twitter profile page, @katebornstein, and clicking on my favorites. The icon is usually a star.★

Thank you, everyone who tweeted to hashtag #stayalive. I did stay alive. And if you're reading this, you did too. I'm so relieved! I still check that hashtag several times a week, if not daily.

I live in a really nice neighborhood in New York City: East Harlem, aka Spanish Harlem, aka El Barrio. It's mostly a working class family neighborhood. There are a few projects. The drug dealers keep the streets safe from petty criminals. My girlfriend and I, and a few other white freaks, have moved in to the neighborhood, and we've been welcomed with open arms. I have lovely neighbors, and I want to thank them for their support

There's one more big difference in this version of the workbook: sex. There wasn't nearly as much sex in the original version. Why? Because even though I was fifty years old, I didn't know enough about sex to be able to articulate it. Then I met my girlfriend, Barbara Carrellas. We've been together fifteen years—so far, we've lasted as a couple the whole time the first version of the workbook was in print. Barbara teaches sex in a way I can understand it. Her books, *Urban Tantra: Sacred Sex for the 21st Century,* and *Ecstasy Is Necessary: A Practical Guide*, belong on your bookshelf—really. Thank you, Miss Barbara.

And thank you to the pug, the puggle, the box turtle, the Maine Coon, the Himalayan, and the Siberian. Your love kept me going the weeks that Barbara was on the road teaching sex, and I was so alone at home writing and so afraid I'd fuck it up.